# ELLiEMENT

## and the
## Material Matter

Bertie Stephens

Published by the Clean Planet Foundation

Published in the United Kingdom by the Clean Planet Foundation.
cleanplanet.com/foundation
Clean Planet Foundation CIC. UK Company Number: 13670829.

ISBN: 979-8-2832242-3-7

London. England.

# DEDICATION

To Mum, Dad, and Barney
for always believing in my ideas,
the big ideas,
and then the even bigger ones.

# Foreword by Stanley Johnson

*Stanley Johnson is a renowned environmentalist, author, and former MEP who helped lay the foundations for the United Nations' and Europe's environmental policy. As Head of the European Commission's Prevention of Pollution division and later Director of Energy Policy, his work has shaped decades of global environmental action. He has published extensively on conservation and sustainability, from The Politics of Environment to Antarctica: The Last Great Wilderness. Recognised worldwide, Stanley has received the Greenpeace Prize for Outstanding Services to the Environment, the RSPB Medal for Services to Nature Conservation, and WWF's prestigious Leaders of the Living Planet Award, among many others.*

~

**W**hen I first heard about Ellie Ment and the Material Matter, I expected a story about science, adventure, and perhaps a little mischief. What I didn't expect was to be drawn into a world so cleverly woven with the very real challenges facing our planet – and to be laughing along the way.

In my years working on environmental protection – whether drafting the original EU Habitats Directive or helping establish the European Commission's first Environmental Action Programme – I've learned that solutions rarely come from the top down. They often begin with curiosity. With a question. Sometimes, with a young person who simply refuses to accept "that's just the way it is".

Ellie Ment is one of those people. Bold, brilliant, and mercifully imperfect, she doesn't wait for permission to investigate. She's clever, chaotic, and completely unafraid to challenge the grown-ups. And what unfolds in this story is nothing short of exhilarating.

What makes this book truly stand out is how it handles one of the most complex tensions I've seen throughout my career: the pull between idealism and pragmatism. These themes – so central to environmental action – shine here through the eyes of young characters who must navigate what is right, what is possible, and what is simply necessary.

This book pulls off something quite remarkable. It makes science genuinely exciting, the problems facing our world accessible, and environmental responsibility fun. Not through lectures, but through story. Through character. Through a wonderfully madcap blend of quantum physics, plastic waste, loyalty, rebellion – and jam jars. It's exactly the kind of edutainment the Clean Planet Foundation exists to champion: a way to educate while inspiring action, curiosity, and courage in the next generation.

Whether you love science, art, sport, or just a cracking good adventure, Ellie Ment and the Material Matter has something for you. More than that: it invites you in. To question. To think. And to believe that change, even on the biggest problems we face, might just start with someone like you.

I, for one, can't wait to see what Ellie does next.

**And I know you will too.**

**Stanley Johnson**. Long-standing international environmentalist and pioneer of Europe's first environmental strategy and programme.

# CONTENTS

Jaliya Gajage

# ACKNOWLEDGMENTS

Cover Art: Farras Raihan
Chapter Art: Milena Vieira

*Ellie Ment and the Material Matter* exists because of the tireless backing and enthusiasm of so many.

From my co-founders of the Clean Planet Group – Dr. Andrew, Adel and Fernando – to the incredible and supportive investors who made this possible; and, of course, to our wonderful team, each of whom spend every hour of every day solving one of the world's most pressing problems.

Then there are the regular *HAPSIE* Comic writers and artists, whose vision for a better future continues to inspire both a new generation each month – and me, too.

Thank you to Lil and Vicky for taking my words and making them far, (far), better.

I am beyond grateful to Stanley Johnson for taking the time to share his wealth of experience with readers by providing the glorious foreword to this book.

To Jon and the team at Palamedes PR – thank you for giving this book the kind of start I thought I could only dream of.

And, of course, to my beautiful wife Steph who helped bring Ellie's story to life through countless chats on our forest walks (and basically any time I wouldn't stop talking about it), as we raise the ever-curious Oskar together.

## The Answer That Solved Absolutely Nothing

Everything that happens in our world has an explanation. Yet not everything can always be explained right here, right now.

And that, for the most part, is perfectly okay.

The beauty lies in the fact that even the strangest peculiarities will be explained eventually.

But if you ever find yourself in the pitch black early hours of the morning, alone in the middle of a forest, with torrential rain hammering your already drenched raincoat, watching your newly built school burning to the ground and the only way to help would be by using the ten jam jars stuffed into your backpack...well, at that point you might start to wonder if this particular oddity would ever be explained at all. And if the flames coming from your school weren't the usual red and orange but instead a roaring purple – yes, purple! - you may think it would remain a mystery forever.

At least, that's precisely what Ellie Ment was thinking when precisely all of that was happening to her...

When these things happen, it's probably best to take a deep breath and remind yourself of all the strange things that *can* be explained in this world.

Take the town of Hapsie, for example. Local litterer

Lucas would always deliberately drop litter wherever he went. He loved it. Even though his mum told him it was wrong. But one day, he suddenly stopped doing it. It was hard to explain.

However, when it was later discovered that Lucas was hoarding this litter to build his own castle made entirely out of rubbish, everything was once again clear. It was a simple explanation that wasn't immediately available when the event originally occurred.

> (A quick side note: The castle eventually fell over with Lucas inside, and he subsequently decided that littering Leafy Park meant fewer food containers smacking him in the head, so began littering again. Sigh.)

Of course there are larger examples, more hygienic ones too.

In this small historic market town of Hapsie, the weather was a constant matter of discussion – as was the case all over England. Hapsie looked quite delightful in the rain, surrounded by lush green hills and with traditional stone houses still standing in its town centre. But why the constant, never-stopping, rain? Well, now there's something the locals of Hapsie (Hapsians) had tried to explain for thousands of years.

When the Romans settled in Hapsie over 2,000 years ago, their explanation was that the rain came from their king of the gods, Jupiter. If they needed more rain to grow their crops, they'd pray to Jupiter. If they needed less rain because clearly their earlier prayers had been far too effective, well, they'd do another quick prayer. Jupiter seemed to listen to the prayers for more rain a lot more than the prayers for less rain. And with that they had their explanation: Jupiter was a very annoying god.

Then came the Saxons. They lived in Hapsie about 1,000 years ago and their first settlers believed rain was controlled by

Thunor (AKA Thor), their thunder god. Like the Romans, the Saxons would perform rituals to start and stop the rain. Like Jupiter, Thunor was also annoying – he was a lot more interested in starting the rain than stopping it. When you're the god of thunder, no rain means no thunder and that means nothing to do. Again, an explanation.

Today in Hapsie, the explanation was all about the water cycle: rivers evaporate, clouds form, rain pours down on Lucas' trash castle, it collapses, and he returns to littering once more. See, two explanations in one there – nice! Today, the science of the rain is considered a more reliable explanation than an annoying god.

But just because people have agreed on an explanation, it doesn't mean it's correct. The Romans, the Saxons and the Hapsians of today would each insist their explanation was right. But who's to say that, in 1,000 years, future Hapsians won't have a completely different idea as to why it rains? The general rule is that if it makes sense at the time, that's probably good enough.

But what was Ellie doing outside in the forest near Hapsie School at two in the morning in the first place?

She'd snuck out of her house while everyone else was far too busy snoring to give a hoot (pun intended) about her nighttime whereabouts.

Why had she left her warm, dry and comfy bed and cuddly gorilla toy, Attenborough? Well, that's simple to answer when you know more about Ellie.

You see, Ellie was a scientist. An eleven-year-old, self-proclaimed scientist, but a scientist nonetheless. Ellie loved science, because with science, everything had an explanation, and for Ellie, that was incredibly important. She had no time for magic, for example. *Eurghhh, magic,* Ellie would often think to herself as she picked up a book about dragons and wands. You see, to Ellie, magic is cheating. "If you can wave a wand to make a feather float, but you can't explain *how* that feather is floating, then what's the point in reading about it at all?" she'd often proclaim.

Ellie would much rather it was explained using science. "Oskar, wearing his favourite red woolly jumper, grabbed his big green balloon and a small feather and rubbed them both vigorously up and down against his chest for thirty seconds. This built up static electricity as electrons jumped from the jumper onto both the balloon and the feather. Oskar placed the feather a few centimetres above the balloon and – SWOOSH! – it floated!" Nice! That's because the rubbing gave the feather and the balloon the same electrical charge, so they pushed away from each other.

Okay, Ellie's version was a little bit lengthier than wand-waving, *sure*. And probably wouldn't sell a million copies if written in a book. But it was certainly more interesting. To Ellie, at least. And best of all, as she was wearing her own woolly jumper under her green raincoat right then, she could perform Oskar's 'magic' trick too! Ellie loved that about science – anyone, from anywhere, could do it if they wanted to. All you needed was a balloon, a sweater and a small feather.

Go on, you try it too.

Well, maybe just get to the end of this chapter first.

> (That said, if you happen to live in Hapsie, the humidity and water vapour in the air might make it difficult. Why? Because static electricity hates moisture, would you believe?)

In short, to Ellie, magic wasn't very useful.

Magic isn't science.

But science *is* magic.

And more importantly, Ellie can do science.

Ellie loved science. She proudly displayed a poster of the periodic table on her bedroom wall. It was no ordinary poster either, neatly embellished with her own notes and thoughts. Ellie could recite the entire periodic table by heart, including names, symbols, and atomic numbers. It was an impressive skill and as you'll see, it would come in handy later in her journey.

But let's not get ahead of ourselves.

Rest assured you don't need to be an expert on it either.

But that was what Ellie was doing in the woods at 2am on a school night: science.

She scurried down the back garden path, huddled over, heading for Hapsie Forest in the pouring rain, backpack full to the brim with jam jars – endless, endless, empty jam jars.

> (By the way, if you happen to be reading this story as a resident of Hapsie, and you've been busy recycling your jam jars over the last year, I'm afraid they never reached the local processing centre. Nope. They were scavenged out of your bin by Ellie. Special mention to the people of 104 Thorn Lane: your endless love for hazelnut spread was a welcome assistance for Ellie's progress. Keep it up!)

The hypothesis was simple, really: everything needs water to grow. But does rainwater at different times of the year and from different environments change *how* a plant will grow? What if a plant only received water from one specific time of year?

In January, when it rained, the air was full of atmospheric gases from Hapsie's wood fires and coal burners. The water droplets might have absorbed these gases before they hit the ground.

In June, the rain from the summer showers fell through

different minerals and nutrients – like pollen or dust in the air – and might have picked them up along the way.

In October, the rain might have landed on microbes from decomposing leaves and organic matter, meaning the rainwater interacted with the soil in different ways.

And as it was October – October 1st – Ellie needed a place with lots of leaves. You'd be forgiven for thinking Leafy Park would be the obvious choice to head to, but while leaves did fall from the sycamore, beech and horse chestnut trees, the Hapsie town council were so efficient in sweeping up these leaves that Leafy Park was, for the most part, leaf-free. Also, it closed at 4pm in the autumn and winter. Everyone in Hapsie found that really annoying – almost as annoying as Jupiter and Thunor.

So that's why Ellie found herself under the tall canopies of the oak trees of Hapsie Forest – there were plenty of leaves on the floor there. Had it not been pitch black with the only light coming from Ellie's faulty headtorch, she would have been able to see a sea of golden, red and yellow leaves. As it was – and gosh she must get that headtorch fixed – Ellie could only really see a flickery faint outline of leafy matter as she stumbled over the forest floor.

Ellie's first task was to use her shovel to dig ten holes, each large enough to fit a jam jar, in various spots around the forest. Digging was much easier in October when the ground was wet; far, far easier than in January, when it was frozen, or June, when the soil was rock-hard dry.

Next, she marked down in her notebook where all the holes were. It was significantly harder to jot notes in your notebook in October when it was raining; far, far harder than on a June summer night, or in January when it's frosty out.

Ellie was determined, however, and began pacing out steps away from a handful of odd-looking trees. Ellie had tried a tape measure rather than steps but it turned out not to be so practical on your own, in the rain, generally in the dark.

"Thirty-four steps from Space Rocket Tree towards Big Ears Tree, away from Large Lump Tree." Ellie spoke out loud as she scribbled down her notes.

Once the locations of the ten jars had been noted, Ellie returned to each hole and buried the jam jars up to their lips, leaving their tops flush with the ground and without lids.

Finally, Ellie needed to cover the jars. Jam jars were fantastic for collecting rainwater, but also brilliant at capturing small insects too. Invertebrates were not part of this experiment and there was no need to sacrifice a living creature by allowing it to fall into a jam jar of certain doom.

Luckily, at the end of last year, Edward McMan of 72 Grumpot Avenue had decided that linen – and only linen – would be his 'thing' for the new year. Linen trousers, linen t-shirts, linen socks – even linen underpants. Edward was quick to purchase an entirely new, pure, natural linen wardrobe.

Even more luckily for Ellie, by the second week of January, Edward had decided that linen wasn't his 'thing' after all. The entire, largely unworn wardrobe found itself on the pavement, awaiting collection by the ever-efficient Hapsie Town Council. The even more efficient Ellie Ment, however, had other ideas. Natural linen, she realised, provided the perfect solution to a bug-free life.

But she left the underpants for the Town Council.

After giving the expensive linen clothes a full wash without detergent, Ellie cut them into circles, ready to place over her open jam jars and secure with string. The fine weave of the organic linen allowed the rainwater – with its dissolved minerals, gases, and other microscopic components – to pass through effectively, while preventing animal mishaps and, importantly, avoiding any future contamination of the water collected in the jars. A practical and scientifically sound choice for Ellie's experiment. Environmentally sound too.

With the October jars safely buried, Ellie set off to retrieve the (hopefully) overflowing September jars.

When she'd buried them on September 1st, she knew if she didn't get her burials completed that night her experiment wouldn't be quantifiably accurate. She needed all jars to be buried at the start of every month and stay there for the whole month of collection, otherwise, "What sort of scientist am I?"

Preparation for the start of a new school year had simply got in the way. Not only was Ellie switching schools, but the school itself was completely new too! A whole new development! Brand new!

It was certainly needed, ever since Head Boy Grant Fry had a wooden beam from the cafeteria roof fall just thirty centimetres in front of his nose. That near death experience for Grant meant the school was grant-ed a revamp. (Sorry, Grant.)

The facts do vary a little depending on who you ask: the official school incident report suggests that Grant had been outside the cafeteria at the time – actually he'd have been at home, probably asleep – as the beam most likely fell sometime between 7.30pm after the cleaners left and 7am the following morning. Grant most probably discovered it on the floor when he arrived early for jazz band practice. But, you know, it had been ten years since then...school kids, rumours, excitement...the near death story was far more interesting.

The school itself had been fundraising for double that amount of time. Building a new school is expensive, and even after both local and national government got involved with funding, it took the sale of a considerable number of cakes, bakes, cookies and jam-swirls to fund a new science block, let alone the rest of the school. I'm not sure how anyone in Hapsie ate that much cake, but somehow the teachers got the school approved. They insisted it was built with brand new, state-of-the-art materials to make sure it was fit for future environmental challenges. It may have taken years to fund the development, but over the summer holidays the school had been knocked down and rebuilt in record time. Brilliant!

But the most impressive thing about Hapsie School was the teachers. Well-regarded as some of the brightest minds around, the teachers of Hapsie School were leaps and bounds above any neighbouring school, or in the whole county for that matter. Ellie felt very lucky to be in the catchment area.

Having trudged through the miserably wet forest, Ellie stood on the edge of the equally drenched road and a large pothole shaped like a Stegosaurus. The Hapsians called it the 'stego-hole'. *Stego-hole?* Stego-bowl more like, as it was filed to the brim with rainwater and…plastic. Food-containers, yoghurt pots, packaging…

*Oh, Lucas!* Ellie thought.

From Stego-hole Ellie had buried the ten jam jars along the side of the road, each fifty paces apart. If she had pulled out her notes, they would have been very repetitive:

#1: Opposite side of the road to Stego-hole

#2: 50 paces towards school along the road

#3: 50 more paces

#4: 50 more paces

#5: 50 more paces

…and so on.

As Ellie walked away having collected the seventh jar, having labelled it like the others with an indelible pen, "September", taken off the linen cover, placed it into a plastic bag for safekeeping, and finally screwed tight the proper metal lid for the jam jar…she was three hundred paces away from Stego-hole, three hundred paces closer to the school, three hundred paces around the bend of the bumpy lane.

The light was different. For some reason she could see a

little more easily. She looked up, to see her brand new school.

Her brand new school, which was now ablaze.

For some reason Ellie's first reaction was to adjust her headtorch. It didn't help in any way. Her torch was too small to have any effect against the light from the flames, even if it wasn't half broken.

There was absolutely nothing Ellie could do. She didn't have a phone (her parents said she had to be fifteen to have a phone – erugh!). She was a good forty-five minutes' walk from home, and shouting out at 2am wasn't going to attract much attention – at least no more attention than an entire school on fire.

So Ellie just stood there, watching.

Watching as her classrooms collapsed in front of her. Watching her dreams of science experiments, records, adventure turn to smoke and fizz up into the rain. Watching the roaring purple flames rip through the ceilings of the new cafeteria.

Wait…*Purple* flames? That's weird, right?

She felt cold now; her rain jacket had given up at least twenty minutes ago, but it hadn't mattered. And then—

"You, there!" grunted a voice.

"Huh?" is all that Ellie could muster as she swung around to see…Master Quinn, the art professor.

Neither of them said anything. As Master Quinn stood watching the school burning down with Ellie, she could see the colour fading from his face. I guess the knowledge that your prized artworks are burning down too will do that. Aside from the roar in the distance the only sound between the two was the chomp from Master Quinn as he munched through a bag of nuts.

Ellie wasn't sure if under her raincoat and drenched to the bone, Master Quinn had recognised her. Given her particularly pathetic performance in art over the first weeks of the term, it was probably better if he hadn't.

"Go home, Ellie," came Quinn.

Oh. So he *had* recognised her.

"Can you call the fire brigade? I don't have a phone," Ellie admitted.

"Nope." And then after a short, confused moment, Master Quinn added, "Me neither."

"How could this have happened?" Ellie wondered aloud.

"It's almost Halloween. Blasted tricksters! It's whizzle-whumping kids."

With that, Master Quinn limped off into the distance, chucking the rest of the bag of nuts down his throat as he left. "Go home, Ellie!" he shouted. "I'll make sure this is taken care of."

Everything in our world has an explanation for how it happens. Yet not everything can always be explained right here, right now.

When the explanation provided made Ellie's face screw up so tight her nose might pop off, well, that was not okay.

"It's not nearly Halloween at all!" she called back. Halloween was almost a month away.

Why wasn't Master Quinn more panicked?

As Ellie remained frozen to the spot, embers still soaring into the sky, her eyes began to adjust to see the silhouettes of other adults walking around the perimeter of the school.

*Who are they?*

*Why aren't they alerting the fire-brigade?*

And:

*What on earth is a 'whizzle-whumping' kid?*

*There was no way kids could have done something this big.*

Ellie always trusted her numbers and Master Quinn's explanation just didn't add up. The thing about explanations, they may exist, but that doesn't mean they are always correct.

Ellie could tell this one certainly wasn't.

Could Master Quinn be responsible for the school burning down? Was he working with these mysterious other adults? Was that the explanation? How would an eleven-year-old, self-proclaimed scientist find out the answer?

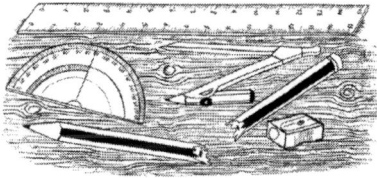

## The Tithe Barn

Ellie sat at her desk, repetitively tapping her foot, and looked down at her current 'work of art' staring back at her. "Hmphh," she mumbled to herself.

*Hmphh* indeed. Her vision of drawing a scientist in a long white lab coat peering into a microscope looked, well, nothing like a scientist in a long white lab coat peering into a microscope. The arms of the scientist looked like the wings of a bird, the rest of the scientist looked like a blob of uneven jelly, and the microscope..? Ahem, to save Ellie's embarrassment it's best we move on. Suffice to say, Ellie could not draw for toffee.

Ellie Ment was, is, and undoubtedly always will be, very smart.

Of course, being 'smart' is very hard to define. It comes in many different forms: the way the school's football team could manoeuvre the ball from their goalkeeper into the top corner of the opponent's net with such ease, or how the school orchestra could flawlessly win the County Festival, means everyone involved must be incredibly smart. But for Ellie, being smart meant that for her last seven years at school – and let's not forget the forty-eight months before that when she was just a toddler – she always had a way with numbers.

$7 + (48/12 \text{ months}) = 11 \text{ years}$.

Ellie could do that sum swinging upside down on the monkey bars in Leafy Park, without pausing for a moment of thought.

Her friend Michael, however, could not do these sums with such ease. No judgement on Michael. Not many people can.

Michael Upperton, who was sitting directly in front of Ellie, sketching away with his black curls drooped over the paper, wasn't like Ellie. Michael was very smart, but in a different way. Michael could create anything he wanted, whenever he wanted, but struggled terribly with sums, long division, or even the most basic scientific question.

'Ellie Ment smart' was Maths and Science, which was neither more nor less important than 'Michael Upperton smart', 'Football Team smart' or 'Orchestra smart'.

It will be smart of you to remember this.

Ellie, Michael, and the rest of Falcon Class sat in the old, creaking barn at the back of the school grounds, one hour into an art exam, and quite clearly it wasn't going well for Ellie. Ellie needed this to go well. She always needed her exams to go well. Not content with being just 'Ellie Ment smart' she wanted to be every other kind of smart too.

Suddenly Ellie's pencil broke.

The protractor, calculator, ruler, compass, and copy of the Periodic Table which Ellie had (for reasons known only to Ellie) also brought into this art exam could not help her here. For this exam she only needed a working pencil, and now that was split in two. She'd gripped it too hard out of pure frustration.

*Gah! Why didn't I bring a spare?!* Ellie scolded herself.

Lack of preparation was very unlike Ellie.

"Michael…" Ellie whispered, with no reply. "Michael…"

"QUIET IN THE BARN," yelled Master Quinn from the front of the barn over his cup of boiling tea. "You have twenty minutes to go."

Ellie studied Master Quinn. He was certainly looking better than when she had met him three weeks ago when they watched the school burn down together. His face was full of colour now, the exhaustion in his eyes no longer there. "But why were you even there?" Ellie muttered quietly to herself, still staring. They hadn't properly communicated since that night; if anything Ellie felt her art teacher was deliberately avoiding her – something she was quite okay with given how this exam was going...

Ellie felt the heat under her shirt-collar rise and her forehead became a little damper than it already was. You see, for all her smartness, Ellie hated exams. It didn't matter how many sums she could do at home, or remember science-facts from a book, or that she knew the periodic table back to front and upside down, for some reason the pressure of testing made Ellie's mind go blank. Always. She took a swig of her homemade lemonade from her drink bottle.

"Why do grown-ups always sit us down to test us?" Ellie would often explain to anyone and everyone that would listen. "Put us in real-world scenarios, then see how we perform!" she would continue, despite 'anyone and everyone' having now walked away or given her a funny look and put on their headphones.

But alas, this was where she was, this was how she was being tested, and Ellie had no working pencil.

*It's the light*, Ellie made excuses for herself. *I can't draw in this light*, she thought.

It's true, the light wasn't perfect. Since the school had burned down all lessons had to be conducted in the Tithe Barn.

The return to school after the fire had been relatively smooth, considering there was no school to return to. Parents can really offer a helping hand when they want their ~~blasted~~

blessed kids out of the house. About one hundred metres away from Hapsie School, where the grounds met the forest, stood the Tithe Barn.

Long after the Romans and the Saxons arrived in Hapsie, the Normans came along. They introduced the feudal system – much to the confusion of the local Hapsians. It was simple, really. Remember all the land and buildings you owned before the Normans arrived? You didn't own them anymore. Now they belonged to the king. Out of the kindness of his heart, the king would let you farm the land (yes, the same land you used to own). But not for free. In exchange for this 'honour' you'd pay a tithe (i.e. tax) – 10% of your crops or wool – to the lords or the church. Hence, the Tithe Barn had to be huge. So the king could fit in all the stuff he'd taken from you.

The Tithe Barn at Hapsie School looked like something out of a fairytale (sorry, Ellie. I know you don't care for fairytales): a massive stone building with a steep, weathered roof, its ancient wooden doors made for giants. Inside, enormous wooden beams arched overhead, making it feel like a cathedral.

In total, there were twelve large rusting iron rings that hung across the beams, installed about fifty years ago. Evenly fitted around each ring were eight light bulbs, the old-fashioned kind, their glass slightly yellowed with age and their delicate filaments glowing brightly within. These bulbs gave off a faint hum and a soft, warm light that felt more nostalgic than bright. Touch one and you'd instantly regret it – their metal bases and thin glass could heat up to a scorching temperature in seconds, radiating heat that seemed to cling to the barn. This is the only reason why they were kept: they helped get heat into the barn.

You could almost picture farmers and monks from hundreds of years ago, busy stacking sacks of grain and hay for their king. It was grand, quiet and full of history – and now it was where all the pupils and staff of Hapsie School would be conducting their lessons (and exams) on rotation until the new school was rebuilt. The only addition being a set of portable loos dumped to the side of the barn.

*Fresh air!* Ellie thought. That would help. Her hand zoomed up.

Master Quinn peered over the book he was now engrossed in. In class, he would always ignore Ellie's hand as he knew it would always have the right answer. Sure, Ellie couldn't draw, but she certainly had read the book on how to draw. One could argue on Master Quinn's behalf (although why anyone would want to do that I do not know) that he simply wanted to give Ellie's other classmates a chance to answer, but deep down even those arguing for him knew he simply wanted to continue reading without distraction.

Quinn didn't speak, he just raised his thick black eyebrows at Ellie.

"Toilet," Ellie mouthed back silently but urgently.

Quinn rolled his eyes. Toilet breaks weren't usually permitted during exams in case pupils were cheating. But he figured Ellie would fail this art test whether she cheated or not. So he flicked his head in the direction of the barn doors.

This was all the permission Ellie needed and she rushed out.

Ellie stood, on the cold early winter day, looking back at the outside of the old barn.

The tall tales of Grant Fry and his acrobatics to avoid the endless beams that fell from the ceiling of the cafeteria were now forgotten. They'd been replaced by legendary anecdotes of 'The Great Fire of Hapsie School' and stories of various students who just happened to be inside the school in the early hours of that morning, dodging flames and debris. The truth of course was that Ellie was the only student who had seen the school burn to the ground. Ellie, Master Victor Quinn and several other figures Ellie saw that night.

"Did Master Quinn start the fire?" Ellie found herself wondering out loud again, before quickly realising this was neither the time nor the place for such thoughts.

Ellie tried to calm her nerves from the exam. *It's only drawing,* she told herself. Then quickly, *Oh dear, Michael would tell me off for saying that.* Three long deep breaths always helped Ellie, whenever it all became too much.

Breath one: Ellie noticed the trees around her. Trees always looked solemn in the winter without their leaves, but these were different. Row upon row surrounding the school and stretching into the forest, they seemed lifeless, their bark a dull, ashen grey as though scarred by the fire. Cracks webbed across their trunks and their branches drooped unnaturally, bending under an invisible weight.

Breath two: Ellie caught in the corner of her eye a colourful flicker of purple light puff out from a heap of leaves to her left.

*Purple?* Surely not again. Turning her head…

Breath three: Ellie looked closer. The embers of the school fire must have been smouldering under the leaves. A pile of singed timber and wreckage had been dumped here from the construction team tasked with rebuilding the school.

Then it clicked…

"Carbon!" Ellie blurted out. Excitedly narrating to herself was a common theme for Ellie, sort of like someone who always sticks out their tongue when concentrating.

She grabbed a large stick from the ground and began prodding around inside the embers. "The charcoal made from the fire is made out of Carbon, which was traditionally used for art and drawings, so it can replace my pencil."

(Thank you, Ellie. That was a very helpful

28

explanation for us all here back at home.)

Grabbing a small rock, Ellie knelt down and hacked away at the edge of one of the timbers until a small chunk flew off onto her lap.

"Perfect!"

And with that Ellie rushed back inside the barn.

Most of the time you don't return from the bathroom with your hands dirtier than when you left, but charcoal was good at marking things. Paper, yes, but also hands. Keeping her hands close to her side, gripping the small piece of charcoal, she headed back to her desk trying not to reveal her blackened palms.

She didn't need to have been so subtle. Master Quinn barely noted her return, his eyes immediately falling back down to the book he was reading.

"Five minutes," he said. It was a lie; the exam would end whenever he finished his next chapter.

Ellie sat back down at her desk and began to draw.

Five stars for the charcoal for making a mark on the paper, but only one star for being able to draw any detail.

Yikes, this was not going well.

Suddenly, "Ellie, Ellie!" hissed from the desk in front. Ellie looked up from her continued disaster. It was Michael.

"Give it here."

Ellie tossed the charcoal piece to Michael.

Out of his pocket Michael pulled an old postcard and rolled it into a long tube. Using some gum that was stuck to under the desk, he glued the tube together and then wedged another bit of gum up one end.

*That. Is. Gross,* thought Ellie as she watched Michael's ingenuity unfold, taking another drink of lemonade from her now half empty drink bottle.

Michael tried stuffing the charcoal piece into the other end of the postcard tube, but it wouldn't fit. Without pause he bit into it, cracked a small piece off and rammed that into the end of the tube.

"There. Makeshift pencil. With rubber!" he whispered as he passed it back to Ellie.

"*THANKS!*" mouthed Ellie.

*This. Is. Brilliant,* she thought. Things can be brilliant and gross at the same time, it turns out. She had two minutes left to finish her art.

Eventually, "Pencils down!" came the cry, as Master Quinn closed his book with a snap. "You can leave after I collect your paper."

The barn had been set up six desks wide and eight desks deep, meaning forty-eight desks were neatly organised inside the barn for this exam. The desks only filled about one third of the space at best, and some dividers had been placed at the back row so other classes could fit in if needed. All the desks were full of relieved Falcon class students whose hands hurt from all the drawing they'd just undertaken.

If someone cared very little for order or direction, there was almost an infinite number of ways you could choose to walk from desk to desk to pick up the completed art works. I mention this because that also means there was almost an infinite number of ways Ellie's desk *wouldn't* be the last one her art teacher got to. But you've guessed it, Ellie's desk was exactly where Master Quinn finished.

Quinn towered over Ellie and peered down over his spectacles onto Ellie's art.

"What on earth is that?" Quinn thundered.

Ellie didn't really have an answer. There was what it was meant to be, then there was what it was. The two things were very different.

Michael stood up from his desk and came over to look at Ellie's finished exam piece too. Michael was a lovely boy, someone always full of optimism, exactly the type of best friend anyone would want. He'd also be willing to chip in with a great comeback to get you out of any sticky situation. But on this occasion his mouth hung open, his eyebrows rose, and the best he could muster was, "Errr..."

Quinn, Michael, and Ellie looked down at the newly completed *artwork*. (The italics are sarcastic.) If it had a title it would be something like: Total Black Smudge and Utter Mess.

Ellie proceeded to mutter a range of different apologies as she gathered up her belongings, frantically stuffing her protractor, ruler, calculator and compass back into her pencil case, grabbing her drink bottle...

...missing her drink bottle...

...and spilling the remainder of the lemonade all over Total Black Smudge and Utter Mess.

The addition of lemonade hardly ruined the artwork, it may have even added to it, but what happened next was surprising for all: the paper began to fizz!

Small bubbles rose from the soaked charcoal lines, creating tiny craters in the smudged blackness of the paper. A soft crackling sound broke the silence, like the faint hiss of a just opened fizzy drink can. Ellie, Michael and Master Quinn leaned in, Michael's eyes wide, as if the drawing itself had suddenly come to life.

"Is that...er...normal?" he asked, his voice teetering between curiosity and alarm.

Quinn immediately stepped in. "No, it is not."

He bent closer, watching as the faint bubbling subsided and left behind a patch of lighter, almost crusty residue where the water had pooled.

"It's reacting to the lemonade," Ellie murmured, reaching

out to touch the edge of the paper.

"Does charcoal normally react with lemonade?" Michael asked.

Ellie shook her head. "No, it does not."

Quinn said nothing but just stared.

"I-uh," Ellie started, a dozen explanations firing in her brain like chemical reactions.

Michael grinned. "Trust you to be doing a science experiment instead of your art exam."

This broke the spell, and as Master Quinn went to fire back, he looked up at Michael, then stopped.

"What is wrong with your face?"

You might think this statement was a little cruel, even for Quinn, unless of course you were actually looking at Michael's face at that moment.

Michael's impromptu support for Ellie and her makeshift charcoal pencil had, like Ellie, left his hands blackened. But unlike Ellie, the smudges stretched all the way up his bright red t-shirt – decorated with the local football team's HAPSIE logo – with the marks settling predominantly on his face. If he'd claimed to have spent a few hours down a local coal mine, it would have been a very fitting explanation for his appearance.

Caught up in the angst of the failed artwork Ellie hadn't fully appreciated Michael's new look. Michael had no idea either, until he picked up Ellie's metallic drink bottle from the desk and stared into it, revealing a new thick black charcoal beard.

If you thought fizzing and crackling paper, and an eleven-year-old with a charcoal beard were going to be the most surprising events of the day, then what happened next will likely leave you flabbergasted.

"Stay right there, Upperton" instructed Quinn.

It's always best to stay right where you are if Master Quinn instructs you to stay right there.

Michael looked up to face Master Quinn. Master Quinn slowly took a few steps to be next to Michael.

He knelt.

He brought out a perfectly folded clean handkerchief and began to gently wipe the charcoal off Michael's face.

"Errr…" said Michael.

This continued in absolute silence, aside from the odd "Umm" and other incoherent stammerings, until Quinn reached into his side pocket, pulled out a small bottle of talcum powder, dusted it onto Michael face, and then continued to use the handkerchief to wipe the remainder of the charcoal.

"Crikey!" Michael exclaimed under his breath.

Crikey indeed.

Master Quinn was renowned for his sharp lines, his thundered instructions, and his distinct disinterest in the students. This calm and caring demeanour he was showing was as foreign to Michael and Ellie as a suntan in December.

Quinn stepped back, inspecting Michael's now pristine face as if he were evaluating a restored work of art. "There," he said gruffly, folding the handkerchief with military precision and returning it to his pocket. "You look marginally less ridiculous now."

Michael blinked, his usual quick wit failing him. "Thanks…I think?"

With that, Quinn turned and left the Tithe Barn, strangely, at least for Ellie, now limp-free, a dramatic recovery from only a few weeks ago when she met Master Quinn in the forests. That's a bit odd, right?

Silence lingered in the barn. It would be almost pointless trying to tell this to the rest of the school. Who on earth would believe them?

So stunned was Michael that he totally forgot about the other strange event that had happened just a few moments

33

earlier: Ellie's artwork, bubbling, fizzing and lightly crackling away at the third desk across in the second row. Ellie quickly rolled it up and stuffed it deep into the bottom of her backpack.

# Chapter Two

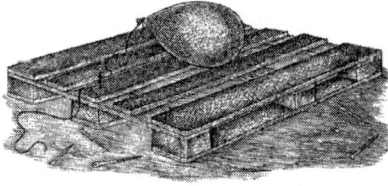

# The Moment That Sparked It All

It was Ellie who broke the spell, her voice barely a whisper. "Well, that was…unexpected."

"Unexpected?" Michael whispered back, despite them being alone in the Tithe Barn. "I thought he was going to summon lightning, not…parent me."

Either way, crazy fizzing paper and concerning teacher behaviour, at least there were no more tests for the day! Ellie approached the barn door, happy to be leaving.

"Ellie? Ellie Ment?" came a voice from behind.

*Oh, what now?*

Ellie turned.

"Oh!" Ellie exclaimed with a smile growing across her face.

It was Professor Lucinda Fialova – the school's head of science – but, more importantly to Ellie, the kindest, most brilliant, most inspiring person she had ever known. The most modest too…With her sandy brown, shoulder-length hair, lilac glasses perched neatly on her nose, and her ever-present black blazer, Professor Fialova looked every bit as warm and approachable as her gentle personality.

This was an interruption worth having. But it came somewhat more sternly than Ellie was used to from the kindly professor.

"Ellie, come with me," Fialova snapped.

"Oh, right, of course," Ellie spluttered as she looked towards Michael with pretend disappointment that they wouldn't be walking home together, but secretly bubbling with excitement that Professor Lucinda Fialova had singled her out.

"Hello, Professor. How are you, Professor? Gosh, you look jolly nice in that outfit, Professor." Ellie was fangirling. It wasn't pretty.

Ellie waved Michael a quick goodbye as Professor Fialova led Ellie Ment to the end of the rows of desks and behind one of the dividers to an empty part of the Tithe Barn.

"I saw what just unfolded," Professor Fialova started, ignoring the flattery.

"Yes, it was the weirdest thing, I've no idea what happened."

Professor Fialova stopped. "Don't you? Huh, shame. Now get on a box."

In the corner of the barn were two apple crates laid next to each other, a gap of about two metres between them.

"Get…on a box?" Ellie repeated.

"Yes. Pick a box and stand on it."

The boxes were identical, so Ellie picked the one that looked slightly less broken than the other, and stood on it. Ellie looked up from the box and saw… well, what was it? A large dirty off-white sheet was draped over…um, something…in the middle of the barn. The sheet was being held up by four large posts; what was under it was anyone's guess…

"Kami!" called Fialova.

Like an actress making an entrance onto the stage, a girl about Ellie's age, with blond hair and blue eyes, came around the divider.

"Take the other box please, Kami."

"Of course, Lucinda."

*Lucinda?!* The girl was on first name terms with Professor Fialova? "Professor, who's this?" Ellie asked as sweetly as she could.

"This is Kami." Professor Fialova was clearly not willing to provide much more. "I've said her name twice already."

"Sure. Of course…Er…does she go to our school?"

"No."

"Er…is she your daughter?" Ellie said, clutching at straws. This was at least an acceptable explanation for Ellie as to why Kami was on first name terms with her favourite teacher, and Ellie wasn't.

Professor Lucinda Fialova looked up at Ellie, gave a caring smile, and then just as quickly responded, "No. Now, pop quiz time!"

Ellie's face, which had already fallen slightly with the introduction of Kami and her familiarity with Professor Fialova, fell further. As we've discussed, it didn't matter how much science Ellie actually knew, in sit-down written tests and quizzes, Ellie's mind would go blank…An exam and then a pop quiz, this wasn't the best of Thursdays for Ellie.

"Is this a trial for the science club, Professor?" asked Ellie.

Professor Fialova thought about it for a second. She glanced briefly at Kami, and then, as curt as she'd been throughout this entire after-school encounter, she replied, "Sure." And added a shrug for good measure.

To an outsider Professor Fialova probably wasn't very convincing, but for someone like Ellie who was trying to make sense of the situation it was at least something to grasp on to. *Okay,* thought Ellie. *Science club – let's go!*

"You have thirty seconds to examine…this!"

Professor Fialova whipped the sheet from off the wooden posts to reveal the mystery that lay beneath.

Two balloons.

Reasonably anti-climactic compared to the large sheet-post contraption Professor Fialova had built to hide them.

A big red shiny balloon on a string floating just under the top of the posts, and a blue balloon, also on a string but lying firmly on the ground.

The balloons were perfectly lit by one of the ancient iron ring light bulbs hanging from the ceiling directly above.

Ellie and Kami stepped off their apple crates and quickly circled the balloons.

There was no question the red balloon was floating, but what about the blue balloon? Was it simply resting on the ground, or something more?

"Can we touch them?" asked Ellie.

"Very lightly. You have eighteen seconds."

Eighteen seconds to what? Throw a party? Float out of here? Pop them? Ellie didn't think so, but she didn't dare ask.

She walked up to the blue balloon and flicked it. It didn't move and gave out a low *pong* in return which echoed across the barn. With this, she caught Kami's change of expression, a raised eyebrow, and noted something.

Kami, who was a good few centimetres taller than Ellie, walked up to the large red floating balloon and did the same. As Kami flicked it, the balloon bounced lightly away, giving a high-pitched *ping* in return.

Ellie tilted her head to one side, moving closer…

"Back to your boxes," said Professor Fialova, exactly eighteen seconds from when she last spoke.

Kami and Ellie trotted back and turned to face their teacher.

"First question. These balloons are made from latex. What are the main elements that make up this material?"

*Okay. Easy,* Ellie thought. *Natural latex is grown from rubber trees. Rubber is mainly hydrocarbons, so the elements are Hydrogen and Carbon…but wait…Professor Fialova didn't say natural latex, what if it's processed…*

"Hydrocarbons," immediately came from Kami, looking at Ellie as she said it. "Hydrogen and Carbon."

"I knew that!" Ellie blurted out.

"You have to say the answer out loud," smiled Kami, with a little too much smile for Ellie's liking.

Ellie was flustered, which wasn't helpful when you were starting off from a position of already-anxious.

"Next question. Why does the red balloon look red?"

A question about light and colours was not something Ellie would normally struggle with, or even think twice about, but her mind had gone blank.

"Focus. Focus, Ellie," she whispered to herself.

She took a deep breath and focussed her eyes and mind on the large, red shiny balloon. Absorbing its size, its tightness, it's…*wait, absorbing, it's—*

Too late.

"Light contains a spectrum of colours, like a rainbow. All these colours together appear to us as white or yellow. The reason the red balloon is red is because it reflects red light and absorbs all the other colours, meaning our eyes only see red." Kami's answer sounded like poetry. She batted her eyelids as she looked at Ellie. "Likewise, the blue balloon only reflects the blue light and absorbs the rest, meaning we see it as blue."

Ellie didn't need to hear Professor Fialova gently congratulate Kami on another question answered correctly; she already knew it was right. Ellie was a scientist. An eleven-year-old, self-proclaimed scientist, but that didn't matter. Ellie loved science, knew science, and yet there Ellie was, not getting a single science question right.

"Okay. Question three," Ellie heard Professor Fialova

say in the distance. "The red balloon is floating. What's it filled…"

Kami shot in. "Helium, Lucinda. The red balloon is filled with Helium. Helium is lighter than air, so it floats." Kami beamed like an angel. "That's right, isn't it? Lucinda?"

Ellie slumped down on the apple crate, not willing to catch the eyes of Kami which she guessed would be looking directly at her.

"Ellie, don't worry," she heard Professor Fialova begin as she walked towards her. "There's really no pressure here to…"

The words of Professor Fialova faded away in Ellie's mind. Ellie was suddenly laser focussed: why now? Why was her mind racing? Something wasn't right!

As Professor Fialova moved towards Ellie, her jacket pocket caught against a nail sticking out of one of the four wooden posts. Her momentum sent it crashing to the ground, dislodging the fixture that held the red balloon in place. The Helium-filled red balloon shot up towards the roof at a great pace.

It all happened in a flash.

"NO!" shouted Ellie within moments of noticing the balloon go.

With a burst of energy, she scrambled off the apple crate towards the balloon, sending two more wooden posts clattering to the ground in her wake. Arms outstretched, she launched herself towards the balloon's trailing string, her heart racing as fast as her feet.

The tips of Ellie's fingers wrapped around the end of the string and stopped it dead in its place.

Ellie stood there, arm up, holding the red balloon. This time she knew for sure both Kami and Professor Fialova would be looking at her.

"That's a bit excessive," snorted Kami. "We could always use a ladder to get the balloon down later. Actually latex has tiny holes, so small you can't see, which means the Helium can slowly seep out, so if we'd left the balloon on the ceiling it would probably have deflated by tomorrow—"

"NO!" Ellie shouted again.

This 'No' came as much as a surprise to the others as the first and it certainly served its purpose of quieting Kami.

"Something isn't right," said Ellie, this time calmer and more thoughtful.

"Go on…" prompted Professor Fialova.

Kami was about to interject but Professor Fialova held up a hand to stop her.

"This red balloon…"

A pause.

"…This red balloon is bigger, more stretched, and shinier than the blue balloon…"

Another pause, slightly longer this time.

Ellie found her flow. "And when Kami flicked it, the sound – the ping – was high-pitched…and the speed, the way it rose…it went up so fast…"

Ellie began to smile as she became more and more certain of herself as she spoke.

"It means the molecules inside are small, very small…smaller than Helium. That's why it rose so quickly. And they're smaller than Helium, which is why the balloon is stretched out more, and the ping was higher-pitched." Ellie took a deep breath as she reached her conclusion. "It's not Helium in here, it's…"

(A quick side note before I let Ellie reach her conclusion. Earlier in the story, I reassured you that you didn't need to be an expert in the periodic table, and I stand by that – don't worry! But one thing that would be useful to know at this time is that the periodic table is a very handy chart listing all the elements we know about in the universe – 118 in total! Most are found in nature (like Gold, Oxygen, and Carbon) while some can only be created in science labs (like Plutonium, Technetium, and Oganesson). The beauty of the periodic table is how it organises all the elements by their atomic number. Helium, for example, is the second element in the table which means there's only one element lighter and smaller than Helium, it's—)

"IT'S HYDROGEN!" shouted Ellie, totally interrupting my flow. But fair enough, this is her story after all.

Professor Fialova smiled at Ellie and began to walk towards her. "And why would that make you cause such a commotion, Ellie? What's so special about Hydrogen?"

"Hydrogen is very explosive," Ellie responded, trying to control her breathing.

The professor broke her gaze with Ellie and turned to Kami. "Is that right, Kami?"

Not so surprisingly, Kami's appetite for long-winded explanations had suddenly vanished. She just nodded.

"Let's see, shall we, Ellie?" Professor Fialova said, redirecting her gaze back towards the girl who was fixed in position with one arm outstretched holding the red balloon.

"May I?" Professor Fialova whispered as she took hold of the string from Ellie. Then, looking up, she said, "It was a good catch. It was only centimetres away."

Ellie and Kami's eyes moved to the red balloon, now hovering just below one of the barn's large iron rings, its eight bulbs burning hot and casting light across the barn.

"Back to your apple crate, Ellie," Professor Fialova said.

Ellie reached her crate and turned. With that, Professor Fialova let go of the red balloon and covered her eyes with her other hand. The balloon instantly rose into the iron ring, brushing into one of the bulbs.

Bang.

(No, sorry…)

BANG!

A blinding flash of light erupted, sharp and searing, as if a fragment of the sun had been released into the room. The Hydrogen within the balloon ignited in an instant. A thunderous crack followed – a sound that seemed to detonate inside every bone, rattling the air with its force.

In that split second, the explosion unleashed a brilliant sphere of yellow-white fire, edges tinged with blue as the Hydrogen gas burned itself out. The heat surged outward like an invisible wave, rippling through the barn.

Shards of red latex and glass rained down onto Professor Fialova. And just as quick as it had started – silence. Kami, Ellie and the shielding Professor Fialova watched the last pieces fall to the floor.

Professor Fialova looked back up at the light fitting, which now only had three of its eight bulbs remaining.

"Hmm…" she reflected. "It's fair to say that was a bigger reaction than I was expecting." Then, turning to Ellie, "I think that's a point for you, Ellie. I also think we better end there for the day, it looks like I've got some cleaning up to do." She cringed.

"Kami, go wait in the car, I'll take you to your house once I'm done here," said Professor Fialova.

Kami did as she was told, but not before throwing Ellie a look that could turn Iodine crystals into vapour.

"Can I help clean up?" asked Ellie.

"No, thank you. No need for a student to be in hospital from cutting themselves. I think I've done enough damage for today."

Ellie was disappointed.

"But do you know the old post office in town?"

"Of course! If you buy the stamps from the post office when you send a letter, Mrs Totterwell lets you pick a printed message where the stamp goes!" Ellie chirped back.

"She's fun like that, isn't she?" Professor Fialova smiled. She looked like her old self again. Like the person Ellie knew her to be about twenty minutes before she walked into the Tithe Barn today. "On Saturday morning, come to the post office and ask Mrs Totterwell if you can see me. We'll need an hour or so."

*AB. SO. LUTELY,* Ellie screamed to herself internally.

"OK. Sure. Saturday morning. Got it," Ellie managed to respond calmly instead. Cool as liquid Nitrogen.

*This is GREAT! A private tutoring session with Professor Fialova?! Maybe she'll provide me with my science club membership card. Or…But wait…*Ellie caught herself from getting carried away.

"But Professor, I lost. I failed the test. Kami won. I mean, I knew the answers, but I didn't—"

Professor Fialova interrupted her. "Ellie, there's understanding science, and there's knowing science. And to know science you need to understand science, so if you're good at the latter, well…"

She left it at that. 'See you on Saturday.'

When she turned to leave, Ellie allowed herself a squeal of delight and a ridiculous happy dance.

*Yay! Science!*

Let's turn away from this undignified display and move on to the next chapter, shall we?

# Chapter Three

# The Elemental Bracers

The big problem about being excited for plans happening on a Saturday when it's a Thursday, is that a Friday neatly slots itself in between those two days. And as Ellie skipped home from the Tithe Barn that Thursday afternoon, Saturday suddenly seemed a very long way away.

Did Ellie have niggling, unanswered questions about who on earth Kami was, why she was so friendly with Professor Fialova, and why *she* got a ride home when Ellie didn't? Sure. Actually that last bit was doubly annoying, given it was raining again. But even the rain wasn't going to dampen Ellie's excitement about one-to-one tutoring with her favourite professor.

*Lessons! On a weekend! What could be better?!*

All evening, Ellie's mind raced with ideas about what she should ask Professor Fialova during their session. All night, she thought about which notebooks and experiment logs she should bring along to show off. In the morning, while brushing her teeth, she debated whether she should assign herself homework on balloons, gases and colours (of course this would also need a presentation). And as she opened her front door to begin her walk to school she—

"Oh, Michael!" Ellie yelped as she stepped from her front door.

Michael was standing right outside it.

If Ellie's mind hadn't been so consumed with Saturday, it wouldn't have been a surprise to see Michael standing there on a Friday. Every Friday morning since they were nine, Michael would take the ten-minute detour to Ellie's house and they would walk to school together.

It was the perfect opportunity for Michael to show off his latest upcycled invention. You see, when Michael wasn't fixing broken pencils during exams, he could usually be found at the local tip, scavenging through the town's recyclables, searching for interesting bits and bobs to turn into even more interesting bobs and bits. "If there's life left in it, people shouldn't bin it!" Michael would cheerfully remind Terry Tip, which is what they called the man named Terry who ran the local rubbish tip. Michael didn't actually know Terry's real last name, and nor do I, so Terry Tip will have to do for now.

Michael's antics were so well-known around school that he'd earned himself his own nickname: Upcycle Michael.

At home, however, Michael was more often summoned from his bedroom with cries of, "Where did you put my scissors?" or "Do NOT put holes in our garden hose to make an impromptu sprinkler! Again!" For while Michael generally found his inspiration in items that had long been discarded, there were plenty of times when the mere fact that someone wasn't using an item at that exact moment was reason enough for him to start prodding and poking it into something new.

This Friday was no different, and Michael stood proudly outside Ellie's door holding something behind his back.

"Oh, Michael! You're here?!" Ellie continued, surprised.

Michael returned the surprise. "Of course I am, you muppet. It's a Friday!" And then without missing a beat, "Look!"

From behind Michael's back came a contraption of some form. That was the thing about Michael's upcycles, their purpose wasn't always obvious at first glance – they were always more of a 'show not tell' type of invention.

"I'll show you, you'll love it!"

As they began to walk to school, Michael decided to both show *and* tell.

"See here, I've used this old fishing rod for a long handle and at the end I've found this amazingly cool old dustbin lid I'm using as a wheel. If I hold the handle at the top, and place the dustbin lid on the ground, it turns as I walk."

"Uh-huh…"

Michael waited but nothing more came from Ellie. So he continued, "Right, well, anyway. As we walk and I push, the dustbin lid turns, and well, you see these twelve plastic cups attached to the outside of the dustbin lid? They make it look a bit like a clock face, don't they? Well, as they turn, they pass by this piece of charcoal I've tied to the fishing rod – I got that idea from you yesterday, thanks for that – the charcoal puts a mark on each plastic cup. Each cup is ten centimetres apart from the next. Oh and because I attached the wheel to the rod with this old screw, every time you walk the wheel moves a little to the left, so it creates a new mark on the cup for every turn. Then, when you've stopped walking, you count the marks on all the plastic cups, multiply by ten, and you can see how far you've walked!" Michael decided it was a good time to draw breath.

He also decided it would be the perfect time to look up to see Ellie's face in absolute awe of his invention.

Ellie's face was pointed firmly forward. She wasn't even looking. No awe. No nothing.

"Maybe you need to see it in action…" Michael persevered, but somewhat less enthusiastically now.

He placed the dustbin lid on the ground about half a metre in front of him and held the fishing old rod with two hands. He began to walk. Sure enough, as he walked, the dustbin began to turn, the plastic cups rotated, the charcoal marked them, over and over again.

Admittedly, it was very clever.

"Anyway, I thought this could help you with one of your science experiments one day," Michael began to say. "I mean, if you need to measure anything, ever."

No reaction.

That was just rude.

"Professor Fialova has asked me to go see her on Saturday. For some private tutoring or something. Isn't that cool?" That was Ellie's reaction. Not what Michael was hoping for.

"I'm sorry? What?"

"I know! She was impressed with what I did or something – even though I don't know how, given Kami answered first – and she wants to see me. What should I ask her?" Ellie continued without noticing Michael's face. If she had, she may have decided it would be better to stop rambling.

"Oh. I guess we're talking about your thing now," said Michael, not bothering to hide his annoyance.

For the rest of the walk they didn't talk about Ellie's thing or Michael's thing, or anything really. Ellie was lost in thought about Saturday, and Michael pushed his upcycled measuring device along, sometimes loudly exclaiming as to how well it was measuring, and how useful this would be for Ellie. Eventually, after getting nothing from his friend, Michael resigned himself to seeing exactly how far it was to school from Stego-hole. (Which, by the way, Lucas Litter had now filled with even more plastic food containers and yoghurt pots – what an absolute littering mess that boy is!) The distance was 184 metres and 20 centimetres, if you're wondering.

Lunchtime was no different. Both Michael and Ellie sat there eating their packed lunches in silence. Even Michael's attempt to draw Ellie from her daydream by fashioning a pencil holder from a used drinks can didn't work.

After school Michael waited to walk home with Ellie but she'd already left. Friday was simply being far too an inconvenient sort of day for her, an annoying barrier between her and Saturday, so Ellie went straight home.

Michael stood around for over an hour before leaving, furious. If he could upcycle Ellie into a better friend, he would.

It's fair to say, Ellie's bedroom wasn't your typical eleven-year-old's room.

We do have a bed, a chair and desk – Ellie must sleep and do her homework somewhere, after all – and, of course, bookshelves, because Ellie loves books. But that's where the similarities with most other children's rooms in Hapsie end.

Instead of books about mermaids, you'll find ones about molecules; the enchanted kraken has been swapped for kinetic energy, and werewolves vanquished in favour of wavelengths.

Forget any dolls or toys; they'd been replaced with remnants of old science experiments which had spilled over from her 'science corner'. Ha – sorry, that made me chuckle. Ellie's science 'corner' was just a pipe dream of her parents. You see, the definition of a corner is a little blurred. If I offer you the chance to bite off the corner of your favourite chocolate bar, there's no real definition as to where that corner ends. As long as you munch the pointy bit where two of the sides meet, then well, technically you're within the rules and can chomp as much as you like, depending on how greedy you are and how much you like chocolate.

Did Ellie's science corner start in the corner of her room? Yes. Did it reach out across the rest of the room, taking up the entirety of the whole room? Also yes.

But that day she had no interest in her science corner.

She was asleep by 7pm – the perfect way to use up the rest of the day. *Why didn't I think of this earlier?* she scolded herself as she moved some jam jars off her bed and tucked herself under the covers.

The problem with going to bed at 7pm, is that you then most likely wake up super early the following morning. Ellie realised this at 6am, but, as she thought to herself while stretching and yawning, *At least it's Saturday!*

The problem with waking up early on a Saturday is that people think they can give you ideas on how to spend your Saturday.

"Ellie!" exclaimed Mr. Ment, AKA Ellie's dad, AKA Phil, as he took a drink of his morning coffee.

"Excellent!" Mrs. Ment called from somewhere upstairs. "You're up!"

This was far too much excitement from them so early in the morning. Why were her parents so happy she was up? This could only mean…

"Road trip!" roared Ellie's dad, heading to the kitchen counter to make sandwiches for all.

Then from upstairs again, but rapidly moving closer, Ellie's mum said, "Your dad and I were only saying last night that we hadn't seen your Aunt Melicia or your cousin Cassie in so long. As you're up so early it makes sense to make the drive! Excellent stuff!"

This, as you'll have duly noted by now, was not the stuff of excellence for Ellie.

She loved her cousin Cassie, and her Aunt Melicia owned an awesome restaurant. But Ellie did not want that today. What could she say in reply? What possible excuse could she come up with? She'd used the (fake) excuse of 'I've got school on Saturday' one too many times to get out of chores/trips/activities with her parents that they were never going to believe a teacher had asked her to their house on a Saturday morning...hmm, tricky.

"Go up to your room and pack an overnight bag," commanded her father as he slapped mayonnaise onto six slices of bread. "Oh what fun!" Ellie could hear him continue as she thoughtfully climbed the stairs.

Ellie did go to her room.

Ellie did begin to pack a bag.

But strangely, and she was sure, quite accidentally, she found that instead of pyjamas, she packed her science notebooks. Her toothbrush was missed in place of her pencil case, and any spare socks overlooked for her safety goggles.

By the end of the packing of her overnight bag, Ellie noticed that – and again, quite by accident – it did in fact look a lot more like the bag she was already planning to pack to see Professor Fialova.

*Hmm*, thought Ellie, *this is quite unfortunate.* She carefully folded her poster of the periodic table into her bag so she could show off her detailed notes to Professor Fialova. *But it would be inefficient to* un*pack everything now.*

And with that, Ellie found her gaze slowly but steadfastly moving towards her bedroom window.

Being naughty was not a characteristic Ellie associated herself with. Pushing the boundaries for scientific excellence? Yes. Sometimes going against the rules to prove her hypothesis? Of course! But outright naughty? That wasn't Ellie Ment. Which therefore was more the surprise to Ellie as she found herself gradually walking towards her bedroom window, slowly sliding up the panel, and completely unintentionally grabbing hold of the branches of the willow tree that brushed against it, finally launching herself towards the trunk.

It was not 2am. Her parents would definitely notice she was missing this time...

As Ellie lowered herself onto the ground and tiptoed over the long-forgotten vegetable patch that ran parallel to the old garden wall, past the mis-matched garden shed Greg Hoggett of Greg Hoggett's Construction had built out of old doors and cupboards (so odd!), she did try to think of the reasons she'd give when she'd return. But her mind kept flicking onto what was about to happen: a private tutoring session with her favourite teacher and an induction into a new science club. Very little else mattered to Ellie right now.

The hop over the garden fence sparked a change in pace too and Ellie began sprinting across the lane towards Hapsie town centre. Luckily for Ellie this was all downhill, largely across quiet country roads, and eventually a long bendy corner ended its turn and there in front of her, just over the River Hapsie bridge, was the cobbled street of the old town centre, complete with stone houses, and timber-framed buildings – a beautiful mismatch of the history of Hapsie, all on one street.

But there on the bridge was Lucas Litter, casually lobbing plastic bottles over the edge.

Even in her excited haste, Ellie (being Ellie) had to stop.

"Lucas!" she cried. "What on earth are you doing? Stop chucking rubbish into the river!"

Lucas thought about this for a moment. "I'm not chucking rubbish," he said. "I'm sending messages."

Ellie frowned. "Messages?"

"Yeah. Message bottles. Down the river. For whoever finds them."

Ellie looked at Lucas. Then at the bottles. Then back at Lucas.

"Lucas, the bottles are empty."

Lucas nodded. "Yes. I'm just sending the bottles. Someone else can add the message."

Ellie was now very angry. "So what you're actually doing

is polluting the river?"

Lucas mulled this over, then nodded. "Yes. I suppose I am."

"Then stop!" Ellie called, furious as she stormed across the bridge. "And you've made me late!"

Behind her, Lucas shrugged and lobbed another bottle into the river.

"You call it pollution – I call it potential," he muttered.

Finally arriving at the post office, it took Ellie a good thirty seconds to get her breath back. Once she had, she straightened her woolly jumper around her waist and opened the door.

At least she tried to, because it was locked.

RATA-TAT-TAT! Ellie knocked on the wooden panel of the door.

No answer.

RATA-TAT-TAT RATA-TAT-TAT.

After what must have been two to three thousand million weeks of waiting, the lock finally turned on the door and a familiar face popped itself into the gap.

"Ah, Ellie!" Mrs Totterwell smiled. "Bright and early, I see."

"Yes, hello, I need to come in," Ellie replied hastily. "Now. Please."

"Of course," said Mrs Totterwell. "Do you have a letter to post?" Her eyes twinkled with amusement.

"Not today! I'm here to join the science club!" Ellie continued as she bustled her way past Mrs Totterwell into the empty post office. "Is Professor Fialova around?"

"Join the…?" Mrs Totterwell asked curiously, and then thinking better of it, "No problem at all, Ellie, she's upstairs. I'll let her know you're here."

And with that, Mrs Totterwell exited through a side door

in the post office that Ellie had never noticed before. It led up a small flight of stairs. Ellie edged closer so she could peer up the stairs but they turned a corner so there was nothing to spy on. *Oh fizz!*

She returned to nosing around the post office, a favourite pastime of hers anyway, as she often waited to post a letter or pick a postmark, a message which gets printed next to the stamp. The standard choice of messages were things like, 'People love a posted letter', or 'Hastily delivered from Hapsie', but if it was quiet, and if you were Ellie, Mrs Totterwell would let you tweak them. 'People love a periodic table' was Ellie's current go to.

She loved this place, and for the most part, Mrs Totterwell loved having Ellie there too. The store was full to the brim with writing paper, stationery, books and board games. Nothing had been updated since the 1960s so the space was still adorned with traditional deep wood panels and posters that were long out of date.

"Hello, Ellie," came the familiar voice of her science teacher.

Ellie turned to see Professor Fialova standing in the doorway. Ellie grinned. But before she could say anything—

"You do understand it's 6:45 in the morning, don't you?" continued Professor Fialova.

"Oh!" is all that Ellie could reply. "Yes, it probably is about that time, isn't it?" She suddenly noticed that Professor Fialova's hair was a tangled mess and she wore a fluffy pink dressing gown instead of her usual black blazer. "Um, sorry about that…"

"It's okay, my fault. I didn't specify a time. Come with me," replied Professor Fialova, with her familiar gentle smile.

Professor Fialova led Ellie up the stairs. As they passed Mrs Totterwell, Mrs Totterwell gave Ellie a knowing look that could only be interpreted as, *You're lucky I like you,* and then closed the door behind her. The narrow stairway went up, turned a corner to the right, and through a door.

"You live here?!" exclaimed Ellie, entering a top floor apartment. "That makes so much more sense than you having a secret lab here."

Professor Fialova pulled out a wooden chair and gestured for Ellie to sit. "Wait here. Let me just…well, give me a few minutes."

Ellie sat down, tossing her backpack to one side. She didn't mind the wait. It gave her a perfect opportunity to take in the room. She was inside Professor Fialova's home!

The flat was small but cosy, with an undeniable charm that felt instantly welcoming. This must be the living room. Shelves lined the walls, packed tightly with books. Ellie assumed most of them would be about science, but she did notice a few cookbooks and novels squeezed in for balance. A small wooden desk sat by the window, cluttered with notebooks, pots of pens, and a miniature model of the solar system that seemed to have lost a planet or two. The furniture was mismatched but warm, the largest item being a faded green sofa that looked well-loved, with a cheerful yellow cushion adding a pop of colour. On the table, a delicate vase held a single daisy, and the faint smell of tea lingered in the air from years of piping hot kettles whistling. On the wall was an artwork of a large owl, with actual feathers of all different types of birds stuck to it.

This was a happy place. Ellie liked it. Although the 3D picture of the feathery owl was a tad strange.

Professor Fialova returned, now dressed, but Ellie noticed her demeanour had changed somewhat. No longer quite as smiley and friendly, if anything Professor Fialova looked quite nervous. Clearly Professor Fialova wasn't a morning person, and Ellie's early intrusion had disrupted matters. Ellie decided she'd break the tension by being the first to speak.

"How long do we have before the others arrive?" she asked.

"The others?" replied Professor Fialova.

"The others, for the, you know, club..." Ellie trailed off. It was clear from Professor Fialova's reaction that no others would be coming.

*That's okay*, she thought, *just the private tutoring then*. Ellie was more than happy with that.

"Listen Ellie. Firstly, thank you for coming round."

"Of course, I—" started Ellie.

"Ellie, let me speak," interrupted Professor Fialova. "Ellie, the way you approach matters, your knowledge and understanding...I mean, for an eleven-year-old..." Professor Fialova hesitated, clearly either not having rehearsed this monologue, or simply struggling with the fact it was still before 7am on a Saturday.

"What I'm trying to say," Professor Fialova continued, slowly finding her flow, "is that in my many years of teaching, I don't think I've met a student who comprehends science in quite the way you do. And in two months of teaching you, you've answered questions, thought through problems, and undertaken experiments in ways that students who've been with me for seven years and beyond have failed to achieve."

"Oh!" was all that Ellie could muster. This was certainly going better than expected.

"And I suppose what I wanted to tell you, Ellie, is that I think you're unique."

"Thank you." Ellie took what seemed like two to three weeks to get each word out.

"I want to help you," the professor said.

"I would like that," Ellie replied, feeling a little giddy.

"I mean, don't get me wrong, there's work to do. Your results in pop quizzes are dire. Remarkably, hideously dire."

Professor Fialova chuckled. "But you notice things that others don't, you see situations unfold before anyone else. Ellie, I want to help you, but I'm not really allowed."

*Not allowed? "*Why not? Aren't teachers supposed to help their pupils?"

"Yes…but not in the way I'm about to help you."

For all the wonderful compliments Ellie had just received about being able to see things, understand things, notice things, she suddenly felt rather silly, because this final line made absolutely no sense to her at all.

"Right," she said, now with huge pressure to come up with something clever. "By joining the science club?"

"What? *Science club?* What science club? Where did you get that from?" replied Professor Fialova, looking a little taken aback and confused. She then shook her head as if shaking out the silly question. "No. I want to give you these."

Professor Fialova reached under the sofa and pulled out a small, dark brown leather satchel. It was tattered and scratched. She placed it lightly on the table. Ellie stood up off her chair and walked over to the satchel. Professor Fialova opened the flap and Ellie peered inside. There was a musky smell about it.

Inside lay two…well, what were they? At first glance, they looked like watches. A silver metal band that could clasp snugly around your wrists, and on top, each had a large, circular sapphire glass face. But unlike a clock face, they were blank, only the tinge of a rich, royal blue glow reflecting in the light. Perhaps they were digital watches that had run out of battery?

Four large metallic knobs were evenly spaced around the glass face, positioned at the top, bottom and both sides, much like the crowns on an analogue watch. Both devices were clearly well used, with scratches and marks covering the metal surfaces. The bands themselves had markings on them, numbers, letters, symbols etched into their metal. The glass faces, however, remained pristine.

Ellie looked at the contents of the satchel, looked up at Professor Fialova, then back to the two silver items inside.

"Umm, Professor Fialova, I know I arrived early this morning, but I'm normally very good with time keeping. And two watches? Seems a little unnecessary."

Professor Fialova, chuckling slightly, replied, "I'm sure you are, Ellie. But these are not watches. These are what we call Bracers. Elemental Bracers."

Twice already this morning, Ellie had responded poorly: once by suggesting that others were going to be joining them, and the second time when she mentioned the science club. Not wanting to face a third embarrassment, she simply sat in silence, waiting and hoping that Professor Fialova would continue with an explanation.

Thankfully, she did.

"They are incredibly special. Not many exist. But I want you to have them."

Ellie couldn't help but smile. "Me?"

"For now. I believe they will help you grow into the scientist you need to be."

Ellie felt tears form in her eyes. She was so happy she could cry. "Thank you." She cleared her throat.

"Erm…What…er…what are they for?"

"Let me show you. Put them on."

Ellie nodded. She slowly reached out and picked up one of the Bracers. "Does it matter which wrist?"

"Either is fine," replied Professor Fialova.

The first was weighty. There was real substance to the Bracer as she looped it over her left wrist and adjusted the clasp on the band to secure it tightly. The clasp snapped shut. As it did, a tingling sensation, a small vibration, flowed lightly down her arms and up into the palm of her hand, then vanished. For a brief moment a wave of exhaustion came over her, then just as quickly as the tingling, that vanished too.

After a moment to appreciate the excitement, Ellie carefully put the other Bracer on her right wrist. She experienced the same sensations as from the first.

Though they were heavy when she picked them up, they didn't feel heavy to wear. They felt good! They felt natural – like she had been wearing them for years. But Ellie still had no idea *why* she was wearing them.

"This isn't a pop quiz, just a conversation now," Professor Fialova began. "Tell me, what elements make up the human body?"

Ellie was relaxed, there was no brain freeze, her mind was flowing freely to her voice.

"96% of the human body is made up of just four elements: Oxygen, Carbon, Hydrogen and Nitrogen," she replied confidently.

"Good," agreed Professor Fialova. "And the final 4%?"

"Well, that's a bit of a mixed bag. The majority of that 4% is made up of seven further elements: Calcium, Phosphorus, Potassium, Sulphur, Sodium, Chlorine and Magnesium," Ellie continued, now in her own element. "But," she continued, "it's also possible to have a further thirty or so additional elements inside your body. But in such small amounts they can often be overlooked, even though some of them are essential."

"Great. So you already know all this. This is where we begin," Professor Fialova said, pacing to the window. "Ellie, these Elemental Bracers allow you to summon the elements in your body. They enable you to conduct science in ways you've never dreamt of. Let's try it out, shall we?"

Excited, and incredibly nervous, Ellie shouted "YES!" rather too loudly.

"Okay, stand in the middle of the room," instructed

Professor Fialova.

Ellie got up from the chair and did as requested, facing the window.

"The more abundant an element is in your body, the easier it is to focus on. Let's start with the easiest ones – that 96%. I think we've had more than enough Hydrogen this week…Oxygen sounds like a somewhat safer start!" Professor Fialova said, clearly thinking out loud. "Okay Ellie, raise your arms in front of you and cross your wrists."

Ellie did so. As she did, the two outer crowns of the Elemental Bracers closest to each other snapped together as if bound by a strong magnetic force. This time, Ellie felt a ripple of vibrations run up both arms, petering off through the rest of her body. There was power here.

"Perfect," said Professor Fialova. "Right, now you need to call out the element you want, so…" She stopped. "Actually, before we continue, can you turn to face the wall?"

"The wall?" Ellie questioned.

"Yes. I think that would be best," Professor Fialova replied, indicating her initial question was purely rhetorical.

Accepting her teacher probably knew what she was doing, Ellie twizzled ninety degrees to the left, arms still outstretched, wrists still crossed, Elemental Bracers still locked together. She was now face-to-face with the feathery owl picture. It really was an odd picture.

"Okay, we're ready," said Professor Fialova calmly. "Ellie, I need you to concentrate. Visualise what you're saying. Really try to *feel* what you're saying. Understand?"

Ellie nodded, though in truth she had no idea what that meant or what was about to happen.

"Excellent. Now ask your Bracers to bring forward Oxygen."

"To do what now?" replied Ellie, trying her best to

unfurrow her brow.

"Try it," was the only further advice offered.

"Certainly," replied Ellie, without any certainty at all.

Ellie thought about it for a good eighteen seconds – just like she had with the balloon – and then, staring into the eyes of the feathery owl on the wall in front of her, and realising she probably couldn't say anything more embarrassing than she already had today, she blurted out:

"Elemental Bracers. Element 8. Oxygen."

Before she could finish her sentence, the glass faces of the Elemental Bracers began to glow pale blue, throbbing brighter and brighter. The very second Ellie finished saying the 'en' of 'Oxygen', a beam of explosive, pale blue light burst out from the glass of both Bracers.

The blast hurled Ellie backwards across the room with incredible force, landing with a soft thud on the faded green sofa behind her.

Dazed, Ellie looked up to find the room suddenly filled with feathers. The owl painting was stripped completely bare. In stark contrast to the chaos that had just erupted, the feathers were drifting serenely, swaying from side to side as they floated to the ground. Ellie lay sprawled across the sofa, out of breath, too stunned to move, her wide eyes fixed on the last feather as it came to rest on the floor.

Professor Fialova turned to look at Ellie, smiled, and simply said, "Excellent. Very well done."

Ellie was going to need some explanation. Panting, she said, "What…what just happened?"

"Well, for one thing you've given me the perfect reason to throw out Mrs Totterwell's ghastly owl-picture." Professor Fialova chuckled again to herself. "And secondly, that's exactly why I had you face the wall. If you'd been facing the other way you'd have been thrown back onto a table and chairs, which hurts a lot more." Professor Fialova frowned and rubbed her lower back. "You can trust me on that one."

"Will I always get blown over like that?" asked Ellie, still not moving from her slumped position, but now resting an arm on the yellow pillow, breathing heavily.

"That part is just simple physics. You know what Sir Isaac Newton said: for every action, there's an equal and opposite reaction."

Ellie did know Newton's third law, but she'd never experienced it quite so up close and personal!

"The Oxygen came out one way, so you got thrown back the other with equal force. Next time, hold yourself properly and you should be fine."

"Oh," said Ellie. *Thank you, Newton.* "But erm…"

Professor Fialova cocked her head to the side. "That explanation is not going to cut it for you, is it?"

Ellie shook her head. "Nope."

The professor sighed and continued. "The Elemental Bracers can draw on the elements within you. If you summon them, they help you bring them out. It takes a certain mind to be able to use them at all, and I saw that in you. It looks like I got it right."

Ellie grinned. Even from her crumpled position on the feather-covered sofa, she felt pretty good about herself.

"And, well, listen Ellie." Within a moment, Professor Fialova's facial expression shifted. The entire way she held her body seemed to morph within an instant from gentle confidence to uncertainty. "Ellie, you are not meant to have these."

"Oh." Then why did she give them to her?

"Under no circumstances do you have permission to have these. You and I will be in significant trouble if…"

Ellie immediately started unclasping a Bracer from her wrist, sensing the immense unease being directed towards her from Professor Fialova.

Professor Fialova raised a hand to stop her. "You *can* have them, you just need to know that you shouldn't have them." She paused. "Is that clear?"

Ellie rolled down her sleeves over the Elemental Bracers, beginning to appreciate the enormity of what had just happened at 7am on a Saturday morning above the Hapsie post office.

"Do *you* have a pair?" asked Ellie.

The professor pulled back her sleeves to reveal another set of Elemental Bracers, firmly clasped around her wrists. Unlike Ellie's design, these bracers were more ornate, their silver bands intricately etched with patterns that seemed to shimmer faintly in the light.

Like Ellie's, the Bracers featured large glass faces, blank to the world yet exuding an undeniable aura of power. The faint glow beneath the surface hinted at their potential, as if they were waiting for the right moment to awaken.

"Some others do, too. But not many people. You can't walk into your local superstore and pick them up," Professor Fialova joked lightly.

"Does Kami have some?" Ellie asked, as much to her surprise as it was to Professor Fialova.

"Of all the questions you could ask me, Ellie, that's what you chose?" Professor Fialova snapped back, a flash of disappointment flickering across her face. "Oh dear, maybe I've got this wrong after all. Jealousy isn't—"

Not wishing for that particular thought to settle in her mind, Ellie decided (very cleverly) to move the conversation along. "I mean…I mean…why am I so out of breath?"

"A much better question, thank you." Professor Fialova's expression lightened. "The Bracers can generate elements themselves, they can pull from the surroundings, but you provide the base. So they've taken that element from you. They've taken your Oxygen. That's why you're out of breath," explained Professor Fialova. "You'll get used to it, hopefully. But you're young, and small. You need to be careful. Here, let me show you how I do it."

She pulled back her sleeves, raised her wrists, and brought her Bracers together, just like Ellie had. "Elemental Bracers. Element 8. Oxygen."

Like Ellie's had a moment earlier, Professor Fialova's bracers began to throb with a pale blue light. As she finished, the glow shot out across the room. But Professor Fialova did not fly back and hit the wall, and no picture was destroyed. Instead, the Oxygen exited her Bracers delicately and under control, swirling through the air as she moved her wrists and fingers in perfect unison.

Ellie felt the new breeze brush against her face, and the feathers on the floor began to flutter. Then, as the wind picked up intensity, the feathers rose into the air, circling as if dancing a routine they had rehearsed for months. It was pure poetry.

With a gentle motion, Professor Fialova lowered her wrists and the feathers floated gracefully back to the floor as the Oxygen dispersed into the room.

"So cool!" Ellie sighed.

She turned to face Professor Fialova. Her teacher's eyes were closed and she was taking calm, steady breaths, far from the chaotic mess that Ellie had found herself in. She took one final long breath and opened her eyes, already looking directly at Ellie.

"Like everything, it just needs a bit of practice." She smiled as she began to pick up the feathers on the floor.

After a moment of reflection, Ellie asked, "Is that why the balloon in the Tithe Barn was filled with Hydrogen instead of Helium? Because Helium isn't naturally present inside our bodies, so you couldn't summon it?"

Professor Fialova, continuing to pick up feathers,

nodded and replied, "Yes, exactly! Gosh, you are smart."

Ellie felt another glow of pride.

"That, and I wanted to see if you would be able to identify it, which you did." The professor smiled warmly at Ellie. "That's how I know you deserve these Bracers."

"But if they're so dangerous to use, why are you giving them to me now?" Ellie needed to know.

"Because quite simply, Ellie, we believe you need to have them now."

"We?"

Professor Fialova paused, thought about how to respond, and eventually said, "We…the people."

That was the start of the American constitution, not an answer to Ellie's question. This time, it was clearly Professor Fialova moving the conversation along before Ellie could dwell on it. Ellie felt the weight of possibility. These devices, capable of harnessing nearly 40 of the 118 known elements – those that made up the biology of Ellie Ment (and you and me!) – were a marvel of science. She took a deep breath. It was slowly dawning on her what this meant: for her, for her science, maybe for something more than that, too. A smile broke across her face. "Thank you…Lucinda."

Professor Fialova stopped picking up feathers, straightened up, turned to look at Ellie, and simply said, "It's still Professor Fialova to you."

# Chapter Four

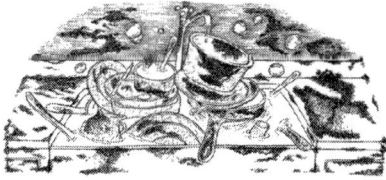

# The Science Of Being A Hero

It's a strange thing, being given a new superpower – especially when, just that morning, you'd only expected to get a cheap plastic membership card to the local science club.

Not that Ellie had anything to compare it to, of course. But, as it turns out, having a superpower gives you quite a lot to think about. And lost in these thoughts, Ellie quickly exited the Hapsie post office, offering a brief, "Bye. See you next Saturday," to a waiting Mrs Totterwell, who had already tidied up the shelves in anticipation of Ellie's usual long browsing session through the stationery range. She would be back next Saturday as Professor Fialova had agreed to meet her again for some training, provided of course she practised herself, in secret.

As Ellie left, a "Bye! Take care out there!" followed her out the door. Was Mrs Totterwell just being friendly, or did she know about her secret too?

Walking down the cobbled street she had joyfully sprinted along barely an hour earlier, Ellie now looked a very different sight. Timidly hunched into herself, she kept checking, over and over, that her sleeves were rolled firmly down over her Elemental Bracers. What a disaster it would be if someone saw her with them so soon.

As Ellie rounded the corner onto the lane leading back to her house, she kept whispering to herself, "This is huge, Ellie.

Totally massive."

By the time she reached her road, the expectations she'd placed on herself had grown somewhat more. "You are now incredibly important, Ellie. You have an obligation to use your science powers to fix big problems. People will be relying on you to do great things. You—"

Ellie stopped. She had reached the front door of her house. A note was pinned to one of the oak panels.

"Ahhh!" She sighed. In all the excitement, she had completely forgotten she'd sneaked out of her house, avoided her parents, would be very late for their road trip, and no doubt in a heap load of trouble.

*Ellie.*

The note began. It was her mother's handwriting.

> *You are a wonderful, brilliant, incredibly intelligent young lady, and we love you very much.*
> *But...*
> *You are also a complete whizzle-whump. Thank you for giving us a good reason to get the willow branches pruned, they've been too close to the house for far too long.*
> *We don't know where you've got to, but we assume you're off doing some science somewhere. We've gone to see your cousin Cassie and Aunt Melica anyway. We'll be back tonight.*
> *Mrs. Bloom from across the street said she'll check in on you. Be safe.*
> *Much love,*
> *Your long-suffering parents!*

*Wowzers*, thought Ellie, purposely ignoring the words of frustration. Alone for the day? And even better, *not* in trouble!

What a Saturday this was turning out to be!

(In case there was any doubt – of course, she *was* in trouble. A heap load of it.)

Ellie then noticed a small arrow in the bottom right-hand corner of the note still hanging on the door. She tore the note from the pin and turned the paper over.

*P.S. If we thought we could ground you, you'd be grounded. However you'd probably still find a way to sneak out at 2am anyway. So instead, here's a list of chores that need to be done by the time we're back:*

       *1. Do the dishes.*

       *2. Sweep the floors.*

       *3. Feed the plants.*

       *4. Clean the bathroom.*

*Love you!*

*P.P.S. We've locked your bedroom window and hidden the front door key under the grey rock to your left. If you've entered the house, we know you've also seen the chore list above. See? Your parents are smart too.*

The commands to undertake household chores certainly did take the whole 'save the world' responsibility thing down a notch or two. Still, Ellie (finally) began to realise it was probably the lightest punishment she could be given and she was grateful.

The one thing Ellie certainly wasn't, was a procrastinator. If something had to be done, then she'd get it out the way, right away. So, within minutes of stepping through the front door she had her sleeves rolled up, ready to do the dishes.

*Are the Elemental Bracers waterproof?* she suddenly wondered. Ellie decided that she would ask Professor Fialova on

Monday, and for now play it safe.

Unclasping them from her wrists felt like removing part of her body – they were so new to her, yet felt so familiar already. Placing them on the kitchen counter, she began filling the sink with warm bubbly water, looking around at what needed to be washed up.

As it turns out, Ellie's dad – most likely with the knowledge that washing up wasn't going to be his responsibility today – had made the sandwiches for the road trip, but then also cooked a full English breakfast for both him and Mrs Ment, with all the fixings included. Fried mushrooms, bacon, sausages, beans, toast, hash browns, scrambled eggs, even bubble and squeak! It had been a feast. A feast that Ellie had eaten none of but would now have to scour clean after.

She began scrubbing the seared bacon streaks off the frying pan, wishing someone had at least let it soak for a while first. Oh dear, imagine if Professor Fialova could see her now? She'd be expecting Ellie to be diligently practising with her Bracers, creating new hypotheses as to how she could expand the scientific horizon, refining her—

"Refining my skills," Ellie said out loud to herself, the bubbly water, and the frying pan. "Hmm."

She slowly placed the frying pan back in the water, dried her hands off with the tea towel and without hesitating picked up her Bracers and clasped them back onto her wrists.

Ellie thought back to how Professor Fialova had calmly summoned the Oxygen to direct the feathers, how she had controlled her breathing and focused on exactly what she wanted to happen. Slowly but surely, Ellie brought her own wrists together, hearing the satisfying thud of the Bracers locking into place once again, savouring the energy that flowed through her. She turned her shoulders to the side and repositioned her feet because there was no sofa to catch her this time if she blasted backwards.

"Elemental Bracers. Element 6. Carbon," Ellie whispered very softly, directing her wrists and words towards the frying pan.

Just as the words left her mouth, the Elemental Bracers began to throb a dark grey, and a slow wisp of dark black light began to radiate from them. Wrapped inside the streams of light, a small, deep black dusting of Carbon powder made its way across to the sink and gently settled on the frying pan.

Ellie took another deep breath. "I did it!"

She reached for the scrubbing brush and dipping it in the water, rubbed it over the frying pan. The fine Carbon particles began acting as a light abrasive, perfect for scrubbing grease and food stains! Within a few seconds the frying pan was gleaming, cleaner than it had ever been!

*Blazing Bunsen! This is going great!* Ellie beamed.

With that, she piled the entire remainder of the washing-up into the sink, locked her wrists together, and excitedly summoned more Carbon!

> (It's worth reminding ourselves here that in small quantities, Carbon will act as a great natural scrubber. Ellie had just evidenced this for herself. Her best friend Michael however had also shown that too much Carbon can create a big mess all over your clothes and face, and Ellie was so excited that she accidentally produced messy-Michael quantities of Carbon. Oh dear.)

After the violent throbs of dark grey light and flashes of dark black matter had died down, Ellie stood back and observed her parents' kitchen. The once-pristine white veneer kitchen was now shrouded in a layer of Carbon – deep black Carbon. The glossy surfaces, once gleaming and reflective, had turned matte and grimy, as though swallowed by soot. Every edge and crevice was lined with a fine black dust. Smudges and streaks marred the cupboards, while the Carbon clung stubbornly to every surface, making the kitchen look less like a place for cooking and more like the aftermath of an experiment gone wrong. Which, incidentally, is exactly what it was.

"Right," said Ellie, as she slowly backed out of the kitchen, taking care not to spread the mess any further. "I'll...er...come back to that later."

Disappointed but not deterred, she picked up the list of tasks and began to look for the next casualty – I mean, chore.

Skip to later that evening: Ellie walked around the house, observing the outcome of her afternoon's work. It was fair to say that even the most optimistic person (which Ellie was, of course) would be hard pushed to be overly enthralled with the results she saw.

To sweep the floors, Ellie had decided to try her hand at Oxygen again.

*Second time around surely must be easier,* she thought.

And, for the most part, she was right. Using her Bracers to blow Oxygen gently across the stone tiles, she managed to create neat mounds of dust and dirt. However, despite her success, her dad's birthday cards on the mantelpiece – and, more unfortunately, Mrs Ment's 250-page geology manuscript – bore the brunt of an unexpected sneeze mid-summoning. With scattered loose papers all across the hallway, Ellie concluded a return to this task a little later would be the best course of action.

Due to some dizziness Ellie was experiencing, the bathroom clean had started quite traditionally: a cloth, some water and a splash of cleaning product. At first the chore was a big success but by the end of Ellie's time in the bathroom there was certainly no cause for a victory parade. Upon closer inspection of the taps and showerheads, Ellie had decided she could make her parents very happy if she also helped remove the limescale and hard water stains.

*Sulphur would be excellent for that,* she remembered. She remembered wrong. Sulphuric acid is perfect for breaking down the Calcium carbonate that makes up limescale.

Sulphur, however, is a bit different, and also responsible for the unmistakable stench of rotten eggs.

As Ellie left the bathroom, with the taps and showerheads just as they were when she started, she couldn't help but notice the foul smell now engulfing the entire house. She was confident the pong would dissipate by late that evening when her parents returned. Probably. Hopefully.

The task that could be celebrated however, was that of 'feeding the plants'. Having filled a jug full of water, Ellie extended her wrists forward and shot a soft blue stream of light into the jug. Within it was Nitrogen, the building blocks of life! Nitrogen helps plants (and you!) grow strong and healthy, giving them their lush green leaves and sturdy stems. As Ellie poured the enriched water onto the soil, she could already imagine the plants standing a little straighter and looking just a bit greener, as if to say, "Thank you!"

With the chores somewhat complete, but importantly the Elemental Bracer practise well underway, Ellie felt it was time to take a well-earned break. She was tired, very tired. Her muscles ached and the dizziness hadn't fully gone away either. The final tidy-ups could happen a bit later.

Ellie went up to her room, sat at her desk, and took out her diary.

Sat 26th October,

Dear Diary,

I'm not really allowed to tell anyone so maybe I can tell you. It will be difficult to explain. But let me try

For someone who loves an explanation, unfortunately I can't share any more of Ellie's accounts from Saturday 26th October, as straight after that Ellie slumped forward and fell fast asleep at her desk.

Head still slumped over her desk, Ellie awoke to find her mum standing over her, arms folded, a look of weary disappointment plastered across her face.

What had once been a cosy family home had, in a single afternoon, been transformed into something resembling a scene from a documentary that Attenborough (her cuddly gorilla) would be proud of (actually, to be fair, both Attenboroughs would have been). The plants Ellie had 'helped along' with Nitrogen enrichment had grown far beyond expectations, as demonstrated by the loud gasp from her mum as she entered her own front door. Combined with the still-lingering sulphurous stench of rotten eggs from the bathroom incident, her parents had returned to find their beloved house not just a tad overgrown, but also overwhelmingly pungent.

Suffice it to say, Ellie spent the entire Sunday cleaning. Properly. No shortcuts, no experimental science, just good old-fashioned elbow grease and an increasingly wrinkled pair of rubber gloves.

Monday brought with it another school day, and while Ellie generally loved learning, she couldn't help but feel that school seriously got in the way of actually doing science right now. History, for example: why dwell on the past when she could be shaping the future?

The walk home from school provided a better opportunity for experimentation. She had spotted a blocked drainpipe at 104 Thorn Lane, water spilling over in the rain. Considering the household had, (unknowingly of course), provided her with most of her jam jars over the past year, Ellie figured a small act of goodwill was in order.

A quick flick through her mental catalogue of elements presented a simple solution: Sodium. Sodium reacted with water, which meant it would help clear the blockage. Brilliant! Except…Ellie had underestimated just how reactive Sodium was. And as it was raining, there was a lot of water. The result? A series of bright orange explosions that shot up the length of the pipe, punching neat little holes all the way down.

It was no longer blocked: fabulous. However, it was also no longer a pipe, so much as a sprinkler system.

Ellie, wisely, did not stick around to admire her handiwork.

By Tuesday, Ellie was looking forward to swimming class, which at the very least would provide a much-needed break from her unfortunate string of minor property damage incidents. But as she trudged and slipped up the muddy hill to the leisure centre, she was greeted by a disappointing sight: a big laminated 'CLOSED' sign slapped across the doors. It turns out no Chlorine delivery meant the pool was unsafe to swim in.

"Why on earth wouldn't you put that sign on the town's noticeboard at the bottom of the hill?" Ellie complained to herself, while also suddenly realising that this was a problem she could fix.

A quick scan of the area confirmed there were no staff members in sight, so Ellie slipped round the back, found the filtration room, and locked her wrists together. The element of Chlorine was inside the human body, but not in its pure form (luckily). Instead it was locked up as Chlorides (which hung around in salty stuff like your tears and sweat), so it was just a matter of summoning it correctly, surely? She muttered the element under her breath and released a soft greeny-yellow mist into the system.

What happened next was…not quite what she intended.

Instead of safely filtering into the pool, the reaction had produced a significant amount of Chlorine gas, a hazardous, highly toxic, emergency-level biohazard. Within minutes, alarms blared across the leisure centre, yellow lights started flashing, and a short while later some people in full protective suits stormed in with ventilation equipment.

Oops.

Ellie watched from a safe distance as the centre was evacuated. Later that day she noticed there *was* now a sign at the bottom of the hill on the town's noticeboard. At least that was an improvement.

Wednesday was a day of caution. Ellie lay low on Wednesday.

She did at one point try to help a young girl named Ike with a grazed knee by summoning Iodine – a great disinfectant – and mixing it with the water in her drink bottle. But after Ike complained to her mum that Ellie had splashed Cola all over her leg (they're both brown!) – Ellie decided to call it quits.

Finally, Ellie found herself on Thursday, October 31st, Halloween. And while Ellie enjoyed the dressing up, she could never quite get behind the endless witches and wizards. Where was the appreciation for actual alchemists? At least they were grounded in some form of science.

Festivities would have to wait, however, because tonight was the start of a new month, meaning it was time for her next round of jam jar placements. She had spent the afternoon scouting locations when she ran into Michael.

"Trick-or-treating," he said. "Tonight. You. Me."

Ellie frowned. "Did we plan that?"

Michael's unimpressed expression suggested that yes, yes they had planned that. Ellie had clearly forgotten. Michael did look fantastic, though. He'd upcycled those long foam noodles from the swimming pool into makeshift spider legs which he wore all along his back. Apparently, the leisure centre had been forced to replace all their swim equipment after an unfortunate Chlorine gas incident.

Ellie nodded thoughtfully. Well. At least she'd helped Michael out in some way.

"Sorry, no trick-or-treating for me this year," she said, patting him on the shoulder. "We can't do everything together."

Michael sighed and adjusted one of his foam legs. "So it seems."

Ellie grinned. "Have fun, Noodle-Man. See you tomorrow."

And with that, she was off to prepare for her night of

scientific adventure.

On reflection, Ellie thought, "Have fun, Spider-Man," would have been a much better comeback, but Ellie never was the best at jokey comebacks. That was Michael's thing.

# Chapter Five

# The Upcycle Uproar

Ellie was tired.

Not only had her notes of 'Thirty-four steps from Space Rocket Tree towards Big Ears Tree, away from Large Lump Tree' not proved to be entirely conclusive as to where her October jam jars were buried in Hapsie Forest, but the ground was frozen, covered in leaves, and the November spot she had planned turned out to be a lot further away than she thought. Oh, and it was raining – but that won't be much of a surprise to you by now.

When she had undertaken her location scout earlier that day, Ellie had totally forgotten Leafy Park closed at 4pm, so she had to walk around it, which had taken ages. How annoying, especially when it meant she now had to do it in the early hours of the morning at the start of November.

To state that the last few days had not been entirely easy for Ellie is quite the understatement. It was less than a week since she'd been handed the Elemental Bracers by Professor Fialova, and while Ellie was certainly practising, she was also beginning to feel very conscious that she'd not put her Bracers to any real scientific benefit. On reflection, she was struggling to work out which of the incidents – the wrecked house, the blown up drainpipe, the swimming pool major environmental disaster, or sterilising of a little girl's grazed knee – she would be telling

Professor Fialova about if and when she was to ask.

Ellie had managed to undertake one scientific success with her Bracers, however. After digging and finding no jar in the middle of a cold forest last night, she became highly infuriated with her flickering headtorch. Again. So she snapped open its front case, ripped out the bulb, held her wrists together, and quietly whispered, "Elemental Bracers. Element 15. Phosphorus."

It needed to be very calm, and not much at all. Phosphorus reacts quickly with Oxygen. But (for once) that's exactly what Ellie was aiming for. The thin wisps of yellow-green light containing the element landed inside the headtorch's case. Ellie slammed it shut and stood back.

It worked!

The Phosphorus reacted with the Oxygen inside the case and it began to glow with a beautiful greenish-white light. Ellie strapped the headtorch back onto her head and for the rest of the night it worked without a single flicker. Maybe she could tell Professor Fialova about *that* next Saturday?

The Phosphorus had run its course but that was okay as the morning light was already up when Ellie rounded the corner to her house. She was cold, muddy, but content that her science experiment would be accurate. Her October jars were stuffed in her backpack, filled to the brim with October's water, and the November jars were planted in the fields beyond Leafy Park, covered in their linen.

In that regard, all was well, until…

"Michael?!" Ellie spluttered as she opened the door to her bedroom.

"Hi!" came back a cheery voice.

"What are you doing here?" a confused Ellie asked.

Michael was not a stranger to Ellie's room over the years,

but when he was in there it was highly supervised and restricted to a chair on the far opposite side of Ellie's science corner. Michael was a major contamination risk. No offence, Michael.

"Er…it's Friday?" Michael said. "And on Fridays we go to school together…dummy." he ended with a cheery insult, as for once he was able to spell it out to Ellie as if he was the science whizz. "You don't mind that I waited in your room, do you?"

"Erm…no, not at all…"

*Well, yes, maybe a little bit.*

"Hurry up!" Michael chivvied her. "We're twenty minutes late already. It's the school trip today, remember?"

"Oh yes," Ellie said with a clap of her hands. "The school trip! To the wetlands! How interesting!"

Ever since the fire tore down Hapsie School at 2am in the morning on that fateful October 1st night, the teachers had to deal with the fact that the Tithe Barn was big, but not big enough to house an entire school. So, for the last couple of weeks, and certainly for the foreseeable future, a variety of school trips had been planned for different year groups each day in order to get some children out of the barn.

Today was the day for Falcon class to visit the Hapsie Wetlands.

And what would Falcon class be doing at the wetlands? Well, that really depended on who would be teaching them. As the school trips were just about getting kids out of the barn, it was up to the teacher to come up with something on the day. When Mr Fry the maths teacher had to take his class to the town's clock tower, he spent two hours trying to come up with maths games solely based on the clockface. It sort of worked. Sort of. But it was slightly easier for him than when Ms Boden realised her PE class would be attending the local cinema. Or for Mrs Dobson when she realised that her history class would be spending the day at the local skate park. The only history to be found there was in the form of ancient chewing gum fossilised onto the ramps. The quick lesson in the history of graffiti was somewhat inspiring for the class, more so when she allowed the sixth formers to 'create their own history' (as they put it) with their own spray cans.

And finally let's not forget Mr Neebles, the English teacher, who had the unenviable task of bringing his students to the county's most thrilling and inspirational location: the local Hapsie insurance office. His plan to link policy writing with poetry was, to put it kindly, not well received. Especially by the customers inside the insurance office who were trying to sign up to a new insurance premium, while also smiling politely at the young child, whom they didn't know, sitting next to them telling them how 'insurance excess' rhymed with 'big mess'.

Today was meant to be the turn of Dr Higton, the school's elderly geography head, and that, for once, would have made perfect sense. But Dr Higton hadn't returned to school after the fire, which everyone found very odd. In fact Dr Higton hadn't been seen around town either. It was a shame as Dr Higton was an excellent geography teacher – albeit incredibly strict. It was this strictness that had meant the students hadn't enquired as to the whereabouts of the esteemed head of geography, as they would much rather have a substitute teacher to take them to the Hapsie Wetlands instead.

But all this is for twenty minutes time. Right now, Michael Upperton was sitting cross-legged on Ellie Ment's bed, unauthorised, and sadly that wasn't the worst thing a tired and wet Ellie was about to encounter…

It all began with an innocent "Look!" from Michael. And with it, he picked up some jam jars. Six of them. Tied together with a belt.

Ellie frowned. "What are you doing with them?" she asked, trying not to panic.

"I'm into an upcycling music phase at the moment. I made some drums with some old food containers and plastic wrap I found in the recycling at home. I thought we could play tunes and march with them as we walked to school today. As you weren't here, I thought I'd upcycle another musical instrument from these old jam jars I found lying around." And with that Michael pulled up a wooden stick – which Ellie immediately recognised as one of her stirrers to mix solutions with – and began bashing jars.

"My jars…" Ellie was in shock.

Each jar was filled with varying levels of water, which meant when clanged at their lips where the lid would go, they made a different sound depending how much water was inside. More water lowered the pitch, and less water went up the scale. It was ingenious, and exactly what Ellie loved about science. Like Oskar's static balloon at the start of our story, she, you and anyone else could create a musical instrument by doing exactly the same.

For the uneducated, you might think that as Michael bashed out the notes to *Twinkle Twinkle Little Star*, Ellie would be enthralled by the cleverness of Michael's upcycle, but if you do think that, then maybe you haven't been following hard enough about Ellie's focus.

"My jars!" Ellie exclaimed a little louder, at roughly the point in the song when she would normally be trying to substitute the line 'Like a diamond in the sky…' with 'like a tetrahedral allotrope of Carbon…'

"Yeah!" Michael continued, happily. "I had to mix up the water a bit to make the notes work at different pitches, but it really works. It's so cool—"

No, it wasn't cool. And what came next was unexpected to Michael, but very expected to all of us.

"MY SCIENCE!" screamed Ellie, immediately thinking

83

she should whip out her Elemental Bracers and blast Michael with a shot of explosive Sodium, but somehow she managed to stop herself.

Michael stopped. He hadn't even finished the first verse but he could tell something was up. He just wasn't quite sure what yet.

He was about to find out.

"YOU JUST DON'T GET IT, DO YOU?" Ellie yelled.

"Er…" was all that Michael could muster.

"Months and months of work, and you just thought you could waltz into my room and mess with MY science?!"

"I didn't think anything really. I just found some old jars and…"

"And…?"

"I thought you were washing out these jars," Michael mumbled. "I just wanted to do something fun. For you."

"Fun?! Why would you think I needed fun?!!!"

"You've been so distant over the last week. You vanish from school without saying goodbye, you barely ask any questions in class, you rush away between lessons. I thought you were struggling with something. I wanted to help. I thought this would be…yeah…fun."

"Fun. Right. I get it. But you don't. You never get it. It's always about fun for you. This is my science, Michael. These are my experiments. This is my fun. That water is key! I spent nearly a year on this. A whole year! It's organised. It's controlled!" Ellie could feel herself going redder and redder.

Michael was beginning to understand that maybe these weren't just old jars. "Ellie, I'm…"

"You're so stupid. You think your arts, music and crafts are clever? They might be *fun*, but they're not going to change the world. Leave it to the smart ones!" Ellie was smart enough however to realise what she just said; that no matter how angry she was, or how bad Michael's mistake was, these words would hurt, and hurt a lot. She already knew she didn't mean them. Not forever. But statements like that can hurt long term, especially when they're simply untrue, and especially when they come from your best friend.

It will be smart of you to remember this.

"I see," said Michael, now very much retracted back into Ellie's bed. Then, after a few more pauses, he stood up, being careful to put the six jam jars down without further incident. "It's probably best I walk by myself. I'll see you at the Tithe Barn." He stopped and turned. "What are you doing with all the jars anyway?" he asked.

"I've told you this, Michael. I've told you so many times, but you never listen, do you? You always want to tell me about your great new upcycle, and never try to understand what I'm doing," Ellie spat back.

"I guess what you tell me always goes over my head. I guess you're right, I guess I'm not very smart," Michael mumbled and turned to leave.

"I'm testing to see if rainwater collected at different times of the year has an impact on how a plant will grow. It's both science and gardening – it's fun," explained Ellie, giving a weak smile. "It's my fun."

"Oh. I see," said Michael again, and then, looking back at all the pots and jars laid out across Ellie's room, "Well, it might be fun, but you're clearly not very good at it." And with that he turned and walked out of the bedroom and slammed the door behind him.

Ellie took in a deep breath, beginning to boil up again at the thought someone would say she wasn't very good at her work. She turned to look at her plant pots, and then quite surprisingly thought, "Is he right?" For what Ellie was looking at was not the scene of someone who seemingly had a handle over an experiment. The plant pots for January to May looked pretty good, but maybe that was just beginners' luck? Because from June onwards her handy work was looking increasingly worse. June had grown, but it was sprawly, July was both sprawly and yellowed – and the less said about August and September the better, because they barely resembled plants at all. October was still too small to judge.

*Plants usually grow well in the summer rain. They can't all be growing badly, can they? This must be something I've done.*

Had all the distraction from the last few weeks meant she'd lost focus? She was normally so attentive to her experiments! Oh no, Professor Fialova had given the Elemental Bracers to a dud scientist who couldn't undertake any science at all!

Ellie didn't have much time to ponder however, as noting the clock on the wall she realised if she didn't leave now she'd be late. She had thirty seconds to slip on a different jumper (it's field trip day, no uniform!) and rub her hands with one of the old linen rags she found. That would have to do.

Closing her bedroom door behind her, she was suddenly engulfed by a complete U-turn on the current mood.

"ELLIE!" her mum called joyfully from downstairs. "Good morning, Ellie!"

"Morning, Mum," Ellie replied.

"Did you sleep in? Don't tell me you're starting to be a teenager already!"

"No Mum, I…" Ellie tried to respond, but was then cut off by her mum, which was super lucky as saying, *I was out all night*, probably wasn't a great reply anyway.

"It's raining again, Ellie, so your dad's offered to take you and Michael in the car. They're sat in there now, waiting for you."

"He did what?! We don't need to use the car for such a short trip!" stammered Ellie back to her mum down the stairs, trying to find any excuse (however legitimate) not to need to share a car with Michael right now.

Ellie slammed the front door of her house shut and sprinted the ten metres to the car to avoid the rain. Assuming Michael would have called shotgun over the front seat already, she jumped in the back. But when she got there she found Michael had also decided on the backseat too. He wasn't trying to be nice; he was just keen not to sit in the front with the full-of-conversation Ellie's dad. Ellie and Michael looked briefly at each other, then stared straight ahead again.

"Quickly now, or we'll be late," Ellie's dad said cheerfully as the two were strapping on their seatbelts.

"I'm surprised Ellie can be late for anything given she wears TWO watches," Michael mumbled under his breath.

The sleeves of Ellie's jumper had rolled up, exposing the Elemental Bracers. With a scowl to Michael, Ellie pushed her sleeves back down and crossed her arms.

After about one minute of awkward silence, Ellie's dad seemingly couldn't stand it anymore.

"So did you two break up or something?"

"DAD!" cried Ellie. "We're not a…thing."

"Yuck," muttered Michael, which, even though they weren't 'a thing', still warranted a harsh look from Ellie.

"Right, sorry," replied Ellie's dad, and the awkwardness continued. But Mr Ment couldn't stand the silence so he said, "What's in your bag Michael?"

"Oh," said Michael. "Nothing."

"Come on, what is it?"

"It's…" Michael paused. "I made some drums with some old food containers. I was going to see if Ellie wanted to play them on our way to school."

"Oh, no! And I ruined all that by offering to drive you both!" replied Ellie's dad, not realising that he totally didn't ruin the probability of this happening today in any way, shape or form. "Well, why don't you both play me a tune now, as if you're walking to school? It will be fun."

"It's okay, Dad. I don't know anything about fun, apparently," said Ellie, turning to make sure Michael fully understood her choice of words.

Quickly followed by Michael with, "No, it's fine, it was a *stupid* idea anyway," turning to make sure Ellie fully understood *his* choice of words.

The journey to school felt interminable, because of the butt-clenchingly awkward silence. But finally – thank fizz! – they made it.

Suddenly, and luckily for everybody, the car screeched to a halt, and "We're here!" came an emphatic cry of relief from Ellie's dad.

They pulled up to the Tithe Barn just as Falcon Class were filing out of it. Ellie and Michael leapt out into the rain to catch them.

"Sorry we're…" Ellie looked up to see the substitute teacher's face looking down on them.

It wasn't going to be a substitute teacher after all.

"Master Quinn!" exclaimed Ellie.

"You're late, Ellie, Michael." Quinn barked back. "Hurry up. We're leaving."

# Chapter Six

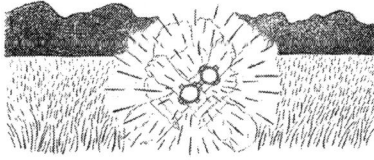

# The Algae Anomaly

Ellie and Michael didn't say a word to each other as they walked from school to the wetlands. But at least the rain ended, the skies cleared, and everyone remained dry. So, that was nice.

In their six years of friendship – including their officially certified four years of *best* friendship – they hadn't really encountered this situation before. Sure, in the past they'd had mini tussles over what to do and where to go, but this was different. This was a fundamental differing of opinions on some very key fundamentals of each other's way of life. And they'd both said some fundamentally mean things to each other. About fun. And, fundamentally, it was very difficult to see who was going to apologise first. Michael certainly had no reason to break: as far as he was concerned Ellie had started it with her insults towards the significance of arts and music. Ellie certainly had no reason to find resolution either: as far as she was concerned Michael's arts and music was the reason her year-long experiment was now ruined. Ellie was also still very aggravated that Michael had pointed out that her science experiment wasn't working, or at the very least her gardening skills were immensely lacking.

Why *weren't* her plants growing? She'd watered them and kept them in the sun as much as her library book on horticulture had recommended. Either way, Ellie was pretty sure if she thought long and hard about it, she'd be able to find a way to blame that on Michael too.

Walking in silence when angry can have its ups and downs. The ups? Well, it gives you time to reflect on matters and think and breathe through your thoughts to find a calming resolution. The downs? Well, it gives you time to reflect on matters and think and breathe through your thoughts to get even more angry about everything. For the whole ten minutes the two walked in silence, reflected and thought, but only just about remembered to breathe, before the group edged out through the trees and arrived at the car park to the wetlands.

The small path ahead would eventually lead them down to the Hapsie Wetlands, though from where they stood, there wasn't a single reed or ripple in sight. You could however look back up the hill, over the tips of the strip of bare oak trees that made up part of Hapsie Forest, to see the school just a few hundred metres above them. Pressing his lips together, Master Quinn turned to Falcon Class.

"This was meant to be a geography trip, so in respect of Dr Higton's syllabus, can anyone tell me the importance of wetlands?"

Angela Pearson, a red-headed girl with freckles, blurted out, "*In respect*, sir? Does that mean Dr Higton is dead?"

Now, Master Quinn didn't have much time for Angela Pearson at the best of times, but he did have time for her parents, Samantha and Toby, whom he had known for many years. So taking a deep breath he said, "No, Angela, Dr Higton isn't dead."

"Do you know where Higo is?" came a cry from the opposite direction, causing Master Quinn to turn on his heel. It was Erwin Ward, a spotty boy with a big grin.

Quinn didn't have any time for Erwin, nor his parents, so was free to ignore him and snap back, "Wetlands! Who wants to tell me about the wetlands?!" And then realising he had a get out of jail card right under his nose, "Ellie?"

It's as if Ellie had predicted Master Quinn would have called on her, as she was already standing there, barely a metre away, arm raised and outstretched, fingers reaching so high they were almost touching his chin. He looked down, then froze.

At the time no one was quite sure what to do. Master Quinn, so full of gumption and confidence, did not move, did not seem to breathe. For thirty seconds he just stood there, staring at Ellie, while Ellie waited for permission to answer, seemingly trying to reach her fingers into Master Quinn's nose. It was certainly awkward. It went on and on and the only sound came from behind Master Quinn – Erwin, helpfully stating to the few class members around him that, "I'm guessing Higo *did* die and he's just remembered."

Eventually, Master Victor Quinn spoke. "Go on. Miss Ment."

Ellie had found the staring match unsettling, but she'd also just been given permission to show off her knowledge. Her mum was a geologist and she'd certainly picked up a thing or two over the years from her phone conversations and articles around the house. Geology and science were closely related, like cousins.

"Thank you, sir," Ellie said. "Wetlands are one of the most important ecosystems on Earth. They filter pollutants out of water and help prevent flooding by soaking up rainwater like a giant sponge."

"Good, now—"

But Ellie wasn't finished.

"But they're not just useful – they're alive!" she continued. "Wetlands are home to thousands of species, from tiny insects to fish, frogs, and birds. They act as breeding grounds, shelter and food sources for many animals. The plants here can survive in waterlogged soil and help keep the environment balanced."

"Exactly, so—" Good try, Master Quinn, but Ellie still

wasn't finished.

"Without wetlands, we'd have more pollution, fewer species and a weaker planet. That's why we need to protect—"

"Enough! Enough geography for today. Thank you," Master Quinn abruptly ended Ellie's lecture. "Now, collect some paper, a palette, brush and paints from Ms Cragg here and go find yourself a spot to paint what you can see. You have two hours. I want to see at least three compositions in that time."

The students, armed with their supplies, filtered up the path and over the grassy knoll down to the wetlands.

After about twenty minutes of sitting on a rock by the edge of the wetlands, Ellie began to realise neither wetlands, nor scientists in labs were her forte when it came to drawing or painting.

*Maybe it's the materials*, she thought. *Maybe it's simply that I don't work well with pencils and paint. Maybe I'm more of a sculptor or a printmaking type of artist.*

She was also realising that she certainly didn't collect enough green from Ms Cragg to depict the view in front of her properly. Sure, she'd expected the bullrushes, reeds, shrubs and wild grasses that surrounded the water to be green-ish, even the water lilies in it…but the water too? The water was just as green as the rest of it.

*How do you make more green? Blue and Yellow. Okay, that should do it.*

As Ellie sat there mixing different concentrations of blue and yellow, wondering if now she didn't have enough blue or yellow for the sky and fallen leaves, she had a niggle. It wasn't going away, and it was a very frustrating niggle.

*Why is the water green?*

Looking up from her palette and accepting that her painting was more akin to modern art than a landscape, she noticed the students dotted around the wetlands, all nose deep in paper and paint. Ms Cragg was nowhere to be seen, probably back at the wetlands café by the side of the carpark – after all she was really only there to support Master Quinn. And where was Master Quinn? Oh yes, with Michael. From across the water, she couldn't hear what Master Quinn was saying to Michael, but by the way Quinn had one hand stuffed in his pocket and the other flailing about, he was either telling him that he'd used way too much paint, or maybe that by sticking actual reeds to the painting wasn't in the brief. Either way, everyone was very preoccupied. Interesting. Very interesting.

Ellie turned to her backpack and slipped out her portable science pouch. *If I'm going to paint the wetlands, it would make sense for me to fully understand what I'm painting. Surely that's what every great artist would do?* She pulled out a metal spoon from her pouch, leant as far as she could reach into the wetlands, and took a scoop of the surface water.

Ellie's science pouch was a beautiful deep green and silver fabric organiser, with pockets on the inside to hold key items. When rolled up, it fastened securely, keeping her test tubes, pH strips, precision tweezers and graphite electrodes neatly in place. It had a little bit of everything in it and Ellie almost never went anywhere without it. In the evenings she'd always enjoyed cleaning it out, replenishing the stocks and formalising her notes in her experiment logs from that day.

Right now, in addition to her scoop, she needed a small magnifying glass and a glass slide. Resting the slide on a rock, she delicately poured the contents of her scoop onto it and peered through her magnifying glass at the green sludge.

"Algae," Ellie said confidently.

She looked up from her glass across the wetlands, and then back down again to her blown up slide.

"Yes, definitely algae…But that makes no sense. No sense at all."

And Ellie was right, it made no sense at all. A wetland such as the one currently being painted by Falcon class often had a high concentration of algae, but only in the summer months. In November?! Not a chance.

Algae would naturally grow rapidly when the sun was hitting it day after day, its warmth stirring the water, feeding the algae like a slow-burning fire. Longer daylight hours meant more photosynthesis, more energy, and more expansion, turning shallow waters into thick green carpets that choked the surface. Even the stillness of summer's air played a role, allowing nutrients to concentrate rather than being washed away by rain or disrupted by fast-flowing currents.

But none of that had happened recently. There had been no scorching summer sun, no long, bright days, no heat radiating off the wetland like a living, breathing thing. Ellie was quite confident that the last few months had been nothing but rain, wind, and cold. Her worn out wellington boots confirmed it.

So what on earth was going on?

Holding a test tube she plucked from her pouch, Ellie delicately dipped it below the surface and scooped up a vial of the wetland water. Next, she removed a thin strip of plastic from her pouch. On the strip were six tiny pads, each treated with a different chemical which, when submerged in water, would react differently depending on what was in the water. Ellie dipped the strip into the test tube filled with the greenish murky water and for thirty seconds gently rotated it, patiently waiting for something on the strip to change. And it did. As she pulled it out, one of the tiny pads turned a deep red. Flicking any excess water off the plastic strip, Ellie pulled out her colour chart to compare.

"Now, this makes total sense," she agreed to herself.

And it did. The deep red colour matched perfectly on the chart with the key for a major contamination of nitrates.

"Exactly like Mum's plants!" Ellie continued out loud.

"Something is polluting the water with excess nitrates, and the extra nutrients are making the algae go wild."

"Do you have a liquid reagent test too?" a gruff voice came from behind her.

So engrossed in her science, Ellie had not noticed that Master Quinn was done with his critique of Michael's work, had forced a smile at Angela Pearson's wild streaks, blankly stared at whatever Erwin Ward had conjured up, and now was standing right behind her.

"I'm sorry?" said Ellie

"Do you have a liquid water test in that pouch of yours?" said Master Quinn.

"Yes, I think I do," replied Ellie.

"It'll be milky white," said Ellie's art teacher, suddenly sounding a lot like Professor Fialova.

"Um…shall I use it?" said Ellie, hesitating with her hand over her pouch.

"You're clearly not doing any art," replied Quinn, looking at the half-hearted green mess on Ellie's pad.

Ellie fumbled through her pouch to find her liquid water test solution and, almost dropping it in her haste, unscrewed the lid and dripped a few drops into the test tube. Gently stirring the test tube around, the drops began to mix with the water. Sure enough, just as Master Quinn had predicted, the wetland water began to react with the drops of the liquid test solution and turn a milky white.

Still holding the vial of water in two fingers, Ellie turned to look in quiet disbelief at Master Quinn.

"Potassium Nitrate. They used to use it in preparing old dyes and pigments. If you want to make them today, you need to do that test to make sure you have the right amount in your solution," Quinn explained.

Dyes and pigments – it made sense that an art teacher

would know about them.

"Right. But here—"

"Fertiliser. It's runoff from the farmer's field. They use Potassium Nitrate to fertilise fields. Makes the plants grow."

"But it's destroying the wetland! The algae is going to starve all the other life in the water."

"Yeah, probably." Master Quinn gave a resigned nod — the same blank shrug of a reaction Ellie remembered from the night the school burned. Was that how he reacted to everything? "Talk to the farmers, but they'll say that without it we will *all* starve. Swings and roundabouts, Ment." And then with a surprisingly loud cry, "Oh, give over!"

Master Quinn's reaction was because it was beginning to rain again, and Quinn had no interest in getting wet in a wetland. "Everyone head to the café, we'll continue from memory there!" he bellowed. And then, direct to Ellie as he turned to leave, "Pack your things, Ment." With that he walked off and Ellie could hear him muttering, "Why Hapsie, why?" as he looked up to the sky.

Ellie was certainly not in a rush. The rain was the same rain that she'd grown up with, spent early mornings with. Ellie was used to the rain. Something was niggling in the back of her brain and her wrists were tingling. If anything, Ellie found herself packing her science equipment away into its pouch even slower than she normally would. Giving the glass slide an extra wipe down, triple checking the test tube wouldn't contaminate the other equipment when it was back in its green and silver pouch.

When Ellie finally turned around to leave she found she was alone on the wetlands. Quinn and the class had rounded the grassy knoll to join Ms Cragg in the café.

*Hmmm*, thought Ellie.

Hmmm, indeed, Ellie.

If you wake up one morning and decide it's your mission to help others, you'll be amazed at how many people around you suddenly seem to need a helping hand. Likewise, if – like Ellie – you ever find yourself with the ability to fix things with science, it's incredible how many broken things will find their way to you.

Or maybe, just maybe, everything needs helping and fixing if you start to look for it. Maybe we all should.

Ellie had the power to fix these wetlands. This would be her science.

She stood at the water's edge and looked around. The tall bullrushes, the wild reeds, the grasses twisting together like a secret maze – and the water. The green, murky, choking water.

Magnesium. That's what she needed.

All living things have a little Magnesium inside them, even us. Magnesium was key to photosynthesis, helping plants turn sunlight into energy. But too much algae had thrown everything out of balance. If she could shift the Magnesium just right, she could tip the scales back toward the native plants. Unlocking the plants' strength to outcompete it. With a precise surge of Magnesium, Ellie could supercharge the wetland's natural filtration powers. Let the reeds and grasses reclaim their ground. Let the algae be smothered, not fed.

The wetlands would breathe again.

Yes, this would be her science.

Ellie gave another look around. Clear.

Adjusting her stance and taking a deep breath, Ellie rolled up her wrists, and – clunk – out rang the glorious noise of her Elemental Bracers locking together. The comforting vibration pulsed through her arms.

The rain was coming down harder now, but it didn't matter.

Ellie Ment, without a moment's hesitation, said: "Elemental Bracers. Element 12. Magnesium."

As she spoke, the Bracers glowed bright silver, the light intensifying as she finished. Magnificent streaks of silver light

97

shot from her wrists toward the wetland.

Just a few metres ahead, the Magnesium ions spread through the water, surging toward the rooted plants and reeds. Their leaves shimmered as the Magnesium supercharged their cells, photosynthesis accelerating like wildfire. In response, the algae began to shrink back, outcompeted and overpowered by the wetlands' reawakened defenders.

"More," she said out loud, and the silver light intensified. The power emitting from her arms increased, the vibrations growing.

"More!" she cried, as the silver bands began enveloping every centimetre of the water's edge.

"MORE!" she screamed as loud as she could, her arms pulsating back and forth now, the energy and force blistering away from her body. Ellie was holding herself firm on the water's edge as a silver light thundered around, bounding off every tree, plant and shrub. Rapidly breaking up the algae.

> (If Angela Pearson had chosen this exact moment to return for her forgotten palette, abandoned on a rock some thirty metres to the right of Ellie, she would have witnessed something truly majestic. An event so surreal, it would have felt deserving of a choir holding a single, long, heavenly note, perfectly harmonizing with the blinding silver light radiating from Ellie. As it was, however, Angela, and the rest of Falcon class, remained blissfully unaware, tucked over the lip of the hillock, happily painting away inside the warm, dry café. Meanwhile, Master Quinn and Ms Cragg counted down the remaining twenty minutes until it was a reasonable time to begin the journey home.)

Ellie collapsed, falling on the wilted and yellowed grasses and shrubs around her. Her legs were cramping, her fingers trembling, but as she lay there on the ground, she slowly opened one eye, then another. Blue. Blue waters.

If Ellie had any strength left in her body she would have given another embarrassing celebration dance. If she had any strength left in her mind, she would have uttered a miniature, yay!

But Ellie was exhausted. She barely had the strength to limp her way back to the café through the rain. Walking in, she slumped down at a table and avoided any eye contact by hurriedly painting on a fresh piece of paper. She didn't have long, as soon after Master Quinn said it was time to leave.

Oh no. Ellie hadn't the strength for the trudge back to school!

"You coming?" said Michael, trying his hand at making peace.

"Nah," said Ellie, realising that this hobble home would require significantly less explanation if it was undertaken alone. But she was also too exhausted to pick her words and tone carefully.

"Right," said Michael, taking offence to this and adding, "Are you colour blind or something?"

Ellie and Michael both looked down at her painting, the green bullrushes, grass, shrubs, and beautiful, blue, waters.

"Oh—" started Ellie, without realising how to explain. But she didn't need to.

"Ment," came a raw voice from behind her.

They both looked up to see Master Quinn, "Feeling unwell, Ment?"

"No, sir?" replied Ellie.

"So you're looking pale and gaunt for no reason then, huh?" snipped back Quinn. Then, "You're coming with me."

"What? Why?!" Ellie shared a panicked glance with

99

Michael.

"Let's call it detention," snapped Quinn.

Ellie wasn't too exhausted to guess that the real reason she was being hauled away had nothing to do with her being late and everything to do with the lush, blue waters she'd left behind her.

# Chapter Seven

# The Material Matter

In a normal school, on a normal day, under normal circumstances, detention would typically take place in the classroom of the unlucky teacher who drew the short straw and had to stay behind to supervise.

Today, however – and for the past month or so since the fire – Hapsie School was not normal. There was no actual school left standing, the students of Falcon class were not at the Tithe Barn, and Ellie was not a pupil that would normally find herself in detention. As it happens, Ellie had never been in detention, but as Master Quinn led her away from the wetlands, in the opposite direction of the roads that wound back up through Hapsie Forest towards the school, she knew this was absolutely not normal.

Michael, however, *had* been in detention, many times. Not because he was particularly naughty, but because the way he was, and how he saw the world, was, unfairly, often considered disobedient (by adults). There's a big difference. Disobedience breaks rules. Michael just bent them into better shapes.

Upcycling his teacher's old textbooks into a beautiful papier-mâché dragon wasn't necessarily naughty. Later realising that those papers had actually been her lesson plans for the upcoming school year – well, unreasonably (he thought) adults considered that rebellious.

It's a fine line between being who you are and fitting into the world around you, and it wasn't something Michael had fully grasped in his first eleven years of life.

However, what Michael did fully understand, was that detention happened at school. So, as he watched Ellie being ushered away, past the disused railway line and towards the derelict glove factory that fifty years ago had been the heart and soul of Hapsie, he knew, without a doubt, that this was not a normal detention.

Michael also knew that no matter the argument, disagreement, or falling out you have with your best friend, there are times when you need to put these things to one side and make sure they're okay.

This was certainly that sort of time.

As Master Quinn led a limping Ellie through the creaking gates of the Old Glove Factory, he told a boy to, "Scram!"

Ellie looked up from the floor where her eyes had been firmly fixed for the last five minutes. The boy (who was not scramming) was Lucas Litter. He was stuffing old crisp packets into the criss-cross of the rusted fencing surrounding the factory.

"But I'm making The Great Wall of Litter!" he replied.

"Get out." Master Quinn didn't wait for Lucas to leave. Instead he marched Ellie through the gates and onto the weed-ridden road that led to the factory that once bustled with activity, and workers, and hope, and gloves.

Michael tucked himself behind an old signalling box and when he considered Ellie and Quinn suitably far enough along, he hurriedly moved along too.

"It's pretty cool!" he whispered to Lucas as they passed each other at the gates.

Lucas, who rarely received praise for his littering, was quite taken aback. "Oh! Thanks. I think I'll—" Lucas replied, but Michael had already scurried on, leaving Lucas looking back at his colourful litter wall with a rare smile of achievement.

"Sir, why am I in detention?" Ellie finally had the courage to ask.

Quinn looked down at Ellie hobbling along with cramps in her legs, reached inside his trench coat, and pulled out...He pulled out a banana. "Eat this." He handed it to her.

It was all very odd, but Ellie, always one to follow a teacher's instructions, did eat it, and instantly could feel her legs un-cramping.

> (Bananas are many things, yellow, squishy, perfect pretend telephones or guns – but they're also a brilliant source of Magnesium and Potassium. And, when you've just summoned as much Magnesium as you can muster from your body to scatter over a large expanse of wetland, well, it's worth remembering that a banana is a well-needed treat to help replenish your body.)

"Feel better?" asked Quinn.

"Yes, much," replied Ellie.

"I thought so," Quinn responded, and then after a short pause, "You're in detention, Ellie, because of your answer to my question about the wetlands earlier today."

Ellie thought about this, mushing up her brow as she did. As far as Ellie was concerned it had been the perfect answer, a textbook response as to the importance of wetlands. Did she miss something out? Did she take too long to reply? She had raised her hand instantly after the question, she had—

"Your wrists, Ment," gruffed Master Quinn without looking back down at her, leading her past the cluster of derelict buildings, rusted industrial chimneys and faded signage from a long-defunct manufacturer. Grime was smeared across every

103

window, pigeon poo left on any flat surface, and ivy crept up every vertical wall.

With Master Quinn not offering up any more information than that, it began to dawn on Ellie what he may have meant; a realisation for the first time that raising her arm up high and answering a question correctly in class may have stupendously backfired on her.

"Oh, you mean my new watch?" And then trying to really cover her tracks fully, "…watch*es*," Ellie cleared her throat. "They're my grandfather's. He passed last year and they…"

Ellie trailed off. Master Quinn didn't seem to be listening. Instead, he led Ellie onto a half-collapsed loading dock, navigating them around the rotting wooden pallets and steel drums. At the back of the loading bay was an old freight elevator, functions long dead. Well, at least the original buttons were. Lifting a flap under a dirty metal box, Quinn yanked a lever to the right. Suddenly the clank of chains and rumble of old motors echoed from under their feet. No sooner than the noise had turned into a low repetitive drone, a platform rose up a few metres in front of them, and Master Quinn led Ellie onto it.

"Hold onto that," he instructed Ellie, pointing to a rusting metal horizontal bar that ran around the edge of the platform. Ellie did.

Master Quinn reached up to jerk a chain above their heads. The platform creaked, jolted, and then shot downwards, out of sight.

('Out of sight' is a somewhat poor use of words here, as in the vast stillness of the Old Glove Factory, there was never really a moment when they were 'in sight' to anyone. Maybe to a pigeon, a newt, a stray cat chasing a terrified rat, or one of the hungry bats and a couple of cute little –

Oh no, wait! I apologise. They were in sight to someone. That person was Michael.)

The lift platform came to an abrupt halt. *How far had they descended? One, two, four storeys?* Ellie wondered. Her eyes were trying to adjust to the change in light, but they didn't have much time to adjust before Master Victor Quinn let out a thunderous roar. A roar that had been building up inside of him ever since he had frozen at the sight of Ellie's outstretched arm at the wetlands, ever since he had glimpsed a shimmer of metal...

"CAN SOMEONE PLEASE EXPLAIN TO ME WHY THIS ELEVEN-YEAR-OLD IS WEARING A BOND OF ELEMENTAL BRACERS?"

There was no response. Who was there to respond anyway? Well, as it turns out, quite a few people indeed.

Ellie looked around. If a human jaw could drop to the floor as they do in cartoons, this would have been the perfect moment for that to happen. Although saying that, it would have also been quite embarrassing too, as about thirty pairs of eyes were fixed on her; *human* eyes, not newts, rats, bats, cats, pigeons or a couple of cute little dormice this time.

There was silence. Everyone stood still. The pause gave Ellie time to take in what was in front of her.

Ellie and Quinn stood at the threshold of what was once the heart of the old factory – the machinery room. But the great iron presses and conveyor belts were long gone, replaced by something far grander, far stranger.

A vast atrium stretched out before them, lined with deep red brick, worn but sturdy, its aged mortar whispering secrets of the past. Steel beams and iron pillars rose like the ribs of some ancient beast, supporting a ceiling that seemed dizzyingly high, at least six storeys, Ellie guessed, though the endless crisscross of walkways and bridges made it almost impossible to tell where it ended and where it began.

In front of them, great oak tables and chairs – the kind you'd find in the grand halls of an old university library – were arranged in long rows. People sat hunched over open books, where just before their arrival hands would have been scribbling in notebooks, eyes flicking between pages.

Beyond the tables, at the far end of the atrium, a small coffee stand sat tucked against the back wall, a warm glow emanating from brass fixtures, the scent of roasted beans curling through the air. But it wasn't the coffee Ellie's eyes were drawn to. It was what loomed above it all.

Suspended walkways and spiralling bridges, twisting metal staircases, all weaving into new chambers on either side. Some of these must have been original – leftovers from when workers needed to reach the massive leather-cutting machines. Others were clearly new, built with a sleekness that suggested purpose rather than preservation.

To the left, one wall looked entirely different from the others. It was covered in books. Not just shelves, but a towering monolith of knowledge that stretched from floor to ceiling, broken only by rickety wooden platforms and ladders that teetered precariously, linking different levels. The gold lettering on the spines glowed faintly in the dim industrial lighting. Some books looked ancient, their leather-bound covers cracked with time. Others were modern, thick tomes with crisp white pages peeking out from between their bindings.

The people in this super cool library weren't dressed like professors. Not like glove makers either. Some wore long coats, some simple jumpers, others had rolled-up sleeves, ink-stained fingers, smudges of graphite or powder on their skin.

Ellie's breath caught. Who were these people? What were they doing in this awesome place? The word awesome is bandied around a lot these days, but this…this was the true definition.

More importantly…

What did this place have to do with her Bracers and exactly how much trouble was she in for wearing them?

A figure rose from one of the desks and walked towards them. They were silhouetted against the streams of grubby light pouring in from the arched windows at the very top of the room.

"Good afternoon, Victor," the voice said. And then turning to Ellie, "Hello, Ellie. Welcome." The voice was warm, comforting. It was Professor Fialova!

Ellie felt so relieved. The professor would explain everything to Master Quinn, then hopefully, to her.

"Welcome, Ellie, to the Material Matter."

"Welcome to the *what* now?" Ellie replied. It wasn't the sharpest reply, but hey, give her a break. She'd had a bit of a day.

"Well, there's one thing for sure," Professor Fialova commented to Ellie quietly as she patted her down and straightened out her coat in front of everyone, "you're not very good at keeping a secret. What do I make that? Six days? I thought we'd at least make it to Christmas."

Ellie didn't respond because she didn't know how to.

Professor Fialova finished by wiping off a smear of mud that ran down the side of Ellie's face and stood back, looking at her. "You look absolutely drained of, wait, don't tell me. Iron? No…" Professor Fialova held out her hand. "Here, hold my hand." Ellie did as she was told. "Okay, now squeeze as hard as you can." Professor Fialova smiled. "Aha!" She reached inside her pocket and pulled out a bar of dark chocolate, broke off a square and offered it to Ellie. "Potassium or Magnesium with that weak grip, but those trembling fingers – Magnesium. Here, have some of this, it will help replenish you."

Ellie had already had the banana, which had helped. But she wasn't going to turn down free chocolate.

"I wonder what you were doing with it—"

"Lucinda!" Master Quinn interrupted harshly.

Professor Fialova, as if she was expecting this, closed her eyes and opened them on Master Quinn.

"Yes, Victor?" she continued just as softly as she had been to Ellie – although without patting Master Quinn down or straightening his clothes.

"Why. Does. Ellie. Ment. Have. A. Bond. Of. Elemental. Bracers. On. Her. Wrists?" Quinn spelled out again, loudly, forcefully.

> (Just quickly – if you ever find yourself in a heated exchange with a friend, or simply can't see eye-to-eye with the person next to you, you generally have two options. The first is to raise your voice, shout back, and show how loud and strong you can be. The second is to remain calm, letting the silence settle around you and using that space to your advantage. You see, people find tense silence far more unsettling than loud rage, so much so that they feel an urgent need to fill it. And that's when they start listening, because they need your words to make them whole again. And that's exactly the approach Professor Fialova followed here.)

"Oh," Professor Fialova said calmly. "Well, without them it will be very difficult for Ellie to undertake the type of science she is truly capable of."

"We've always made it very clear that children do not have or use Elemental Bracers outside of these walls. Very clear." Master Quinn's voice was slower now, and quieter. (See? Not shouting back helped bring the conversation back down to a manageable level! It really does work!)

Professor Fialova took a little time to choose how to reply. "You're right, we did," she finally responded, and then, without meaning it in any way, shape or form, "Whoops."

Master Quinn didn't know how to respond to that. Professor Fialova had stolen all the volume from his argument and left him only with logical retorts, of which she was also not willing to engage properly. He tried a different tack: concern.

"There are many reasons we don't allow kids to use Elemental Bracers, Lucinda. But the number one reason is, well, look at her!" Master Quinn said, masterfully turning the argument in his favour.

> (This is lesson number two in arguing, and something that Master Quinn is very good at: if you find yourself losing a discussion, then remember, you are not debating with yourself, but with someone else. Find what's important to them and use that to your advantage. In this instance Master Quinn knew Professor Fialova cared very much about Ellie.)

Master Quinn had asked everyone to focus their eyes on Ellie, not that many eyes weren't already glancing over in this direction already. "Are you going to drain the life out of another one of your...prodigies?"

It worked. Professor Fialova was on the back foot. Her charming smile had vanished. There was a knowing glance that everyone but Ellie clearly appreciated. Master Quinn's words had hit home.

The adults were now talking as if Ellie wasn't standing there, mouth still filled with chocolate, eyes wide, trying to work out what the hell was going on. Because it sounded like Master

Quinn had called her a prodigy. Which was so cool! But it also sounded like a previous prodigy might have…*died?*

Less cool.

Now, here was a silence that needed filling. And there was one 'prodigy' who felt like it was time to fill it.

"Professor, what is the Material Matter?" asked Ellie

Professor Fialova began answering Ellie while still looking at Master Quinn, her face crestfallen.

"The Material Matter is an organisation of people who want to and can make a difference," Professor Fialova began to explain. "Quite simply, we deal with matters of material importance."

"So, you're like a government agency?" asked Ellie.

"Erm…we work *with* the government but we don't have their…" Professor Fialova trailed off, then decided to restart in a different direction.

"Everything you see around you is from the minds of those who care deeply about the world we live in but also see it collapsing around us. The polluted rivers, the vanishing forests – all warnings we can no longer ignore. Here, we work not just to dream of solutions, but to create them and make them reality. We build, we innovate, we fight."

Master Quinn decided to step in. "And we don't let others know about what we do, until it's done. Which is why we shouldn't be letting an unrelated child in here."

"Thank you for that mansplaining, Victor," said Professor Fialova. "Ellie, inside these walls the brightest minds use science to fix the world's problems."

"You're like, the last stand?" Ellie suggested, as if she was narrating a movie trailer.

"We're, like, the last stand, and we're, like, the *only* stand," Professor Fialova returned, tenderly mimicking Ellie's sentence structure. "Governments are restricted. Compromised towards any cause. They know these serious problems exist but these problems are always for tomorrow, for someone else, for a date long in the future. The politicians need votes now. They only fix what's on people's minds today. If they take decisions that clean the air from dirty fumes, but it means factories will be shut down and jobs will be lost, they hesitate. If they restore forests, but it raises food prices by removing farmlands, they delay. Every solution comes with a consequence, and those in power always fear the backlash more than the disaster itself. So, they push it forward – to tomorrow, to next year, to the next election. Always later. Always too late…" Professor Fialova trailed off, her face wistful and a little pained.

Master Quinn decided he'd lost the battle for now and ended Professor Fialova's speech. "That's why we're here. The brightest minds. Using science, without restriction, hidden away, to develop the solutions for our futures."

Ellie stood, chocolate long since swallowed, not knowing how to react. Her first thought, she couldn't say out loud: *Oh. My. God. Am I part of a secret science club, after all?* The second thought she shouldn't have said out loud…

"But you're an art teacher!" she blurted out.

Master Quinn didn't appreciate what she was implying by this comment. But due to a glance from Professor Fialova, he kept his response constructive.

"Yes," he replied. Constructive, but very short.

Professor Fialova helped lengthen it. "There's only room for one science teacher at Hapsie School, Ellie. And anyway, you don't think there's science in art? How very naive. Different pigments? Chemistry. Perspective? Mathematics. Sculpting? Engineering. Restoration? Well, that can go as deep as X-rays, Carbon dating…Ellie, don't be so quick to judge based on a label. There's science to art, just as much as there's an art to undertaking the best science."

(Oh, that's the third rule of arguing – find a way to compliment your opponent, and they'll slowly become your friend again. In this case, Master Quinn forgot his point for just enough time.)

"Now, let's show you around." Professor Fialova decided this was a fantastic moment for the awkward standoff at the entrance to the freight lift to move on. "Where's Kami?"

*Kami?* thought Ellie. *No, no, no, no. Kami was here too?*

But before she could protest or ask any questions on the matter, another voice was heard from one of the tables. "She's in the Matdev laboratory, I'll make sure she's on her way."

Ellie looked up. What on earth? Mrs Totterwell? The post office mistress?

"Hi Ellie! Now, this is one thing you absolutely can't be adding to one of your letters to your family," she added brightly, as if she was standing behind the counter helping Ellie choose a custom postmark for her envelope, rather than meeting her in a secret, underground, organisation of top scientists.

"Yes. Of course!" replied Ellie, then turned back to Professor Fialova. "Is everyone in Hapsie in the Material Matter?"

Professor Fialova chuckled. "No, Ellie. In Hapsie, there are about a hundred of us, maybe fewer. The hardest part isn't just finding people, but making sure everyone else doesn't get suspicious." She sighed. "So we all have a second, real job, to help within the community and distract anyone else from noticing."

"But Mrs Totterwell?" Ellie asked. "A post mistress?"

Professor Fialova nodded. "Turns out, the best way to communicate without being tracked is by good old letter. Anything digital is far too easy to hack in to. A custom postmark or two can really speed things along if you know the right people. Plus, she's a real whizz when it comes to the admin."

"So are all our school teachers at Hapsie part of Material Matter?" asked Ellie.

"Mostly," Professor Fialova admitted. "There may be a couple who aren't that I can't remember right now."

"So the fire at the school. With all this, with everyone here, you weren't able to stop it?"

"Even we have to sleep, Ellie," answered Professor Fialova, not noticing Ellie turning to tilt her head towards Master Quinn who she knew from that night at 2am was certainly not asleep as the school burned with purple flames.

Master Quinn decided to clear his voice and lose eye contact just at that very moment. How very convenient.

"Ah, Kami!" Professor Fialova perked up. "Show Ellie around, will you?"

And before Ellie could say to Professor Fialova that she would rather be shown around by anyone else than the girl who resoundingly (and overly-confidently) beat her in a pop quiz, Kami replied, "Of course, Lucinda, I'd be happy to." So that was that. And there was Kami on first name terms with Professor Fialova again.

Kami led Ellie away from the elevator shaft through the oak tables, where all eyes continued to follow them both, and into a brick archway which led out of the main hall.

"Sorry, can you slow down a little? I still haven't fully recovered," Ellie asked Kami, wishing she didn't need to show weakness.

"Oh. Of course. Are you injured?" said Kami.

"No. Well, not really, I guess. I'm just short of a few elements from using the Bracers," Ellie replied. And then, trying to show that she really belonged at her new secret organisation, "You know how it is."

113

"You have Elemental Bracers?" Kami said.

(The question Kami asked could easily be interpreted in two ways. The first would be surprise that Ellie had Elemental Bracers when Kami didn't. The second would be surprise that Ellie *also* had Elemental Bracers. The second would mean they were equals…Ellie realised then and there from Kami's tone of voice that it was the first example. Kami *didn't* know how it was, not really.)

Ellie pulled back her sleeves to reveal the beautiful metallic bands, the sapphire glass faces tinted blue in the warm light that blended with the natural rays seeping through from the rafters.

"Don't we all have them at the Material Matter?" Ellie queried.

"I've had a go with some. But I don't have my own, no," was all that Kami volunteered. And then, looking closely at the markings etched onto the bands of Ellie's bracers, "Gosh! Are those…" But she didn't finish, just turned and walked forward in silence.

*Are those* what? Ellie wondered, but regretfully didn't ask right then and there. She was feeling too pleased with the current situation to ruin it. Kami might be on first-name terms with Professor Fialova, but Ellie had the Elemental Bracers. As far as Ellie was concerned, that made them even. And when it came to disagreements, Ellie had made sure to level the playing field with something Kami clearly valued. The Master Quinn strategy worked well here.

"So, I guess you go to Patterbridge School?" Ellie asked, now willing to make small talk with someone she considered her equal.

Patterbridge School lay on the north side of Hapsie, further upriver, where the small hamlet of Patterbridge met the water's edge.

"Yeah," replied Kami. "My dad is part of the Material Matter and I've been coming here for quite a few years now. They all said they saw something special in me. And well, here I am."

Ellie noticed a hint of sadness in Kami's voice and was about to ask more when she inadvertently let out a cry of wonder as they exited the archway into another large area. "Wow! What's that!?"

She was staring up at a huge green wall. A towering indoor, upright...*garden?* Everywhere she looked, plants were climbing, sprawling and twisting around carefully designed metal frames, their leaves shimmering.

The air was thick with humidity, the scent of damp earth and fresh vegetation filling her nose. In the middle of it all, a network of translucent tubes headed in every direction. The roof here was glass, dirty glass, but just clean enough to let natural light pour in over the endless stream of plants.

"It's amazing, right?" Kami said. "That's our vertical farm. It helps the Material Matter grow plants, fruits, vegetables, herbs to replenish themselves and increase the nutrients within their body if they use their Bracers."

"It's incredible," said Ellie, thinking back to her bedroom where Michael had earlier that day, in what seemed like a lifetime ago, pointed out to her that her own plant-growing techniques were failing miserably.

"If you grow them vertically like this it uses way less space, needs 90% less water, doesn't need pesticides, and isn't affected by seasons. More food, less waste, no pollution," Kami said proudly. "Winning on so many levels! The Penruth outpost built it for us two years ago."

Ellie stopped, both because she needed to ask a question,

but also to give herself more time to appreciate the marvel in front of her.

"There's more?" she asked.

"More plants? Or more people? 'Cos, yeah! Both! We call them outposts," Kami explained. "There are Material Matter outposts all over the world. Each tends to focus on different areas. In England, there are three. There's Penruth on the southwest coast, they focus on ecosystem restoration. So that could be re-wilding trees, geoengineering, artificial photosynthesis, things like that. That's why they could build this for us."

"Go on," Ellie said in absolute wonder.

"Then there's another up north, I'm not 100% sure where it is as I've not been, but they focus on new energy generation and resource efficiency. Like synthetic fuels, new ways of harnessing the wind and sun."

"And us? What do we focus on?" interrupted Ellie, clearly not being able to receive information as quickly as she needed to satisfy her growing astonishment.

"Oh, we focus on new, sustainable materials, circularity, areas like that. So, inventing biodegradable packaging, making sure your waste goes back into the system. Your new Hapsie School, the material it was built from, we invented it! That's where I've been helping Mr Hoggett—"

"Mr Hoggett? Greg Hoggett of Greg Hoggett's Construction?" Ellie was dumbfounded. Her parents said he was a complete wheeler-dealer and couldn't be trusted to build an outhouse let alone a futuristic school building.

"Yeah, him. He actually owns the Old Glove Factory. He bought it off the council years ago. They keep trying to issue enforcement orders to buy it back and build apartments but it's amazing how many protected bats, newts and badgers pop up at the right moment. He certainly has his crazy schemes, quirky ideas. But he's pretty darn smart and resourceful too!"

"You're kidding me?" Ellie smiled. "My parents asked him to build us a garden shed. And he did, but it was made from old doors, kitchen cabinets, filing cabinets, basically a mismatched jumble of everything. I mean, technically, we got a garden shed, so…" Ellie sniggered.

"As I said, resourceful." Kami laughed back. "But you know, what we've been doing here is incredible. Greg has developed a building material made from recycled waste. It's amazing – just as durable as concrete and bricks, but using stuff that would otherwise be discarded. That's what your new school was made from!"

"Until it burned down," Ellie quipped.

"Right. Well. It wasn't indestructible. Not many things are. If vandals want to burn something down, they pretty much can."

"Who would want to burn down a school?"

Kami shrugged. "Mr Hoggett was devastated. But he said we regroup, we rebuild. We keep going. He's not here today, but I can show you the workshop where we invented it."

With that Kami led Ellie away from the vertical farm, towards Mr Hoggett's workshop.

"You said we focus on the circularity here? That's upcycling, right? Repurposing things that are waste into something new?" asked Ellie as they walked towards two big metal doors at the end of a brick passageway.

"Yeah, pretty much." Kami nodded as she pushed open the doors into a workshop.

"I have a best friend who would love that," said Ellie, instantly forgetting how much Michael had upset her that morning.

"Ah, it's a shame you can't tell him then!"

"Oh right, yeah, sure. Why is that? Wouldn't it be great

to show everyone what you're – I mean, what *we're* doing here?"

"You'd think so, right? But big ideas scare people, and not everyone wants that," Kami explained.

"I guess that makes sense. But Michael would love to see this. It would show him how smart he is."

And with that the metal doors slammed behind them as they entered the Matdev laboratory.

As it happens, Ellie was right. Michael did love seeing what he was seeing. Having found an old stairwell where he watched Ellie and Master Quinn descend, Michael had bashed open a door in a desperate bid to follow them.

He crouched at the edge of a metal walkway at the top of the atrium, looking down, the oak tables very small at the bottom.

"What on earth?" he said, far too loud.

"Hey! You!" shouted a voice from across the gangway.

Clearly Michael wasn't as well-hidden as he'd thought.

The Material Matter

# Chapter Eight

## Stefon Back

**W**hen you're hiding, desperately trying not to be seen for fear of being kicked out of, well, wherever it is you're not meant to be, you're always kind of expecting an angry, "Hey! You!" to be shouted at you eventually. But a *cheerful* "Hey! You!" is something you're *not* expecting to hear. And when that "Hey! You!" is followed by, "Wanna hang out?" and a boy about the same age as you, with a joyfully-bouncing black Afro, wearing a colourful hoody, waltzes over to you, totally unfazed by the fact you're there – well, it actually turns out to be rather comforting.

"Erm…sure?" Michael said cautiously.

"Awesome, man!" the boy continued. "I think one of the upper Reaction Rooms is empty. Let's go chill there."

"Sounds great," said Michael, hoping it was the right thing to say. And then decided to add a sly, "Awesome, man," to try and fit in.

The boy led Michael down the gangway, saying, "I'm Stefon, Stefon Back. Great to meet you." He didn't worry about lowering his voice or anything. It was pretty reassuring to Michael, who moments ago thought he was in deep trouble. "I like your t-shirt." Stefon was eyeing up Michael's bright red top underneath his unzipped coat with the HAPSIE logo pushing through. "I went to see the Hapsie soccer team for the first time the other week. They're…great?"

(Ahem. That's Stefon being polite.

The Hapsie team is…not great.)

"Ha – yeah I'm pretty sure our school team could beat them. I don't play much but I love watching football – er, I mean, soccer."

"Nice, man," replied Stefon as he opened a door to lead them into a Reaction Room.

"I'm Michael, by the way, Michael Upper— Woah! What is this place?" Michael said in wonder. The room wasn't overly big, about the size of your average classroom, but it was lined entirely with silver metal plates, across the walls, floors and ceiling. Across them you could see scorch marks, dents and all different types of residues. If these metal plates were ever shiny, the shine had long gone. In the centre there were what looked like targets. At the sides of the room were tables holding large glass boxes, about the size of your kitchen fridge. Some of the boxes had what looked like colourful gasses inside, others looked empty. And then, quite contrastingly, there was a snack table. Apples, bananas, nuts, cheeses, spinach, eggs, pumpkin seeds, an eclectic mix of all sorts of food.

"This place? Have you never been in a Reaction Room before?" Stefon said, as if he was asking if Michael had never been in a kitchen before. "Have you not looked around this building at all? These rooms are everywhere!"

"Yeah, I'm…I'm not really meant to be here." Michael finally admitted, then waited to see what that meant for their new friendship.

Stefon paused. Gave Michael a look up and down, and then as if nothing had happened said, "Nah, me neither. But here we are."

Michael wasn't totally sure if his 'I'm not meant to be

here' was the same as Stefon's. He doubted Stefon had snuck inside in search of a kidnapped friend. But if Stefon wasn't going to mind, then he wouldn't fret about it either.

"My dad came up with some interesting theory, so now we're spending a year in Hapsie," Stefon told him. "We moved here a few weeks ago."

"You're American, right?" asked Michael.

"Yeah. Brooklyn, baby. New York born and bred." Stefon stated, thumping his heart.

"Cool! You don't meet many Americans in Hapsie!" Michael grinned.

"It's been a bit of shock." Stefon tipped his head to one side. "Hapsie is nothing like New York, I can tell you that. I was meant to start school a few weeks back but it burnt down or something."

"That's my school! You're going to Hapsie School?" asked Michael, loving the idea that he had made a new friend.

"Yeah! Nice, man!" said Stefon. "I'm being homeschooled for now. After the fire my mom and dad wanted to make sure everything settled down. They say I'll join after Christmas."

"So, your dad is part of…" said Michael, before realising that he had no idea what was going on here. "All this?"

"Yeah. And my mom," replied Stefon. "The Brooklyn outpost focuses on Quantum Science & Advanced Physics. They deal with quantum energy, superconductors, advanced computational models, material manipulation using quantum properties…you know, stuff like that."

Michael nodded along. The nods however did not mean he understood a single word of what Stefon just said. He decided again to be candid. "I'll be honest, all of that went over my head. Sorry. I'm, er, not very smart."

Stefon frowned and smiled at the same time. "Don't

speak about yourself like that, man. Sure you are. Everyone's smart in their own way."

"Not this type of smart!" said Michael. He thought of Ellie. She was exactly this type of smart. But where was she? Where had Master Quinn taken her?

"Are your parents part of the Material Matter too?" Stefon asked.

"The *what?*"

"Aw, come on!" Stefon laughed. "You're not smart, yet you're inside an outpost of a secret science organisation focussed on bettering the world, standing in the Reaction Room, with seemingly no adult aware that you're here. Sounds like you're pretty smart if you're able to do that." Stefon was clearly enjoying himself.

"Yeah, well, I just followed someone in. My friend Ellie." He felt a pang of worry. "Do you think she's okay?"

"Sure! She'll be totally fine in this secret underground maze that no one on the outside world knows about."

This did not make Michael feel better. "I'd better go and look for her."

He turned to go but Stefon said, "Wait! I'm kidding…I think. Don't you want to see what this room can do?"

"What *is* this room?"

"I'm glad you asked," said Stefon with a grin. "This is where they practise with their Elemental Bracers."

There was a pause as Michael looked blankly at Stefon and Stefon looked curiously at Michael. And then, with a cheery smile, "Oh man, you really don't know anything about this place, do you? Ha! This is fun."

Making sure the door to the Reaction Room was fully closed, Stefon walked back to Michael. "Look!" he whispered, rolling up the sleeves of his hoody.

The cuffs momentarily caught and then sprang back to

reveal two shiny metal bands with blue-tinted glass faces.

"Oh!" said Michael, suddenly feeling relieved he was able to contribute to the conversation. "Ellie has those too!" He was starting to wonder why Ellie had the same watches as this American boy he'd only just met.

"Well, there we go!" said Stefon, stepping back happily. "Your friend's mom has Elemental Bracers and is therefore part of the Material Matter. You know a lot more than you think you did! Nice!"

"Her mum?" said Michael, even more confused than he was two minutes ago – which was already pretty confused.

"Yeah, you said your friend's mom has—"

"Not her mum. My friend Ellie. She's my age."

"Interesting. That's new…" Stefon commented after a slight pause.

"So how come you both have the same Elemental watch-type-thingies?" asked Michael.

"Elemental Bracers, they're called." Stefon held out his wrists to show them off again. "These are my dad's actually. I've…borrowed his because he doesn't use them much. But I've found them quite useful."

"They're not watches?" Michael checked, pretty sure what the answer would be.

"Watches? Nah! These are way cooler than watches. They allow you to conjure up any element inside your body and fire it out. Everyone uses this room to practice."

Michael blew out a long breath. "Blimey!"

"Yeah, totally. When you see it in action it's awesome. Last week I watched them conjure up things like Ammonia and Methane to help with some research. It looked like laser beams shooting out of them!"

"So they're a bit like a magic wand?" Michael's eyes lit up. Unlike Ellie Ment, who lived and breathed science, Michael had always been drawn to the world of myths, dragons, and enchanted swords – fantasy tales that whisked him away whenever he read them.

Stefon chuckled, shaking his head. "Well, if a magic wand was real, actually worked, and was powered by the fundamental laws of the universe instead of fairy dust and wishful thinking…then yeah, you could say it's like that."

"Awesome!" said Michael, inadvertently using Stefon's phrase. "Show me!"

Stefon deflated a little. "I can't."

"Oh." Well, that was an anti-climax.

"They don't work for everyone." Stefon sighed. "It takes a certain mind to be able to use them properly or something, and I guess mine isn't quite like that…well, not fully…"

Michael was impressed all the same. "It still sounds pretty amazing to me. So, there's this group of secret scientists with their wand watches—"

"Elemental Bracers," Stefon corrected

"Sure. With these Elemental Wands," continued Michael, "and you're apparently able to do the coolest stuff to make a difference to the world. And," Michael's face fell, "and I'm here making drums out of plastic food containers." He trailed off, dumping his backpack on the ground. "I thought my upcycling was helping the world by keeping waste out of the trash, making it useful again. But as it turns out, I'm barely making a difference at all. What a waste of time."

There was a long pause. Michael felt pretty pathetic.

Stefon picked up the plastic drum that had fallen out of Michael's backpack, tossing it from hand to hand like you would a baseball.

"So, you like music, huh?" he asked.

"Yeah. A lot," Michael replied, flatly but truthfully.

"And you want to make a difference?"

"That's mostly why I upcycle," Michael explained.

"But you don't think you can make a difference because you're only doing music and arts?" Stefon tried to clarify.

"Seemingly so." Was Stefon just trying to rub it in now?

"Hmm..." Stefon replied. "Well, I think you need to meet Ethel."

"Who?"

"Oh, you'll love her, she's great!" Stefon's eyes were twinkling with excitement.

Michael was sure Stefon was about to head for the door to find Ethel but he didn't make any attempt to leave the room. Instead, once again, he pulled up his sleeves to reveal the Elemental Bracers.

"I thought you said you couldn't use them," Michael pointed out.

"I said, I couldn't *fully* use them. I can't blast out elements or anything, but I've worked out something pretty cool of my own. That's why I keep swiping them off my dad. Here, hold my hand."

It was a bit of a strange request, especially as they'd just met, but they seemed to be getting along pretty well, and Stefon oozed a super-fun confidence that Michael really enjoyed. Michael grabbed hold of Stefon's hand.

"Let's go meet Ethel," said Stefon. "Warning, this might be a bit strange."

He closed his eyes, held his arms tightly by his side, concentrated very hard, took a breath, then under his breath began muttering.

"Step up, take one step back, we are travelling to the past, to the world of white and black..."

The Elemental Bracers began to throb white, then black, slow at first but then more rapid. Blinding light and darkness strobed across the room. Tugging on Michael's hand, he and

Michael took a big step backwards. The flashing light became more and more bright, faster and faster, so much so that Michael had to force his eyes shut to avoid the blinding light and the blinking rapid interludes.

Then the flickering stopped.

After a moment, Michael opened his eyes.

Stefon's face was looking at him, smiling from just a few centimetres away. "You good?"

"Er, yeah, I think," Michael replied.

Behind the smiling Stefon, Michael could see there were no longer metal plates across the walls. There were no targets. No snack table. Instead there was wood. Lots of wood. Smooth, polished and stretching high above him. Rows upon rows of seats in a perfect semi-circle, each carved and rigid, their edges softened by years of use. A colossal structure loomed ahead. Towering pipes lined the far wall, their metal dull and silent for now.

*A pipe organ?* Michael swallowed. The air smelled strange: varnish, old paper, a trace of something burned into the wood itself over years of performance and presence.

"Crikey. Where are we?"

"Where are we?" echoed the happy voice of Stefon. "*When* are we, more like."

"What?"

"We're in 1914, I think. At least, I hope," Stefon said with a chuckle. "Where are we?" He looked around. "I'm pretty sure we're in London. The Royal Albert Hall."

"Right. Makes sense," Michael said, though none of this made any sense at all. "Those wand bracers of yours really are magic, aren't they? Did we just…time travel?!"

"Firstly, it's physics, not magic," Stefon corrected Michael with a pointed finger. "And secondly, no. Time travel – at least as much we know – is impossible. That *would* be magic," he concluded. Oh no wait, he had one more point. "And thirdly, I'm really glad that worked! I've never done it with someone else before! Thanks for being my guinea pig." He gave a wry smile and started to walk down a row of seats in the direction of the pipe organ.

"Wait! Hold on," said Michael, scurrying after him.

Stefon stopped and turned. "What's up?"

"We're in 1914?" Michael tried to clarify.

"Yep!"

"But we also haven't time travelled?" a confused Michael checked.

"Nope. That's right. No time travel. Impossible," Stefon confirmed.

The two stared at each other as they had done on the gangway when they first met, and then again inside the Reaction Room. But this time it was Michael who broke the silence.

"Then you're going to have to explain," he said. "And please do so as if I'm not very smart at all," he added, realising that whatever Stefon was about to say would most likely go right over his head.

"Haha, it's all good. Follow me, I'll explain on the way." And with that, he jumped over a couple of rows of seats which led towards the exit of the Circle.

"So, first things first," Stefon began. "No time travel. Nada. Zip. None. It might look and feel like we're in 1914, but in reality, we're still in today. Got it?"

"Go on," said Michael, hoping that if Stefon continued he might actually get something, anything.

"All right, cool. The next thing to understand is that everything around you is connected. The water you drink? The same water dinosaurs drank. The air we breathe? The same elements that Shakespeare inhaled. The Carbon inside you was once part of a tree, a woolly mammoth, maybe even a Roman soldier! The dirt under your feet has been part of everything before."

Stefon paused at the top of a grand stone staircase, winding downwards and dimly lit by gas lamps. He turned to Michael.

"You love to upcycle, right? Turning one thing into something else?"

"Yes! Absolutely." Michael nodded.

"Well, that's basically how the universe works!" Stefon grinned. "Everything is constantly being reused and reformed. The atoms in your body were once something else, just like an old food container became your drum kit. When you eat a carrot, it stops being a carrot. Its elements break down and become part of you – a human. Everything changes form."

"I get that," said Michael, relieved to realise he did actually get that. "But eating carrots might help my eyesight but doesn't let me see 1914."

"Don't get ahead of yourself," Stefon warned. "I'm just setting the foundations."

He led Michael further down the steps into a curving hallway.

"Right," he continued, "here's the big idea. Atoms don't have memory – not the way we do – but they have patterns. They've existed in different states over time. And under the right conditions, they can be nudged into revealing a past state, like an echo."

"We're standing in…an echo?" said Michael.

"Exactly! A visual echo." Stefon's voice bounced off the curved walls as they walked. "Think about when you're in a cave. You shout real loud, and your voice keeps bouncing back. But the present you isn't shouting anymore. You've moved on. What you're hearing is the past you – an echo of what was already said."

Okay, that actually made sense. Amazing.

"That's what this is, except instead of sound waves, we're working with matter itself."

Michael started to smile. This was so cool.

Stefon continued explaining. "Scientists call it Quantum Superposition and Wave Function Collapse theory."

"Oh." Michael's smile faded. "That suddenly sounds complicated again."

"Yeah, scientists love making simple things sound complicated. It makes them look clever." Stefon chuckled. "But I've worked it out! The principle's easy, because everything has already been anything so all the atoms, particles, and electrons in the world *could* therefore exist in multiple possible states. But the moment you observe them, they collapse into a single, fixed form. So, if you know how to interact with them, you can guide them to collapse them into a *different* form, a past form. Like, say, back to how they were in *1914*."

Michael thought for a second. Then his face lit up.

"Wait! So that's why we had to take a step backwards? Because you can't observe the particles change as they shift? If you did, they get 'stuck' in the wrong form?"

Stefon stopped in his tracks and turned, grinning.

"My man! Look at you, figuring out quantum mechanics! Yeah, they actually call that the Observer Effect. Shut your eyes, step back into the moment, and let the Elemental Bracers do their thing. But don't watch while it's happening or the particles will freeze mid-change. Trust me on this: it gets messy."

Michael nodded, absorbing it all.

Then a thought hit him.

"But what about the butterfly effect?" he asked. "If I change something here, wouldn't it change the future?"

Stefon's face fell. "Aw, man, we were doing so well!" Then his expression softened again. He was only joking. "What did I say? We're *not* in the past. Not really. If something happens to an echo, it doesn't rewrite history. If you filmed yourself doing something, then deleted that film, you don't delete yourself in real life. It's the same thing here. What you're seeing around you is a reconstruction – a quantum imprint of what once was."

He grabbed a stack of paper leaflets from a nearby table and threw them in the air. The pages fluttered around them. Then he picked up a paperweight, tossed it at a glass vase, and watched it shatter into a thousand shards.

"The small ripples we make in the echo are enough to change it *now*, but the wave flows around it. If we came back here again another time, it would be exactly the same as before, unbroken. We're not big enough to change an echo. Look around you, it's huge."

Michael was about to nod when he noticed something. Stefon was rolling up his sleeve, revealing a fresh, raw cut along his forearm.

"Where did *that* come from?" Michael asked.

Stefon winced and shrugged. "Hapsie Roman guard. Last week."

Michael stared. "Wait, you can get hurt here? You could *die* here?"

Stefon gave it some thought. "Hurt? Yes. Die? Hadn't thought about it like that before," he admitted. "Yeah, I guess you *could.*"

Michael swallowed. "And if you *did* die here? If this is just an echo, but we're really in the present, then what happens?"

Stefon stared at him for a second. Then he smirked. "No idea," he said. "I suggest you don't die so we don't have to find out."

And with that, he pushed open the heavy doors beneath a sign saying 'Backstage'. He let out a proud, "We're here!" And there they were.

The Royal Albert Hall, even in 1914, was, is, (and probably always will be), an open and semi-circular stage. There are no wings or side exits like a traditional theatre. Those on the stage can be seen from almost any angle by the audience members. The only thing blocking a complete circle is a giant pipe organ that dominates the back of the stage. Michael had seen this pipe organ from the Circle, but now they were standing at the back of the stage next to it, the pure scale and grandeur overwhelmed him.

Looking up, he suddenly realised for the first time that they weren't alone.

An orchestra, all men it seemed, were sat waiting, instruments at the ready. They wore tailored suits, all black…wait…hold on a second!

"Stefon!?" Michael exclaimed.

"Shh!" Stefon hissed. "They'll hear you."

Michael was staring at Stefon. "Your…your hoody, it's lost all its colour. Everything's lost all its colour!"

"Ha – it took you that long to notice?" Stefon smiled. "An echo will lose its colour first, then slowly the detail diminishes. The further you go back the grainer it gets – echoes can fade. I mean, you can go back pretty far until it's noticeable, but after a while, it's a pretty awful experience, just fuzz really. Colour though? Fades very quickly. You might sometimes get the odd splodge sticking around here and—"

A shadow crossed over Stefon and he stopped mid-speech.

A stern-looking man with a big bushy moustache and wearing suit tails was standing over them.

"Ahh, darn it, I knew we shouldn't have spoken."

Michael was worried. This man might only be an echo, but he'd seen the scar on Stefon's arm. Echoes could hurt.

The man tilted his head to one side, straightened it again, and cleared his throat. "Here you are, young fellows," he pronounced in a very posh, BBC accent. And he handed them each two wooden drumsticks with a soft pom-pom end.

Michael accepted it gladly. He was out of his depth with Elemental Bracers, but musical instruments? Bring it on!

Stefon on the other hand looked a little more annoyed.

"Drums again!" Stefon sighed. "I really thought I'd get the piano this time. I've been practising with Beethoven."

"You've been doing *what*?!" exclaimed Michael. "You can interact with people? They're cool with that?"

"Yeah, man. Just like chucking that vase, you can play with the ripples, and because you're the anomaly, they tend to gravitate towards you a bit. The echo seems to like a bit of variation. Mostly friendly, unless you're a Roman guard who doesn't want to let you in of course." Stefon rubbed the scar on his arm. "Come on, if we don't play, they'll only get annoyed." Stefon pulled himself onto the stage.

Michael led the way to the two large timpani drums. This was his time to shine.

A silence fell over the Royal Albert Hall as a lady wearing an elegant suit – a long skirt, high-collared blouse, and a fitted jacket –walked onto the stage towards the conductor's box. Over the top of her suit, a tightly wound kimono brushed against the music stands as she walked. She held a baton in one hand.

"That's Ethel," Stefon whispered. "She's a musician. Like you!"

Michael grinned at being defined as a musician like any one of these people.

"We have five minutes left," Ethel commanded. "We will get *The Boatswain's Mate* down, or we may as well not perform at all tomorrow." Ethel raised her baton. "From the top. Again."

To Michael and Stefon's left a man holding a large tuba rolled his eyes and sighed. "The top? Really?"

"Do you have an issue, Mr Barrington?" Ethel snapped from the conductor's box.

Mr Barrington didn't reply, simply turned his eyes back to his sheet music. No less annoyed or content than before.

"Do they not like her?" Michael whispered, holding his wooden mallet above the drum.

"Come on, man. She's a woman in a position of power in 1914 England. What do you *think* is going on?" Stefon side-eyed Michael while facing Ethel. "She might be a musician like you, but she's certainly got a lot more against her than you ever will. Now watch."

With a flick of her wrists the orchestra lifted the instruments up and within another flash, the strings of the violins started filling the Royal Albert Hall. It was playful, joyful, majestic. The sound travelled across the hall, filling the empty seats with pure bliss. In perfect harmony, the entire violin section brought the music to life.

Michael stood, wide-eyed. He was in a full symphony orchestra, playing the drums, in the Royal Albert Hall! It was a dream, but it wasn't. It was real, but it wasn't. Or was it? Well, it felt real, and that was enough.

Suddenly, with a shout of, "Now give it some passion!" from Ethel, the trumpets and rest of the brass section put their instruments to their lips and joined in. Short, quick notes brought the feeling of glorious hope and expectation. Ethel's baton moved with energy and purpose, the rising melodies of the violins contrasting with the deep resonance of the cellos. The clarinets and oboes danced and weaved with intricate harmonies. The horns exploded into life, driving power through the piece, and then—

"You there. Come on! Time to play it like you mean it!"
Ethel was pointing directly at Michael and Stefon.

It was time for the percussion.

Michael and Stefon began thumping their timpani drums in unison as the tension rose and rose. With a final cry of, "Three, four. Give me power! This is a battle, not a tea party!" the flow of the music swelled to its splendorous crescendo.

Michael began to laugh. This was spectacular – a far cry from this morning when he was planning on smacking his upcycled food container on a walk with Ellie.

And then, with the same passion and force that had flowed throughout, Ethel brought her hands together and just as fast, apart. Stefon followed Michael's lead as they gave a drum-roll. Before…silence.

They waited. No one moved.

Ethel pursed her lips, ran her tongue across her teeth.

Did she like it or did she hate it?

"That will do for today," she said. "Thank you, everyone. I will see you all tomorrow. Just like that please."

*Just like that.* She *did* like it! Michael was thrilled!

Ethel stepped down from her conductor's box and very quickly exited the stage.

"Where's she going in such a hurry?" Michael asked Stefon. Didn't she want to stick around and talk to the players for a minute?

"I'll show you. It's the second reason why we're here. Let's follow her."

Pushing her way through a door at the back of the Royal Albert Hall, along a corridor and onto the cobbled streets of 1914 London, Ethel hurried off. Michael and Stefon followed.

"Watch it!" Stefon shouted to Michael, holding him back with one arm. It was a good call because just as he did, a horse-drawn carriage rolled past centimetres from their toes, with a man in a top hat and tailcoat shouting something indistinguishable at them.

"Argh!" Michael yelled.

"Let's not test that 'if I die here' thing so soon, yeah Michael?" Stefon laughed.

Ethel began hurrying along the back streets of London, wrapping a long woollen coat over her suit and kimono as snow lightly began to fall. As they jogged to keep up, Michael had questions, many questions. "Do you know her?" he puffed as his breath started to show in the air.

"Who, Ethel? Yeah, I guess, we've met a few times now."

"But she didn't seem to notice you," continued Michael.

"Oh, well, yeah. I know her, but she doesn't know me, of course. As far as she's concerned, in this echo, we've never met. I do have a theory that if I keep going back to the same echo the ripples I make will leave a dent, but I'm still working on that one. Quick! Round here!"

Ethel had turned a corner and was heading towards a noise. Shouting. As she exited the narrow street, she pulled something out of her bag – a roll of paper? Ethel began to unfurl it. Michael could read the word, 'Deeds'. Just that?

No, she kept unrolling:

*Deeds, Not Words!*

"What does that mean?" Michael asked. "What's going on?"

"You'll see," Stefon told him.

Ethel stepped into a paved square where a huge crowd of women stood. There was shouting, banging, commotion. Around them stood policemen in full uniform, occasionally shoving back the women who they felt strayed too far outside of a reasonable area.

The two boys pushed their way towards Ethel, who was standing in the middle of the crowded protest. Michael grinned at her. She furrowed her brow at him, having absolutely no idea who he was, of course.

Stefon had to shout to be heard above the din. "Michael, meet Ethel, Ethel Smyth. Musician. Composer. Conductor…and a leading suffragette."

Ethel Smyth nodded at them but then pushed her way to the front of the crowd, losing Stefon and Michael in the jostling and bustling. It was loud, it was chaotic, but it was a powerful and united force. Signs, posters and handmade placards were everywhere you could see:

*Votes for Women!*

*Equality Now!*

*Freedom for Women is not a Crime*

Ethel reached the front of the crowd and greeted another woman, who stood on the steps of an imposing building wearing a long coat and gloves, her eyes burning with intensity.

"That's Emmeline Pankhurst," Stefon shouted to Michael as they jostled to get a better view.

"No! *The* Emmeline Pankhurst? Wow! That's incredible!" replied Michael, at equal volumes above the ever-growing noise from the crowd.

"I love this bit," said Stefon, like he was re-watching his favourite movie.

Ethel stood next to Ms Pankhurst and raised a rolled-up scroll of paper. Just as she had done inside the Royal Albert Hall, she pushed her hands forward. But this time she sang, she sang loudly, powerfully. She was not alone; a chorus of voices from the crowd began singing with her. It was forceful, passionate, beautiful. The vigour of unison echoed off the walls of the buildings, and together the women edged closer towards the police line.

Michael and Stefon were shoved from left to right, the women around them lost in purpose, in anger, in need for a fairer society, for the right to vote – together in song.

Michael had arrived in 1914 thinking music and art couldn't make a difference, but in that moment, listening to the women sing, he saw that his art had the power to lead movements, to inspire revolution.

"You better duck," Stefon said calmly.

Just as quickly as the song had broken out, a loud crash was heard to the left of Stefon and Michael. A stone hurtled through the window of a nearby building. With it, two policemen violently grabbed a suffragette and dragged her away, smacking her with a baton for no apparent reason.

"What's happening?" Michael shouted to Stefon.

"In this case? What needs to happen..." Stefon shouted back. "We better get—"

A wayward stone struck Michael's cheek, slicing it. Michael let out a cry of pain and fell to the floor.

"Michael! Are you okay?" Stefon called, pushing to try and close the gap between them both. "It's time we left!"

He hurdled himself over to Michael and took his hand. Michael grabbed it tight, desperate not to lose him in the surging crowd.

Stefon closed his eyes and muttered under his breath. "One step back. Here I'm done. Back to the present, echoes, be gone!"

Michael and Stefon were hurled backwards as the Elemental Bracers blinked bright white light and darkness across the scene, strobing violently, just like on their arrival.

There was silence. There was calm. There were two dishevelled boys sprawled across the floor of the Reaction Room. There was blood dripping from the cut across Michael's cheek.

Slowly they uncurled themselves from each other's grip, knelt on all fours, and very unsteadily got to their feet.

At last, a very out of breath Michael had the ability to speak. "All of that just to show me that music and art can make a difference?" he said, holding a tissue to his cheek before accepting he'd probably had worse cuts from his own failed inventions.

"Yeah," replied Stefon. "You seemed a little unsure before."

They both broke out in laughter.

"You see," Stefon said, "art and music can be just as smart as maths and science."

The mention of science made Michael think of Ellie. He suddenly realised his mission to rescue his best friend had somewhat taken a side turn.

"Oh gosh. Ellie! I totally forgot she's been kidnapped!"

"Kidnapped?" Stefon echoed, still laughing. "If she wasn't kicked out immediately, then she'll be in safe hands, don't worry about her." Stefon looked Michael up and down. "You on the other hand…you better find a way out of here without being noticed."

"Right. Sure," said Michael, still not quite so certain Ellie would be okay. Master Quinn certainly hadn't rolled out the red carpet for her when they arrived.

He turned to leave the room through the great metal doors.

"See you around?" Stefon asked Michael.

"Yeah! If you ever want to hang out again, I've always wanted to learn more about Van Gogh," Michael casually hinted.

"Ha, let's see. Can't have you losing an ear as well as a cut cheek." Stefon grinned.

Michael turned to leave.

What a day.

But Ellie! He needed to find Ellie!

## Chapter Nine

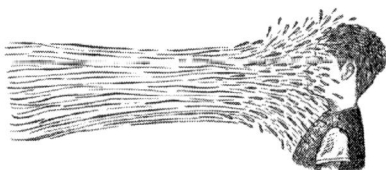

# Compounding Friendship

Ellie opened her eyes. A big grinning face greeted her.

"Argh!"

"You're safe!" Michael announced.

"What time is it?" Ellie asked groggily. "How did you get in here?"

"It's obscenely early!" the merry voice came back, far too cheerfully. "Your parents let me in. I'm so glad you got back safe! I was so worried!"

Ellie could see a faint light pushing through her curtains, so she knew it was just late enough for the winter sun to have risen, but yikes, her body and mind were still exhausted from the last 24 hours!

"Can we talk now?" Michael asked.

Realising Michael was not going to go away until he had closure on yesterday's argument, Ellie decided there was likely no better time to get it out the way. Maybe she could even roll over and get a bit more sleep afterwards. She wearily sat up. "Sure, Michael, where do you want to start?"

"Er, okay, cool…umm, so…" Michael stumbled.

To help get it over with, Ellie decided to play both parts of this chat: "Ordinarily you'd begin by saying sorry, and then I'd say I'm sorry, then—"

"Huh? What? Oh! No! I didn't want to talk about that! I

want to talk about your detention!" said Michael, suddenly full of confidence.

"Michael!" Ellie sternly replied, somewhat now annoyed again about their argument.

"Fine. Okay. I'm sorry. All right? Now can we please talk about your detention," Michael pleaded.

Ellie was having none of it. She'd just managed to get an apology out of Michael! "And whyyyyyy are you sorry, Michael?"

"Yes, yes, yes, I entered your room without permission – er, twice now." Michael grimaced. "I touched your science equipment when I wasn't supposed to. I potentially contaminated one of your science experiments. All bad, very bad," Michael reeled off, proving to Ellie he knew exactly what he had done at the time was off limits. "Although I don't take back the bit about you not being very good at the gardening. Your plants are shockingly bad." He looked towards the windowsill where the sprawling, yellowed, wilted pots planted from June to September were fighting with the curtain, and more pertinently, fighting for their own lives.

"Noted on that – thanks for reminding me. And thank you, apology accepted. I also apologise for saying music and arts aren't as important as maths and science," conceded Ellie. "That was not nice and it's not true."

"Yeah, yeah, now let's talk about your detention," said Michael, relishing his newfound confidence in his own smartness.

"I can't," Ellie replied. "Sorry, Michael, I really can't talk about it. Even to you."

"Hmm…Well, I may have been in detention once or twice, so can I at least try and guess what it was about?"

"Sure, if you want to," said Ellie, grinning to herself about how little he knew.

"Okay, well, how to put it? My guess is that your

detention took place down an elevator shaft at the Old Glove Factory, where you were introduced to a secret science organisation called the Material Matter, each of whom also have Elemental, er, somethings – the same ones you wear on your own wrists – which can summon elements from your body, like Methane and Ammonia." Michael stopped to draw a breath, realising that (a) that was probably all he actually knew about the organisation, and (b) that was probably enough for now too.

> (I'm not sure about you, but if you've ever been tasked to keep a big secret, and you desperately want to keep that secret, but also just as desperately want to shout it to the world, well, having the glorious realisation that you can now chat about not one (i.e. Elemental Bracers) but two (i.e. The Material Matter) of these secrets you're being forced to keep, and not just with anyone, but with your best friend…well, that's quite something.)

Ellie lunged into Michael and gave him a massive hug around his waist. What a relief, even if she wasn't quite sure why or how he knew. For a split second she wondered if actually all detentions happened at the Material Matter – but that moment passed quickly and she realised that it was a silly idea and Michael (being Michael) must have found out another, more Michael-y way.

Still hugging tightly, Ellie (being Ellie) had to correct Michael about the Bracers. "I can summon elements from my body in their purest form, like Oxygen and Carbon. But Methane and Ammonia are not—"

"Methane's what farts are, right?" asked Michael.

"Yes Michael, Methane is what farts are," Ellie confirmed.

"Yeah, he definitely said Methane," re-confirmed Michael, smiling.

Ellie let go of the hug and quickly pushed herself off Michael. "*Who* said?"

Then just as quickly she yelled, "WAIT! I can do compounds too!?"

And without a second moment for further thought, and certainly before Michael could finish his question of "What are compounds?", Ellie clamped her wrists together and shouted, "Oxygen. Hydrogen. I mean, $H_2O$. That makes...WATER!!!" Ellie's left Bracer throbbed a pale blue for Oxygen, her right Bracer lit up in light pink for Hydrogen, and simultaneously they shot out two streams of light which met together and blasted a stream of soft blue light containing water right into Michael's face, blowing him backwards, soaking the end of her bed and some clothes dumped on the end too.

"OH YES!!!" cried Ellie. "YES. YES. YES. Why didn't she say this in the first place?!"

Slowly, Michael picked himself off the drenched bedsheets, using his t-shirt to wipe his face.

"Right. Great. That's a thing you can do now." He laughed, trying both to appreciate and comprehend his best friend's new skills.

But just as he finished speaking, another blast of water shot out (as directed by Ellie) and blew him backwards again, head over heels off the end of Ellie's bed.

"This. Is. Brilliant!!!" Ellie cried out in glee. An impressed, but slightly less amused, Michael picked himself off the now soaked floor.

"MICHAEL?!" Ellie called.

"Yes?" Michael responded, covering his face with his hands in case another jet was heading his way. Luckily (for now) there was a pause.

"Grab the jar instrument you made. It's on the floor down there," Ellie instructed.

Not daring to do anything that would seem like he was questioning Ellie, Michael, with his black curls drenched and pressed firmly against his forehead, started fumbling around on the side of the bed for the six jam jars he had fastened together with the black belt. "Here!" he said and held them out to Ellie.

"Okay. Watch this." Ellie held her wrists together again. "Quicklime is Calcium Oxide – that's Calcium and Oxygen combined together. Elemental Bracers, Quicklime!"

This time one Bracer throbbed white, another pale blue, and with the streams of light meeting in front of her hands, a much fainter blue light was emitted and with it the compound of Calcium and Oxygen flew through the air towards the jars.

As the Quicklime hit the water, it did what Quicklime always does when it hits water: it reacted, violently. The water within the jars immediately began to bubble and fizz, and then Michael let out an almighty, "YARRRRRRR!"

The cry wasn't overly surprising to Ellie, because bubbling and fizzing aren't the only thing that happens when Quicklime hits water. Oh no, heat – immense heat – is generated, too. With scalded fingertips, Michael threw the jars into the air, freeing them from their belt grip, jars and water going everywhere.

"WHAT ELSE?" cried Ellie in absolute joy, potentially the first time she'd ever been happy to see her science corner contaminated.

But before Michael could think back to what Stefon had said, Ellie was one thought ahead of him.

"That's right, Ammonia…Ammonia…Ammonia," she mulled. "That's Nitrogen plus Hydrogen. Okay, Elemental Bracers. AMMONIA!" and as Ellie held her wrists in front of her, Bracers firmly clunked together once again, the left Bracer throbbed the deep violet glow for Nitrogen, the right Bracer light pink for Hydrogen, and together the streams of light merged into a perfect lilac which brought Ammonia into the bedroom.

> (Now, Ammonia is a compound that LOVES to dissolve in water vapour; the same water vapour currently steaming up from all over the room via the boiling hot Quicklime solution which was no longer contained in the six jam jars. So—)

"SCARPER!" Michael shouted as loud as he could, and rightly so. The white fog now filling the room, spawned by Ammonia gas mixing with the rising water vapour, tingling their eyes, was spreading rapidly. Ellie and Michael pelted out the room, clattering into Ellie's dad who had arrived to determine the seriousness of the commotion he had heard from the kitchen downstairs.

Phil Ment's eyes followed the pair as they rushed down the stairs; he then turned to the bedroom. The soaked bed, the fizzing and bubbling pools of water all over the carpet, the white clouds of fog edging towards him. Phil clamped his lips together, nodded, and remembering just exactly who he was the father of, slowly closed the door and muttered, "Nope…nope, nope, nope," and turned to walk back down the stairs to try and forget about it and enjoy the rest of his Saturday morning coffee.

Ellie and Michael looked at each other, then a broad smile spread across the faces of both best friends, and Michael said, "I know where we should go."

Disappointingly for Ellie, Professor Fialova had had to cancel their private session for this morning. She'd told Ellie earlier in the week that she had forgotten she had a Material Matter to deal with. So wherever Michael thought they had to go, especially as it was going to be related to her newfound secret, well, it would be a welcome distraction.

Michael and Ellie ran down the icy roads of Hapsie towards the town centre. Ellie, not wanting to lose a moment of practice, fired Sodium and Chlorine in front of them as they ran, the resulting compound creating salt which made the roads and paths slip-free as they ran.

On the way, Michael tried his best to explain to Ellie what had happened to him and Stefon the afternoon before. Although Michael could still barely make himself believe what happened, so trying to make someone else believe wasn't as easy as he had hoped.

"You're trying to tell me you time-travelled, Michael?" snorted Ellie midway through his story.

"No, we didn't time travel, we just went to 1914, inside a visual echo of the past. He called it Quantum, er, Quantum Soup?"

"Quantum Soup?" asked a confused Ellie

"Yeah, you know, where atoms and elements can be in different places at the same time, but only when someone looks at them do they go into the place you want..." Michael attempted to explain.

"Oh...Quantum Superposition?" Ellie corrected.

"That's it! Stefon used his Bracers to step back in time, but not actually in time, it was just an imprint of time. And I saw it, I saw it all! 1914, Ellie, the Royal Albert Hall, a lady called Ethel Smyth..."

Ellie stopped. "This boy, Stefon, had Bracers?"

Michael stopped too. "Yeah, well, I mean, he had nicked his dad's. He said couldn't do what you do with them, but he could do this non-time-travel-thing-that-certainly-felt-like-time-travel, thing."

"How did he do it?"

"Well, he sort of held his arms by his side, thought really

hard about going somewhere, and asked them to take him there," said Michael.

"And you could go anywhere?!" Ellie prompted.

"Apparently," said Michael, not really knowing the answer to that.

"Okay then," said Ellie, and she held her hands by her sides, closed her eyes, thought really hard about going somewhere, and said, "Elemental Bracers. Take me to the year 1914 and Ethel Smyth."

Nothing happened.

"Oh no, wait! We had to step backwards," said Michael. "So do all that, and then take a big step backwards."

So Ellie did all that again, but this time added a big backwards step onto the side of the road.

Nothing happened.

"Hmm…." Michael considered. "Then I have no idea. But it really did happen! Mind you, we did all this in one of the Reaction Rooms."

"The what?" said Ellie.

Michael responded proudly, "They're amazing! They are made for practising with your Elemental…magic wands. More importantly, they have snacks! Come on, I'm freezing here!" he protested, as his soaked clothes were turning to icicles in the frost, while Ellie scowled at him for linking her scientific marvel – her Elemental Bracers – to magic wands.

Ellie and Michael ran through the town centre, clambered over the disused rail track, and through the gates of the Old Glove Factory. They reached the freight elevator, but Michael didn't stop. Instead he continued into the concrete building where he'd snuck through before.

"Michael!" Ellie called after him. "Where are you going?"

"Er, inside? It's this way," said Michael.

"We can go in the elevator. I'm a member, remember?"

said Ellie.

"Right, but I'm not!" Michael reminded her.

Ellie thought about this for a second. "You can be my guest! Members surely are allowed to bring guests." She wasn't overly confident on this matter, but she for sure wasn't going to be sneaking into the headquarters on her first time entering alone. "Anyway, what are they going to do? Kick out their newest recruit?" she ended, with even less confidence as the initial thought on this matter.

Ellie unveiled the lever of the elevator just as Master Quinn had done, yanked it, and the rumble of chains whirred into motion. She and Michael descended into the darkness and came to a thumping stop at the entrance to the large atrium.

Four people close to the elevator, previously deep in conversation, turned to look at them. Ellie couldn't quite make them out at first, but decided confidence was key.

"Hello, er, fellow members, we're just here to do some practising in the Reaction Room," she announced as if she was entering a gym and telling the receptionist she'd be using the treadmill today.

"UPPERTON? YOU TOLD UPPERTON?" shouted one of the people. Ah, it was Master Quinn. "Ellie, if you can't be trusted—"

"She didn't tell me! I already knew! I followed you in here yesterday!"

Master Quinn had no reply.

"Well," said Professor Fialova with a hidden smile, "I guess this one is on you then, Victor."

At that moment Ellie noticed they were all dressed the same. They had smart black trousers with a bright yellow stripe running up the leg, then tailored jackets buttoned up with at least six or seven buttons. Like the trousers, a yellow stripe ran down the back and diagonally across the front.

151

"What are you guys wearing?" enquired Ellie, wondering if she needed to get fitted for a Material Matter official uniform at some point.

"As I mentioned, Ellie," Professor Fialova told her, "I have a Material Matter to be dealing with today. We are off north. Come on. I'll tell you more about it on the way."

"Absolutely not!" interjected Master Quinn. "We're already babysitting one kid, given Reverend Cal is bringing Kami. We're certainly not having two."

"Three," Michael added quietly.

This time it was Professor Fialova who was firm to reject the notion that Michael would be included on this impromptu field trip. "Sorry, Michael. We really can't—"

But Ellie was having none of it. "Michael's coming too! Come on, Michael!" and she led Michael towards the large oak tables.

Professor Fialova, Master Quinn, Reverend Cal and Ms Boden, the school's PE teacher, who together made up the original four bodies, watched Ellie lead Michael into the centre of the atrium.

Professor Fialova waited for them to get a suitable distance away before calling, "Ellie, Michael, if you're really set on coming, you should at least go in the right direction." She gestured back towards the freight elevator before adding, "and would someone please get Kami."

Moments later Kami rushed to join them, mouthing "Sorry, Dad!" to Reverend Cal before sharing an excited glance with Ellie. Ms Boden yanked the lever further right and the elevator started to shift and move again, but this time further downwards.

As they began to descend, Professor Fialova looked at Victor Quinn, smiled and said, "Kids, hey?"

As expected, Master Quinn did not share Professor

Fialova's amusement and turned his face away to look firmly into the encroaching darkness. All he had to say in his usual gruff humph of a voice was, "Where is he? He's going to make us late again!"

To which Professor Fialova simply let out a long sigh. "He'll be here."

It was only Kami who spoke prior to the elevator coming to an abrupt halt a few moments later, a quiet whisper to Ellie. "We're heading to the Foundry! Eek!"

## Chapter Ten

# The Foundry

Ellie wasn't quite sure what to expect as the lights flickered on at the end of their rather short downward elevator ride, but anyone listening to her exclamation of, "Oh!" as in, *Oh, is that it?*, would have understood that her anticipation of 'the Foundry' was significantly greater than what she saw in front of her.

What she saw in front of her was a low, narrow rock tunnel, no wider than a car, no higher than a doorway an adult might have to duck to get through. The rough walls and ceiling had clearly been hastily chiselled and hacked away from the bedrock beneath the Old Glove Factory. Ellie was right to react the way she did. It wasn't very impressive at all.

"Is...is *this* the Foundry?" Ellie whispered back to Kami.

"This?" Kami smiled. "Ha—no, this is just how we get to the Foundry!"

At this point, anyone listening to Ellie would have heard an, "Ah!" as in *Ah, that makes so much more sense!* At least, they would have, had the sound not been drowned out by the clunk of a large lever as Master Quinn pulled it down from the wall.

As soon as he did, a low hum rumbled from the stretch of darkness to their left. Silently, yet somehow gracefully, the oldest, most rickety, rusting orange metal railcar rolled into view. The railcar itself must have been over fifty years old, never maintained, and looked as if it could fall apart at any moment. It had no roof, just bars at the side, except at both ends where panels had clearly been added to protect whoever or whatever was inside from the rush of cold, damp air that now surrounded Ellie.

Inside, equally old and rusting metal seats lined the railcar, twenty-four in total, split into four blocks of six. On the left side, two sets of seats faced each other with a small walkway in between. On the right, two single seats mirrored the layout. At the very front, a single forward-facing seat stood before a set of levers. And at the very back, an open space clearly intended for cargo.

But for every patch of rust, broken screw, slight hole in the floor she saw, it did not reflect what Ellie heard. There was no clank of metal, no scratch of wheels on the track that ran beneath the railcar into the darkness of the tunnel each side. No, it was…well, it moved without any sound at all.

"Come on, come on!" a bright Reverend Cal instructed everyone.

Michael and Ellie took a double seat in one of the blocks facing forward, and Reverend Cal and Kami sat facing them. Professor Fialova opted for the single seat facing forward to the right of Ellie, while Master Quinn and Ms Boden went to the front of the train by the various levers, deep in discussion as they examined a small brown piece of parchment.

"It's called the Smugglers Passage," said Kami. "It's how the glove factory owners managed to bring in dyes and leather in ways that weren't fully above board," she explained. "The tunnels supposedly stretch all over the country, hundreds and hundreds of miles of them. They were all carved out over a twenty-five year period when the factory, and others like it, were in their heyday. Then the factories closed down and the tunnels were forgotten. But not by the Material Matter – we've repurposed them. No one really knows how far they go."

"So cool!" said Michael, loving every second of his unauthorised entry into this secret organisation.

Then, breaking Micheal's glee, a "Where is he?!" came from Master Quinn again. "If he's not here in one minute we're going without him. We can simply start a point down."

That last part of his sentence didn't make much sense to Ellie or Michael.

Suddenly the rumble and clank of the freight elevator started up and the platform rose up and out of sight. A short pause later, the chains began whirring again and down came the platform again bearing a man who was struggling to hold an exceptionally large cardboard box.

"Sorry, sorry, sorry!" came a muffled voice from behind the box. "But you're all going to thank me! Aha! We'll be taking home the prize this year!" And with the voice came the box, with two short stubby legs poking out from under it. The person wobbled its way onto the rail car and sat down in front of Professor Fialova, dropping the heavy box in front of him. "Ahhhh! That feels so much better," came a slightly clearer voice.

With the box now firmly on the rusted floor of the railcar, the man behind it was a lot more visible. A rotund man, with a thick round nose and a crescent of brown hair retreating rapidly towards his thick neckline, leaving his vast, shiny forehead behind. Ellie instantly recognised him as the man who had spent three days smashing together her parent's makeshift garden shed: Greg Hoggett, of Greg Hoggett's Construction.

"Ah, where are my manners?" he exclaimed, and proceeded to shake everyone's hand immediately around him, while also not really caring who they were or whether his shakes and polite, 'hello, hello, hello' were coming across as sincere or not. At Kami, he did add a little extra, happier, "Hello!" and then he sat down again and started rummaging through his large cardboard box, paying no attention to the fact that Master Quinn (the only member of the party whom Greg had decided not to acknowledge or shake the hand of) was sitting there staring at him. A few moments later, Greg pulled out a small milk carton, popped the straw through the metal foil, and began sucking. Mouth full of straw and milk he offered a carton to the others, who all just shook their heads.

"Silly, silly. You need to be prepared!" he spluttered in between slurps.

"I've had enough of this," grunted Master Quinn from the front, and he shoved the first lever. The railcar began gliding forward into the darkness of the outstretched tunnel.

"Keep your arms inside the railcar at all times, everyone," called Ms Boden.

For a good thirty seconds the railcar hurtled silently along, rapidly accelerating, more and more, quicker and quicker, but never with noise. If you could have seen them, the rough rock walls would have been a blur.

Breaking the silence to her right, Ellie heard a small whisper of, "Phosphorus."

With the words, a yellow-green glow from two Bracers provided some relief to the darkness. Looking down to her right, Ellie could see four large lanterns that lit up the railcar, the Phosphorus reacting with the Oxygen inside, exactly as it had done with Ellie's headtorch. From her seat Professor Fialova began passing the lanterns to the areas of the carriage where they sat, providing an eerie glow to their journey.

"Don't waste it!" Greg Hoggett said, leaning over to Professor Fialova. "Here, wait…" and he rummaged in his cardboard box and pulled out a pot of tuna and popped off the lid, offering it to her. "Replenish!" he urged as he pushed the tin further and further into her face.

Professor Fialova politely declined (many times), and Greg, shrugging at her total stupidity, poured the pot of tuna down his throat and went back to sucking on his second (or was it third?) carton of milk. "At least have some water, everyone." He passed bottles of water out from his box, with everyone politely taking them and putting them down by their feet.

"It's so old, but so quiet!" said Michael.

"Yes!" said Reverend Cal. "We upgraded it quite a few years ago now, it's made quite the difference."

"How does it work?" Michael asked.

"Magnets! Magnetic levitation, to be exact. We put electromagnets on the bottom of the railcar, which repel the metal of the tracks. We're actually floating right now, completely friction-free!" Reverend Cal explained as the railcar rushed through the tunnel. "With no friction holding us back, we can reach immense speeds. Gravity still pulls us down, of course, but the magnetic force is strong enough to keep us suspended, so we glide rather than roll." He grinned. "It really is quite magic!"

Hearing the word 'magic' again, Ellie pulled a face and turned to Michael to remind him, "It's not magic, it's science!"

A curious Reverend Cal tilted his head to one side, and as if he was giving a sermon on an average Sunday, asked Ellie, "What's the difference?"

Ellie thought for a moment. "Science is governed by laws of our universe. Magic is…well, you can't explain why magic works in books. There's no logic or explanation to it, it's just silliness."

Reverend Cal calmly replied, "And can you tell me why gravity works the way it does? Why the railcar wants to be on the ground rather than floating in the sky?"

Ellie could not. She had read theories on to *how* it worked, what it could do, and where it was stronger or weaker. She knew what changed the effect of gravity, like an object's mass. But *why*? Ellie couldn't explain why.

"Er…" was all that she said.

"Then perhaps, Ellie," Reverend Cal said, "the difference between science and magic is simply whether or not we've figured out the explanation yet."

"See! I told you those Bracers were wands!" Michael turned and joked to Ellie, while keeping a side eye on the rest of the group in case they too berated him for it.

"Ellie, we all live in this world," the Reverend explained. "As you say, we all abide by the same laws of the universe, experience the same peculiarities and oddities of things we can't explain. I'm a man of God. But the only difference between myself and say, Lucinda here, is how we think it all began. That's it. Otherwise, we all need to do our best for the world based on what we have in front of us."

He trailed off to look over at Greg Hoggett who was stuffing Brussels sprouts into his already overly engorged mouth.

"And what we have in front of us today," he continued, as Greg decided that there was still space to stuff some beef jerky between his lips (there really wasn't), "is, well, something I'd much rather not be doing. But alas Dr Higton isn't around, and no one else was willing to volunteer."

Ellie fumed as she thought this over, but before she could respond to either of them a cry of, "HOLD TIGHT!" came from the front, a lever was pulled, and everyone was flung to the left as the railcar changed tracks again. The remainder of Greg's Brussels sprouts slapped Michael in the face before continuing their flight into the darkness of the tunnel behind them.

Michael, wiping exploded sprout residue from his face, having largely not been following the preceding conversation asked, "And what is it we're actually doing?"

"The games!" Kami said excitedly.

"Huh?" said Michael.

"We call them the Foundry Games, Michael," Professor Fialova interjected. "Quite simply, because they take place in the

Foundry." She continued, "Originally, the games were nothing more than a way for the overly confident men of the Material Matter to flaunt their so-called strength and skill against one another…"

A voice from the front continued the explanation; it was Ms Boden. "But that was well over forty years ago. Today, women are involved too, and we all challenge ourselves, to make sure we stay focussed and sharp. Each time, at least on these shores, one of the Material Matter outposts is responsible for designing the games, and the other two compete in it. This time around we're competing against Penruth. And God help us for whatever crazy plans the buffoons at Glenmorgan have decided to test us with!" She raised a hand to Reverend Cal by way of an apology for using the Lord's name in vain.

With that, the humming died down, the rock walls were no longer a blur, and the railcar came to a sudden stop. "Last time they arranged it we only sustained one broken arm, which was an improvement," said Professor Fialova, who picked up her coat and walked out of the railcar.

The others followed Professor Fialova off the railcar, stepping into a wider platform area, still without any frills or furnishings, just scraggy rock. Greg Hoggett, tipping a bag of nuts down his throat while somehow simultaneously spooning yoghurt into his gullet, picked up his now half-empty box of snacks and foods and toddled off after them.

"Where exactly are we?" Ellie asked Kami as the three children walked down the narrow walkway towards an opening.

"No idea! We're deep underground, the only way in or out is through these tunnels. There's no phone signal, no GPS, nothing that you can use to track. But we're north, somewhere up north."

"BUT NOT NORTH ENOUGH!" suddenly came a bellowing Scottish voice from the end of the platform. A large, burly man with a big bushy beard, donned in an even larger red and black velvet jacket, stood smiling at the arriving party.

"Who do I see there? Lucinda? Of course, Lucinda! Victor? I wouldn't have doubted it! Joanne? Welcome my lovely and gosh, Reverend Roland Cal? Greg Hoggett? Well, Hapsie certainly has brought quite the team this year!" The voice echoed off the walls as it continued to bubble out of the large presence silhouetted against the light of the wider corridor beyond him.

"And I see you've brought your kids? Interesting choice. I recognise Kami of course, hello dear. But these two, these two are new to me. Lucinda?"

"Barry, meet Ellie. Ellie, meet Barry McBain," responded Professor Fialova.

Barry looked down from his great height, then knelt and patted Ellie on the head. "Hello dear, are you interested in science too?" and without letting Ellie reply, "Wonderful, wonderful." Next, Barry MacBain turned to Michael, frowning somewhat at his damp clothes and tousled black curls which had taken the brunt of Ellie's soaking earlier. "And who does this one belong to?"

"He's with me," said Lucinda. "He's interning. His name is Michael."

Michael gave a sheepish grin.

"Interning? Is that even a thing we do?" Barry questioned.

Realising that there was no helpful follow up to this for her, Professor Fialova decided to ignore the question. "So, let's get on with it, shall we?"

"We're ready for you. Oh it's a good one this year! You'll love it," said Barry, and led the group along and out of the platform area into a network of rock corridors, turning back to Professor Fialova simply to say, "Interning? Really, Lucinda?"

Professor Fialova just smiled back.

162

"Everyone, welcome back." He gestured towards Ellie and Michael. "Or for some of you I guess welcome for the first time. Welcome to this year's Foundry."

"OH!" said Ellie – this time as in *OH MY, THAT'S QUITE SOMETHING!* as she arrived at the end of the corridor that led to the view beyond.

The Foundry stretched out before them: an enormous underground cavern, most likely a disused mine. Its vastness swallowed the light from overhead lanterns that swung precariously from thick iron chains. Hanging high above the centre loomed a brutal gauntlet of obstacles.

At the highest point, two side-by-side tunnels of intertwined metal shimmered with waves of heat, where unpredictable jets of fire shot from hidden nozzles, licking through the centre of the tunnel in random bursts.

If you had been skilled enough to make it to the end of the tunnel alive, you would have had the chance to pick one of the bridges of crumbling rock slabs that dangled above the abyss, each stone visibly different in its stability from the one before or after, as if daring competitors to make a wrong step.

Beyond that, two towering metal pillars with jagged steps spiralled downwards, sparks crackling from the surface of each step. The only way through was to wind yourself carefully down the steps…yet Ellie guessed that if you touched one you'd get an electric shock.

Hot under the collar from the pressure so far? Well, you would have been in luck – a roaring wind tunnel waited to cool you down, a force so strong it sent any rock dust spiralling violently through the air as it crumbled from the ceiling above. Of course, you could have chosen to avoid the wind by reaching for the horizontal ladder at the top of this tunnel; it just would have been a lot easier if each rung of the ladder wasn't frozen ice-cold.

The penultimate obstacle saw a platform leading to a landing point on the ground about five car lengths away, with a fire roaring across the entire gap. It was impossible to jump across, and your fate was all but certain should you hit the fire below.

If you had made it through all that (but how was anyone's guess) then you would have almost completed the course. Almost. Your final task was to fuel a small flame at the end of a fifty-metre sprint, which would, in turn, ignite a large banner in your outpost's colours.

"Crikey," was all Michael could say. He turned his attention to the ground below them.

Around the edges, wooden benches had been bolted to the stone, filled with around a few hundred spectators, all wearing outfits similar to that of the Hapsie team. But instead of yellow stripes, a crimson red ran across their tops and bottoms. Their voices were hushed, their eyes locked onto the monstrous course above. Some leant forward in excitement. Others watched with quiet apprehension.

In the centre of the floor, a massive cauldron rested, as big as the fountain in Leafy Park where in the summer twenty or thirty children would play and splash. It was filled to the brim with a yellow, glimmering liquid. In the middle was a massive stone decagon statue, a towering ten-sided pyramid stretching up to a single point.

"Oh my God."

It was all Reverend Cal could say as he looked on, raising a hand to Professor Fialova in silent apology for his own use of the Lord's name in vain, although Ellie wondered if it was actually a small prayer. His reaction wasn't overstated. In just a few moments, he, along with Professor Fialova, Master Victor Quinn, Joanne Boden, and Greg Hoggett would be up there. Ellie didn't fancy their chances. If she were them, she might have even said a prayer too.

They glanced to their right, where five members from the Penruth team, with green stripes along their black tops and bottoms, looked on, the colour in their faces matching their stripes.

This was no game. This was real. And there was no easy way through it.

The Foundry Games were upon them.

# Chapter Eleven

# Games

"The rules are simple, as always!" boomed Barry MacBain from the floor of the Foundry. He needed no microphone, his thunderous voice already recoiled off the walls of the vast cavern and filled the ears of the few hundred expectant onlookers in their black outfits with red stripes.

"Each challenger will go head-to-head with another, five challengers per outpost, and up to five rounds. Complete the course by igniting your outpost's flag and it's two points for your outpost; or if you can't, simply finish further ahead than your opponent for one point."

Barry MacBain stopped, letting his voice fade away into the furthest reaches of the cavern. "Ingenuity and resourcefulness will always be greatly rewarded," he said. "But there shall be no direct attacks on your fellow challengers. No using your Bracers against your opponent." MacBain paused, so everyone took in his words. "These games are about succeeding for yourself, not bringing others down." He let out a resounding roar to finish.

A loud rolling thunder rose from the benches where the members of the Material Matter's most northern outpost stomped their feet in approval.

"No one else gets to watch?" asked Ellie, turning to Kami as they made their way to a free bench at the bottom of the cavern. She looked around at the sea of red stripes. "Where's all the Hapsie team's support?"

"Tradition," replied Kami. "Well, sort of. The competing outposts are only meant to send their five challengers. The outpost who designs and arranges the games then have their members as the spectators. I think I heard once upon a time things got a little out of hand and a mass brawl started between the spectators of each competing outpost. You don't want to be in the middle of a Bracer Battle, I hear it's very messy. Colourful, but messy."

Sitting down, Ellie, Michael and Kami looked up at the gauntlet above them. A towering inferno of twisted metal, hanging chains and sparks. "So, er, why are we allowed to watch?" asked Michael.

"Well…" Kami thought aloud. "We're probably not meant to be here, but I'm guessing that it's because we're kids, we don't have Bracers ourselves, and none of us would've taken no for an answer." She smiled at them both, just as Ellie tugged down on each sleeve while Kami gave her a look that clearly said, "Oh yeah, I forgot, you do!"

"Your dad's going to be okay, right?" asked Ellie

"Yeah," replied Kami, and then, "I really hope so. I mean, he's very clever." Before ending with, "I mean, he's my dad, right? He's got to be okay." Suddenly the reality of the situation seemed to bury Kami's earlier excitement of attending the games.

Ellie put an arm around her and Kami leaned into it.

Ellie turned to Michael to give him a glance; Michael returned the same alarmed expression. But soon their attention was taken by movement on the floor. "Look! They're there!" Michael called over the growing rabble of voices and murmurs.

Following Michael's finger, Ellie saw the ten challengers, five from Hapsie, five from Penruth, slowly make their way towards the centre of the Foundry where the great cauldron stood. For Ellie, Michael and Kami it was easy to determine who was who despite the great distance. Master Quinn led the Hapsie challengers, the only member walking with confidence. Behind him Professor Fialova and Reverend Cal were in deep conversation, and finally Joanne Boden was desperately, and increasingly less politely, trying to refuse all manner of foodstuffs that Greg Hoggett was trying to pass her from his cardboard box, while he simultaneously munched on what looked like a large broccoli tree in one hand and a raw steak tucked under his arm.

"Dad! Dad!" cried Kami from the benches. It was endearing, but also entirely hopeless, as her voice faded away, soaked up by the rabble of Glenmorgan Outpost spectators that sat in front of them.

"Where are they going?" asked Michael, leaning across to question Kami.

"It's called the Diffusion Drop," Kami explained. "It selects which order the challengers will compete in. It means you don't know who you're going up against." She pointed towards the great cauldron. Each of the challengers had evenly spread themselves around its wide lip. They held up their arms and Ellie could see a clear, open beaker in each fist, filled to the brim with a colourless liquid.

"Challengers!" barked Barry MacBain again. "On my word you will make the drop!" He paused to build the tension. "NOW!"

As commanded, each of the competitors tipped their beakers forward, releasing the liquid into the yellow waters of the large cauldron. As the beaker's liquid dropped into the cauldron instantly the colour around the liquid changed into a beautiful bright green, ten striking pools of green in front of each challenger.

"What on earth?" Michael exclaimed. "How's that

happening?"

"It must be an acid of some form inside the beaker," Ellie started explaining. "As it hits the alkaline waters of the cauldron it lowers the PH level. My guess is that's Bromothymol solution in there, and it's reacting with the acid, changing the colour to green."

"This is the best bit," said Kami, fixated on the pool that belonged to her father.

As the trio watched, the pools began to shift. What started as a thick circle of green began to twirl, twist in the water, swirling into beautiful patterns as it moved away from the edge of the cauldron.

"It's diffusing towards the centre," Kami explained. "Whoever's swirl reaches the centre of the cauldron first will go first."

From a distance it was a beautiful sight. Ten pools of ferocious green rapidly moving through the yellowish waters, leaving a green trail wherever they went. The cauldron was big enough that the individual trails wouldn't mix, and from afar each swirl created its own unique glorious patterns as it diffused through the liquid, spinning, branching, but bit by bit moving towards the ten-sided statue at the centre.

The spectators watched the first swirl hit one of the ten sides of the statue. As it did, the chemicals at the base of the side turned a bright pink, rapidly moving up to the tip of the pyramid.

"Tegan Roscarrock!" announced Barry from his viewpoint at the edge of the cauldron. "You shall be the first of the challengers for Penruth!"

Michael gave a large cheer! He was the only one.

Kami immediately cut him off. "That's not good for her, Michael!" Kami hissed.

Michael cringed.

"Going first is never a good idea for the Foundry Games

170

because you have no idea what you're really up against."

"REVEREND CAL!" screamed Barry, his excitement growing. "You shall be the first of the challengers for Hapsie!"

Kami's father's stone side of the decagon had lit up in pink. Ellie tightened her grip around her friend's waist.

"Oh no!" murmured Kami.

"It'll be okay," Ellie reassured her. "As you say, he's incredibly smart."

Kami nodded slightly and glanced up at the looming course that burned and sparked above her father.

One by one, the ten sides of the statue turned bright pink. And one by one Barry MacBain announced the order in which they would be competing. For Hapsie, Reverend Cal was to be followed by Joanne Boden, before Professor Fialova and then Master Quinn would take on the gauntlet. Hapsie's final challenger was Greg Hoggett, who was eating an egg when he heard the news.

Two metal platforms on long iron chains lifted each team high up into the roof of the Foundry, where they met together before they ground to a halt and the challengers stepped onto the starting platform, looking like flying insects to Ellie who squinted up at them from below. If you were scared of heights, the design of these Foundry Games was not for you. If heights weren't the issue, but you had even the slightest hesitation about being blasted by flames, electrocuted, knocked off balance by hurricane-force winds, being frozen solid, or navigating a firepit five car lengths wide, well, these games also weren't for you.

"Look! Who are they?" asked Michael, noticing a group of about twenty people marching out from a doorway and spreading themselves across the floor of the Foundry.

"Marksmen," said Kami, keeping her eyes firmly fixed on her father.

"Marksmen…as in, shooters?" said a concerned Ellie,

but a booming voice interrupted her.

"Members of Glenmorgan!" hollered Barry MacBain from the bottom of the cavern. "Our challengers are ready. But are you?"

Cheers erupted from the benches. This time Michael decided to wait until Ellie or Kami cheered before he followed. With Ellie now holding Kami's hand for comfort, and Kami's other hand clasped in her lap, Michael decided that now was probably a good time to stay quiet.

"First up, it's Tegan Roscarrock of Penruth versus, Reverend Cal of Hapsie," Barry announced to the crowd. "Challengers, I ask you to step forward and ready yourselves. Should you make it through the first obstacle unscathed then I wish you all the best with the rest of the course." At this point Barry let out a roar of laughter. He was enjoying this – the whole of the Glenmorgan outpost were enjoying this. "At any time you can of course choose to stop, but if you forfeit first then the point will be awarded to your opponent. Oh and remember, no attacking your opponent! The game is to challenge yourself, not each other. Good luck everyone. We begin in 3…2…1…"

Reverend Roland Cal shook his head as if shaking out the madness around him. Professor Fialova placed a soft hand on his back as he walked forward. Kami's dad and Tegan Roscarrock stood in front of their first obstacle. Each had a long criss-crossed metal tunnel in front of them, with a thin strip of even flooring down the middle. Along the tunnel nozzles were pointed at them, ready to shoot out fire as they made their way along.

A large explosion from down below signalled the start of the games!

Immediately the two closest nozzles on each side of the metal tunnels shot out a burst of fire to where Roland and Tegan were standing, still on the starting platform, neither yet inside the metal mesh tunnel just a few metres in front of them.

"Elemental Bracers. $H_2O$. Water!" screamed Tegan, crossing her wrists.

Roland saw his two fireballs hurtling towards him, saw Tegan's reaction and also crossed his wrists, Elemental Bracers binding together, and shouted, "$H_2O$. Water!"

It all happened so quickly.

The fireballs did not extinguish themselves. They spread.

The enraged fireballs engulfed Teagen, scorching her shoulders and wrists, blowing her further back onto the starting platform. She screamed.

At the same time, the enraged fireballs engulfed Roland, blistering his chest and wrists, blowing him sideways and off the starting platform. He screamed too.

And he fell.

He fell the full height of the cavern.

"DAD!" yelled Kami as she watched her father fall.

And then.

"ELEMENTAL BRACERS. OXYGEN," came a roar of four marksmen from below. Blasts of blinding pale blue light shot upwards towards Kami's father.

*So that's what the marksmen are for!* Ellie realised.

The Oxygen slowed his fall.

Slowing, slowing. Thud.

Kami leapt from the benches, threw herself past those laughing spectators and ran across the floor of the Foundry towards her father. Ellie was a step behind her.

"DAD!" Kami cried.

Reverend Roland Cal turned to look up at his daughter, scorch marks across his chest, his hands singed black. "I'm fine, Kami. I'm fine. They caught me," he comforted her.

"Your hands!" sobbed Kami, hugging her father.

He did look rather awful, Ellie thought.

"I'll heal," replied her dad.

Ellie knew their mistake. They'd used water, but they were obviously oil-based flames. Water just spread them…

"How's Tegan?" the Reverend asked.

Kami clearly didn't care at all how Tegan was, so just hugged him tighter.

Ellie looked up to see Tegan picking herself up from the platform, hobbling over to her four team members, breathing deeply, holding their hands. Kit Lamorna of Penruth walked over to her, held his wrists together and muttered something under his breath. A bright metallic-grey light edged out slowly and onto her hands, which Kit then guided up to her face.

"They must be using Zinc," Ellie said thoughtfully. "It protects the skin and helps it regenerate."

She brought forth her own Bracers and, focussing her mind, shot the same metallic-grey Zinc streams onto Kami's dad's hands and chest. No one else really noticed; the spectators were too wrapped up in congratulating themselves about the spectacle that was unfolding around them.

"WELL, WELL, WELL!" Barry MacBain hollered to the crowd. "It looks like we've really got the games underway, haven't we? But, er, neither challenger stepped foot onto the first obstacle, so unfortunately, I can't actually award any points."

The crowd booed but he waved them silent.

"Next up, Joanne Boden of Hapsie versus Morwenna Pascoe of Penruth! Let's begin!"

This time both Joanne and Morwenna were more prepared. Firing shots of Carbon Dioxide from their Bracers at the fireballs that roared towards them they suffocated the flames, immediately extinguishing them. Easy, of course, if you knew what to do.

Now out of the metal tunnels, both stood on the edge of a bridge, with its creaking, cracking unstable stones ahead of them.

Kami muttered to Ellie, "I think it's limestone. What do you think?"

Joanna must have had the same thought as Kami and rushed towards the bridge. Each step Joanna took was a risky game as to whether the stone would support her. Morwenna quickly followed on her own bridge to the side. Quick steps were key and then – CRACK – a stone gave way.

"CALCIUM!" commanded Joanna, firing her Bracers downwards.

It worked!

"You're right, Kami!" Ellie cheered.

The Calcium fused with the Calcium Carbonate makeup of the limestone, holding it in place. Sharing a glance backwards to Morwenna, and Morwenna nodding in full understanding as to what was needed, the challengers began making their way across the bridge, reinforcing their footing as they went.

About ten metres before the end of the bridge, Joanna froze.

Morwenna, catching up with her on the bridge to her right, called over, "Are you okay?"

"I'm done," Joanna cried back. "I'm out. If I use any more calcium it'll weaken my bones. I feel like I'll break one just by taking a step. Go on, the point is yours."

Morwenna nodded, and with a soft, "Better luck next time," took a step forward. But as she turned back and saw Joanna just a few metres behind her, she hesitated.

She held up her hands and smiled. "I'm not going any further. One point is enough for me."

"A POINT FOR PENRUTH!" Barry bellowed from below. He clapped his hands together, forcing a grin, but his voice lacked its usual energy. "Onto round three! This is exciting! Although, let's have something slightly more…competitive this time, shall we?"

Professor Fialova was readying herself at the platform at the top of the Foundry. Just as she was about to step forward to take on the metal tunnels, she turned to Greg Hoggett who was preoccupied with funnelling prawns into his throat. She snatched a milk carton from his grasp.

"I'm so nervous!" Ellie proclaimed as she took her seat back with Michael.

"She'll be fine," Michael said without any confidence.

Within a few minutes both Professor Fialova and Jenna Trenouth had overcome the first two obstacles and reached the third, learning brilliantly from those who had gone before them. A vast metal pole, the height of two buses standing end to end, stretched downwards to another platform. And the way to get down? Spiralling each metal pole were small metal steps, each sparking electricity.

Jenna Trenouth observed the metal and sparks and the small platform. Ellie guessed she'd have to divert the electric current. Bringing her wrists together, Jenna summoned, "Elemental Bracers. Carbon." Out shot a stream of black onto the first step then onto the floor.

It was a very clever idea. Carbon, especially graphite, can reroute and hopefully ground electric currents, allowing the electricity to take the easiest path to the floor. With this, Jenna leapt on to the first step, and then—

CRACK!

It clearly wasn't a very clever idea! Jenna jolted before being thrown backward, her body flailing through the air.

For the second time that day a commotion came from the marksmen below. The shouts and blue streams of Oxygen caught Jenna before she landed, slowly letting her down with a gentle thud.

"OSKAR'S BALLOON!" screamed Ellie from her seat, not that anyone other than Michael could hear her in all the delight of the Glenmorgan spectators.

Michael did hear her though, and turned to Ellie, "You what?"

"You remember! *Oskar's balloon!* Why can Oskar make his feather float, Michael?"

Michael thought back to the many times Ellie had tried to explain to him about a feather and a balloon. "Because he owns a big green balloon?"

"Right!" said Ellie. "And what does he do with the balloon?"

"Um, rubs it on his woolly jumper?" said Michael, hoping he was remembering correctly and at least helping a little.

"Exactly!" said Ellie, believing both she and Michael were on the same page.

They weren't.

"Ellie, you're gonna have to spell this one out for me," Michael finally said, as nodding along with her was beginning to feel a tad awkward.

"The pole, it's not a live electrical current, Michael, it's static electricity."

"Righhhhttt. Clever!" responded Michael, finally nodding along for real now.

"And why would Oskar struggle to make static electricity in Hapsie?" continued Ellie, much to the disappointment of Michael who believed this particular test to be over.

"Because…" attempted Michael.

"Because…" Ellie started.

"ELEMENTAL BRACERS. $H_2O$. WATER!" cried Professor Fialova from the top of the cavern.

It was not overly clear to everyone else whether Lucinda had overheard Ellie and Michael's conversation (most likely not given the noise and great distance) or if she was also thinking of Oskar's big green balloon (highly improbable too) but either way,

177

Ellie and Professor Fialova were aligned in their intellectual processes. Firing a fine water mist over the steps as she worked her way down, the static charge dissipated safely into the air making the steps safe – well, at least as safe as small spiralling metallic steps on a tall pole suspended in the middle of a giant cavern can be.

And as it happens, that's not very safe at all. Midway down, the water vapour had made one step particularly slippy. She fell and Professor Fialova found herself being caught in a bubble of Oxygen from the marksmen below. But unlike Jenna Trenmouth, the professor had earned a point for Hapsie.

With the scores tied at 1-1, and only two challengers left from each side, Barry MacBain was nothing short of ecstatic. The tension was building beautifully and the next set of challengers – Master Quinn and Lowan Carlyon from Penruth – were now well underway.

After slowly and painfully mastering the first three obstacles, Master Quinn was the first to reach the wind tunnel. Choosing to face the wind at the bottom, rather than the ice-cold rungs of the horizontal ladder above, he stepped inside. A ferocious blast of air slammed into him. The bottom of the tunnel roared like a storm in a canyon, its unpredictable bursts twisting and hammering from every angle. Quinn dug his heels in, trying to hold his ground, firing Oxygen from his Bracers to deflect the gusts. Then, with a final gale-force blast, Quinn lost control. The wind hurled him backward, sending him stumbling off the tunnel's platform, straight into the metal pole he had just climbed down. The pole which had already begun recharging with static electricity. The moment his hand slammed against it, a fresh jolt of charge snapped through him, his body jerking sideways before he was flung towards the cavern floor below.

Lowan Carlyon watched the entire disaster unfold. He barely had to move. All he had to do was remain standing on the wind tunnel platform. Lowan raised his hand announcing that he had no intention of attempting to get two points for Penruth by completing the course.

"2-1 to Penruth!" The scores were announced.

"GLORIOUS. JUST GLORIOUS!" Barry MacBain wiped away tears of joy. "With just one point in it, and on to our final round, any outpost could still win or lose! My, this is even better than—"

Barry MacBain stopped suddenly.

He raised his hand to his shoulder and touched something warm.

Wet and warm.

Wet, warm and smelling revolting.

Wet, warm, smelling revolting, and full of sweetcorn chunks, prawn scraggs, milk curds, broccoli residue and steak ends.

He looked up.

As he looked, picking up speed from its starting position thirty metres or so above him, another bout of wet, warm and revolting hit him in straight in the forehead.

"EURGHHHHHHHH!" came a groan from far above which echoed around the underground cavern.

Eurgh indeed.

Greg Hoggett lay over the edge of the starting platform at the topmost point of the Foundry and finished throwing up the entire contents of his day's nourishment. Greg waved to whoever would see him, whoever wasn't laughing at Barry MacBain, to suggest that he was very much done, very much out, very much *not* going to be challenging at all today.

Greg rolled himself off the platform onto the lift and flapped his hands in the air to be lowered back down to the floor, still groaning and retching as he did.

Slowly, thoughtfully, Barry MacBain wiped himself down

179

with the jacket of a spectator, and then without a further moment of pause stormed back into the centre of the stage.

"GREG HOGGETT. YOU ARE DISQUALIFIED," he thundered to the crowd, a statement that didn't trouble a heaving Greg any more than he already was. "WHICH LEAVES ME NOTHING ELSE TO SAY THAN: THE WINNERS OF THE FOUNDRY GAMES ARE—"

"WAIT!" came a voice a few metres in front of him.

There was a small figure standing by his legs.

A small girl.

A small girl called Ellie Ment.

"I'd like to compete," she said.

Oh dear, Ellie. Don't do it!

# Chapter Twelve

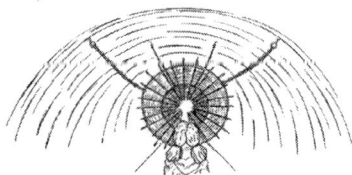

# Flames

"What?" Barry looked down, quite taken aback as to how or why anyone felt it appropriate to interrupt him, let alone when he was in full flow in front of a packed audience during the Foundry Games.

"I'll do it," Ellie whispered softly.

"I'm sorry? I couldn't hear you."

"I'LL DO IT!" shouted Ellie, far louder than she needed. "I'LL BE THE FINAL CHALLENGER!"

A patronising sneer ran over Barry MacBain's face.

"Oh!" he shouted. And then with his own roaring, knee-slapping laughter, "Oh! Oh! Oh! How wonderful! How adorable!" Barry MacBain turned to the crowd. "Ladies and gentlemen, this is exactly what the Foundry Games were made for, to demonstrate commitment from our members, testing our passion for the cause and hardships ahead. And who better to show it than this young lady here, ladies and gentlemen? This here, er...what was your name again?"

"Ellie, Ellie Ment." Ellie scowled.

"Ah yes, Ellie." He roared with patronising laughter, which was swiftly followed by the same laughter from the spectators.

A hand placed itself softly on her shoulder. "Come on, Ellie," said Professor Fialova, who had hobbled over to where they were.

Ellie looked at the limp in Professor Fialova's stride, then across to Master Quinn, clutching his arm at the far end of the Foundry. She swung her head around to Kami and her father, locked in a tight hug.

These were her people. This was her team.

She wasn't going to let their efforts go to waste.

This was about showing what they could do. She wouldn't let them fail. She had to prove she had what it takes.

"LET. ME. COMPETE!" she shouted, and then more steadily, "I'm a Material Matter member, I have the right to step in for Hapsie."

Barry MacBain knelt down in front of Ellie. His tone changed, and he became quiet yet still somehow audible to the engaged ears that surrounded the cavern. "You may be somehow part of the Material Matter, young Ellie, but only those with Elemental Bracers can compete, I'm afraid." And with a final patronising pat on the head, Barry MacBain stood up to announce the winner.

"THE WINNERS OF THE FOUNDRY GAMES ARE—"

"AHEM," said Ellie, rolling up a sleeve.

Barry MacBain paused once again mid-sentence. He didn't move his head, instead he just peered downward, straight past his nose, straight to Ellie's wrists. Under his breath he muttered, "Gosh, are those…?" and then stopped. He turned towards Professor Fialova and just as quietly repeated, "Lucinda, are those…?" but once again he stopped himself.

Barry's eyes turned back to Ellie who was staring daggers at him. A wry smile spread over his face. He grew taller, more pompous, and then was back in full flow. "SHE WEARS A BOND OF BRACERS, EVERYONE. SHE IS A MEMBER. THEN WHO AM I TO SAY NO?"

A cheer erupted from the benches. There would be a final challenger after all.

"Hey, Barry?" Ellie taunted him. 'You missed a spot." She pointed to a chunk of puke in his hair and skipped away towards the lifting platform.

Professor Fialova followed. "Ellie, Ellie, you don't have to do this. You shouldn't do this!" It was useless. Ellie stepped onto the platform, turned to face Professor Fialova, and holding onto a chain support didn't say a word as she was hoisted into the air. "Ellie!" Professor Fialova called, her trembling voice lost in the heights of the cavern.

It's fair to say Kit Lamorna was just as surprised as anyone else that an eleven-year-old was on the starting platform next to him.

"They want me to challenge a kid?" he muttered to himself. "A whizzle-whumping kid?"

Ellie turned to Kit and, realising that the art of condescension was just as strong by adults even when thirty or so metres in the air, she simply replied, "The game is to challenge yourself, not me." Then, without another word, she turned to face the enormity of the flame-throwing metal tunnel ahead of her.

Ellie was a long way away from her jam jars now.

A loud bang signalled the start of the final round. Kit rushed forward, and as he did a fireball flashed towards him. Skilfully, at complete ease, he extinguished it with a shot of smoky blue-grey light as the Carbon and Oxygen mixed from his Elemental Bracers to form Carbon Dioxide.

Ellie's legs were like jelly, but she somehow found the ability to move forward. The first fireball was hurtling towards her so she raised her wrists, clunked together her Bracers, and felt that surge of vibration and power run down her arms. Ellie was just in the process of summoning her own Carbon Dioxide when…when the fireball flew straight over her head!

(Now, the Material Matter members from the outpost from Glenmorgan who had designed this course were an interesting bunch. Talented, exceptionally bright minds, minds that were focussed on creating new ways of generating clean energy. They had helped improve the world for the better in many different ways. They were however also of a certain disposition where they believed themselves to be one step higher on any ladder than anyone else. To them, the other outposts were inferior – especially those from Penruth who focussed on whimsical activities such as growing trees and restoring ecosystems.

With this type of mindset there was no doubt that when they stood back and admired their completed design for the Foundry games, they truly believed they had accounted for every eventuality, every twist and turn that could possibly catch out, test – and most likely hurt – any challenger that set foot on it. And for the most part, they had. There was only one problem: they hadn't taken into consideration the fact that a petite eleven-year-old might also take part.)

Ellie stood and watched as a second fireball flew over her head, and then a third.

Oh. Easy peasy.

Ellie began to slowly walk her 1.38m self down the metal tunnel as the fourth, fifth and sixth fireball followed the others, whooshing harmlessly above her. As she walked, she turned her head to her left to watch Kit Lamorna battling fireball after fireball in his tunnel. She was sure at one point Kit had glanced across in panicked confusion as to why Ellie was calmly standing in the tunnel watching him, but if he did it was only for a flicker of a moment, before another fireball shot towards him to be extinguished. Ellie reached the end, calmly, collectedly, unburned-ly.

Carefully she placed her foot on the fragile stones of the bridge ahead of her. Nothing happened. Nothing would happen: the 32kg weight of Ellie Ment had no impact on even the most fragile stone. Ellie calmly walked across the bridge, taking a look back at one point to see a slightly scorched Kit blasting his first shot of Calcium at a random stone in a desperate bid to help secure it in place.

Onto the statically charged metal poles, and while even eleven-year-olds are still very much susceptible to electric-shocks, a fully refreshed Ellie Ment had absolutely no trouble in using her Bracers to summon water vapour as she daintily spiralled down the metal steps, her size 2 shoes fitting perfectly into the small metallic footholds.

During all this, on the ground there was quite the commotion. Barry MacBain, the course designers, and the rest of the Glenmorgan spectators had not necessarily wanted to see this particular eleven-year-old be harmed, but the Foundry Games were about competition and pushing oneself to further the implementation of science. They'd certainly wanted to see a competitive race to conclude the games. This was an insult to the Foundry Games as a whole! But Ellie couldn't see this or hear this, and quite frankly she couldn't care less what they thought, especially as she lightly jumped herself off the final metal step and onto the platform for the next obstacle.

*Wind tunnel down below or ice-cold horizontal ladder above?* Ellie thought to herself as she pondered how to navigate the fourth obstacle, an obstacle no one had yet conquered. There wasn't much need for lengthy pondering. Ellie climbed up a support pole with ease and began swinging herself from bar to bar, just like she would most days on the monkey bars at Leafy Park.

> (Oh, the ice-cold bit? If you felt that would be a problem then clearly you haven't touched the metal framework of the playground during the winter months. This wasn't cold, this was just how it was for all the kids around Hapsie as their parents watched on sipping and warming their hands on their rapidly cooling coffee mugs.)

Below Ellie's feet the wind tunnel roared pointlessly. Elegantly somersaulting herself off the end bar and onto the platform that led to the final obstacle, Ellie was feeling pretty pleased with herself. *This is all going rather well!* she thought. Turning back, she could see Kit was still going, slowly but steadily, now edging down from the top of the metal pole, blasting shots of weakening blue water vapour from his Bracers as he did, exhausted from the two previous obstacles he'd just overcome.

Ellie turned to examine the final obstacle.

*Oh fizz,* she thought.

It was a fitting reaction. Being an eleven-year-old certainly wouldn't help here. The end of this obstacle was about five car lengths ahead of her. In between was nothing, nothing except a drop of around ten metres into a roaring fire pit.

There was nothing to duck under, nothing to step onto, nothing to daintily manoeuvre around, and certainly no monkey bars to swing herself breezily across on. Nothing but flames. For the first time, the reality of the situation crept over Ellie. She was frozen and had no idea how to move forward. She wouldn't have the ability to build her own bridge with the amount of Calcium inside her, or the breath to use her own Oxygen to lift herself up.

This was, quite simply, an impossible task.

Ellie turned back. Kit had reached the bottom of the metal pole and was now considering whether to tackle the gale-force winds below or ice-cold horizontal ladder above. Ellie looked out to the spectators around her. They were loving this! Finally the stakes had risen, the course had matched its challenger.

All eyes were on Ellie.

Perhaps Kit would fail in the gale-force winds, just like Master Quinn had. She would have earned one point, and the outposts would draw 2-2. Would that be enough?

She looked back. Eyeing up the horizontal ladder above, Kit had summoned a cloud of metallic-grey from his Bracers and was passing his hands through it.

*What was it?* Ellie squinted, trying to focus on the cloud of light and dust. *Oh!* Ellie suddenly recognised the colours from earlier: Zinc.

*That's clever* thought Ellie, and it was. The same element that Ellie had used to help regenerate the skin on the Reverend's burnt hands would also be the perfect short-term protection against the ice-cold rungs of the ladder. Kit jumped up to the first horizontal bar and began moving himself from rung to rung, towards Ellie.

What was Ellie to do? There must be something! In the corner of Ellie's eye, a frantically waving red blob caught her attention. Squinting again into the distance she saw it was Michael. He was mouthing something to her. What was it? He was so far away.

*Art-art-art*

"Art?" said a confused Ellie out loud. "Oh! Master Quinn!" she exclaimed, frantically searching out the whereabouts of her art teacher down below. She found him. But Master Quinn had his back turned and was paying little to no interest in her progress.

What could Michael mean? Ellie looked back to where Michael was mouthing the same word over and over, and now also gesturing, he was gesturing…

"Oh!" Ellie suddenly realised.

"OH!" she reacted on her second consideration of Michael's idea.

"Oh," she disapprovingly concluded on a third reflection of her now very clear understanding as to what her friend was trying to indicate.

"Oh, Michael, really?" she finally disappointedly said out loud. But she knew he was, at the very least, not wrong.

Kit was nearing the end of his monkey bars. If she was to retain her lead advantage it would be now or never.

Ellie Ment ran across the platform towards the firepit as fast as she could and then jumped. She leapt as hard as she could into the abyss.

(Now, let's take a moment to pause please and have a think for a second: how far can you jump? The length of an average car? Probably not. In fact, the furthest a human has ever jumped is roughly the length of two average cars, so it's likely a safe bet you'll be somewhere between no cars and two cars in your distance. And Ellie, not being a long jump world record holder, would most likely fit into that same bracket as you, and certainly not the required length of five cars to overcome the gap in front of her. That's exactly why, as Ellie launched herself off the platform, the spectators screamed. They were here for fun, and that fun would probably have a dramatic downward curve if they had to witness the total incineration of an eleven-year old child.)

Everyone screamed – except for Michael, who sat expectantly.

As it turns out, our assumptions were correct, Ellie couldn't jump the length of even one car, and within a metre or so of the platform's edge she began hurtling downwards towards the fire pit below.

As it turns out, Ellie knew this was about to happen, and bringing her wrists together in front of her as she fell, she cried, "ELEMENTAL BRACERS. CARBON, HYDROGEN. GIVE ME METHANE."

Ellie's left Bracer throbbed black for Carbon and her right Bracer throbbed pink for Hydrogen, uniting in a dusty-pink stream of light which shot out in front of her towards the flames. As Ellie plunged headfirst closer and closer towards the fire the methane suddenly ignited and a roar of controlled fire and force shot downwards, which threw her upwards at breakneck speed. There's good old Sir Issac Newton's third law again!

In front of everyone, Ellie had just experimented with her own rocket-propulsion. Flying with the force of…farts.

"OH YES!" cried Michael, thumping the air. "YES, YES, YES!" and then turning to the benches beside him, "Methane! It's what farts consist of – quite flammable, you know!"

Ellie landed with a thud onto the ground of the cavern. Looking up, she could see the flame she needed to expand to ignite the banner above. No more obstacles, just a short sprint and a quick blast of explosive Hydrogen onto the flame to win two points for Hapsie, two points which would win the Foundry Games.

THUD.

Kit Lamorna landed a few metres in front of Ellie. Turning to her he said, "Nice idea, kid! Very smart!" and then started to sprint forward, towards Penruth's flame and banner.

Ellie lifted herself off the floor and sprinted after Kit. As it happens an eleven-year-old's legs were no match for an adult's, and no matter how much Ellie pushed herself, the distance between her and Kit was widening with every step.

With ten metres to go, Kit raised his wrists and with a deep cry of "HYDROGEN!" his Bracers began to throb pink.

It was now or never. Ellie was too far away from her flame to reach it with her own Hydrogen blast, but potentially close enough to Kit to neutralise his stream of elements.

Ellie knew if she could just combine some Chlorine with Kit's emerging Hydrogen shot it would create Hydrogen Chloride, a non-flammable gas. It wouldn't burn. It wouldn't explode. It would shut the whole thing down cold. The flame wouldn't expand, the banner would stay exactly how it was, then she could race ahead and win.

With one last push forward, Ellie let out an immense scream. "ELEMENTAL BRACERS—"

Ellie tripped and stumbled.

"OH FIZ—" She just caught herself in time to add, "CHLORINE!"

Her Bracers throbbed with light, the vibrations rattling through her body. It stung more than it ever had before. As streams of light shot towards Kit, she felt a power unlike anything she'd experienced, a searing heat coursing through her wrists and out into the blinding light ahead. And with that, Ellie landed on the floor with an almighty cry, unable to see whether her plan had worked.

She heard Kit scream. He was screaming in immense pain.

Did she get it wrong?

Was Hydrogen Chloride not a neutraliser after all?

No, Ellie was sure of that. It was, it definitely was.

Then why did it happen?

Why was there that blinding flash?

Why was there a violent explosion?

Why was Kit lying there, burnt all over?

Ellie lay on the floor, staring up as Kit writhed in pain in front of her. Marksmen and spectators sprinted over to help him. Various lights streamed from their Bracers, cooling the flames, aiding the burns.

*Oh gosh*, she thought as she lay there, alone. *What have I done?*

"ELLIE!" a voice rang out. It was Professor Fialova. "What did you do?"

"I don't know! I don't know!" Ellie shouted over the chaos.

"What did you summon?" Professor Fialova demanded.

Ellie had never seen her look like this before. "I just wanted to neutralise Kit's Hydrogen," Ellie gasped. "I tried to make Hydrogen Chloride."

Professor Fialova froze mid-step. "With Chlorine?"

Ellie nodded. "Exactly. So it would react with his Hydrogen."

The professor didn't respond. She just stared at Ellie, her lips slightly parted, her face showing the thoughts that spun in her head.

"It was bright yellow, Lucinda."

Ellie looked up. Master Quinn was standing over her, his pupils narrower than she'd ever seen.

Bright yellow? That wasn't right.

Ellie swallowed. "No...it can't be. When I summoned Chlorine before it was greeny-yellow."

"Before?" asked Quinn.

"At the leisure centre, they were short of—" Ellie started to explain.

"Ellie, *you* were responsible for that Chlorine gas leak?"

Professor Fialova asked.

Ellie didn't need to reply or nod; her eyes said enough.

Master Quinn knelt, running his fingers over the scorched floor, dissolved surfaces. His expression darkened. He turned to Professor Fialova. His voice was quiet, but it carried like a thunderclap.

"Lucinda. This wasn't Chlorine. This was Fluorine."

"Fluorine?" Barry MacBain's voice boomed across the arena. "FLUORINE?!" He strode closer towards them, his heavy boots echoing. "IMPOSSIBLE! Are you insane, Victor!? Do you even hear yourself?"

But as he lowered himself to the ground, his protests died in his throat. He too saw the impact. Whatever had just happened had corroded deep into the floor.

"I meant to say Chlorine..." Ellie said with a whimper. She might have, but what had come out of her mouth, stumble and all, had sounded an awful lot like Fluorine. Oh no...

"How long has she had access to these Bracers?" MacBain demanded, looking up at Professor Fialova and Quinn.

"Just under a week," the professor murmured back.

"Oh my," said MacBain as he exhaled sharply. For a long moment, he said nothing. Then he turned to Master Quinn, his voice dropping to a whisper.

"Victor, if she has the skill to summon Fluorine within a week..." He swallowed. "What else can she do?"

Fluorine. A gas so reactive, it couldn't exist freely in nature.

In the body, it was barely there at all, just minute amounts chemically bound as Fluoride – stable, safe, locked away in bones and teeth with extra electrons, just like Chlorides were.

But Fluorine? Pure Fluorine? Element number 9?

*That* burned through metal, shattered glass, and could rip apart water itself.

"What's going on?" Ellie asked, feeling more than a little terrified.

Professor Fialova sighed. "No beginner should be able to summon the Chlorides from their body as pure Chlorine. And even those with many years of practice can barely summon the traces of Fluorides in their body as pure Fluorine." She hesitated, before adding, "You can see what can happen."

"It was a mistake, Professor. I promise. I tripped. My Bracers must have misheard me. I was trying to neutralize the Hydrogen."

Professor Fialova stared at Ellie.

"What does this mean?" Ellie asked.

"It means everyone will be scared of you, Ellie. Very scared."

# Chapter Thirteen

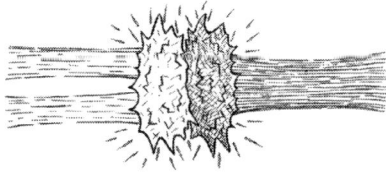

# Blame

Ellie sat silently in the railcar waiting for Master Quinn and Joanne Boden to determine which levers they would pull to take them back to the Old Glove Factory.

As the faint hum of the magnetic levitation began and the railcar lifted a few millimetres above the old tracks, Ellie folded her legs into her chest and wrapped her arms tightly around her. She was still sore from the vibrations which, just thirty minutes before, had stung through her entire body. Her mind was still replaying over and over the sight of Kit Lamorna writhing on the floor.

No one else was talking, no one was even willing to share the faintest eye contact with anyone else.

But Ellie's mind was racing. It was clear from the reaction of everyone at the Foundry that the result of the games was no longer the talking point. *It was probably for the best anyway*, Ellie thought. Ellie neither finished the course, nor was further ahead than Kit when everything happened. If there was going to be a result, it would probably have been a win for Penruth. Ellie had even heard murmurs of her being banned. The game was to challenge herself, not attack the opponent. That was against the rules.

"It wasn't my fault. I didn't mean to. I wasn't aiming for Kit," Ellie mumbled to herself, half hoping someone would hear her, react to her, tell her everything was going to be okay.

But no one did. Was it because of what Professor Fialova said? Was suddenly everyone scared of her? Why? Because she could use her Elemental Bracers in ways beyond her years? Surely that was a good thing.

As mentioned, Ellie's mind was racing.

Kami and her father had retreated to the back seats, still wrapped in each other's arms.

Professor Fialova sat, deep in thought, on the far side of the carriage, with Michael across from Ellie. Michael had tried to put a hand on her leg, mutter something quietly to see if she was okay, but he too was shocked by it all and didn't know what to say.

It was such a quick journey home, but like this it would feel like an age.

"So, er…" came a voice from behind Ellie's shoulder. "So, er…" it came again. A less green and more human-coloured Greg Hoggett squeezed himself down onto the chair next to Michael, facing Ellie. "So, you know, if you can summon Chlorine from Chlorides, and you can muster up the smidgins of Fluorides you have in your body and turn them into Fluorine…you know…" He paused and leaned into Ellie. "You know, we all have traces of Gold in us…" he whispered.

"Greg?" came Professor Fialova's voice from behind him.

"Ah. Well," said Greg, clearly annoyed that his whispers weren't whispery enough. Then, turning back to Ellie, "Think about it." He winked.

It was odd, but Ellie welcomed the conversation. Someone was at least acknowledging her, no matter what the subject matter. If Greg was willing to talk, to break the mood, then she didn't want to let the opportunity slide.

"The garden shed you built us is still standing," she said,

instantly regretting that this would be her conversation starter. Across the railcar Professor Fialova gave a light smile. Anyone who'd passed Ellie's house over the last year had inevitably stopped to stare at the contraption which screwed old doors and cupboards together to call itself a shed.

"What's that? Well yes, I mean, it should. It's a shed!" replied a slightly taken aback Greg.

Ellie thought it best to move the conversation on. "Kami mentioned to me about the amazing new building material you created."

Greg Hoggett would never turn up an opportunity to talk (positively) about himself. "Ah yes!" he replied as the railcar jolted through a junction onto another track. "Concrexio! It's going to revolutionise the building industry. We found a way to convert old waste, wastes that are already going to landfill, and turn them into a recycled, durable building material. It uses so much less energy to manufacture than anything else."

"It sounds amazing," replied a very impressed Ellie. "Concrete uses so much water and needs an enormous amount of energy just to produce the smallest amount. If you've found a way to replace that, it really could transform the entire industry! Not to mention the planet. It would do a world of good for saving water and the environment."

Michael had perked up his ears at the idea that this was potentially the ultimate upcycle.

"Yes, this is the joy of the Material Matter, Ellie. We can change the world for the better," replied Greg.

"If only you had used it to build our new school, it might not have burned down within a month!" Michael suggested, feeling that if there was a conversation about upcycling, he should be part of it.

"We did," replied Greg shortly. "It was our flagship project."

"Oh, well…bad luck," joked Michael.

Ellie wanted to kick him.

"But science is about learning," Greg said with a shrug. "Any issues we encountered there have been improved, and it's now much more, let's say, vandal-proof. You know we've already got five more projects under way using it. Think of all the waste no longer going to—"

"We're here," came a grunt from the front. And they were. The railcar had halted back at the same dingy rock basement from where they had left a few hours earlier.

The troupe of exhausted, hobbling and frail challengers – with Kami supporting her father, and Michael following on behind – made their way to the freight elevator and the familiar rattling of chains and grinding metal brought them all back up to the atrium of the Hapsie Material Matter's headquarters.

The oak tables were lined with the most wonderful-looking foods and drinks. Banners and decorations were hung inside the atrium in the same colours as the stripes on their uniforms.

A large celebration was expected for their return.

But there was no expectant crowd waiting to celebrate their efforts, win or lose.

In fact, there was no one at all.

It was all rather odd.

Where was everyone? A party of some form had clearly been planned.

The enormous atrium stood desolate. Ah no, there were two people sat chatting on the oak tables – or at least they *had* been chatting until they stepped further into the atrium. The men had now got up and moved towards them, but they weren't celebrating, they weren't enquiring how they did at the games.

*What is going on?* Ellie wondered. *Was everyone just about to jump out and shout 'Surprise'?*

"Ment," said Master Quinn, turning to her, blocking her way forward. "Ment. I need you to hand me your Elemental Bracers," he commanded.

"What! Why?" Ellie replied.

"You're dangerous," Master Quinn responded. "You're dangerous. You're a liability. And a child. You have taken no responsibility—"

"Dangerous?" snorted Ellie, still in shock. "I'm good at this! That's what I am. As far as I understand it, I'm skilled beyond my years!"

"Good?" Master Quinn scowled. "GOOD?" he shouted, towering over Ellie. "What are you good at? Burning people? Endangering innocent people with toxic gas? What exactly, Ellie, are you good at?"

The rage that emptied from Master Victor Quinn filled the atrium, and it was all turning, pointing itself at Ellie.

"Yes, you've shown you can use the Elemental Bracers in ways most people never could. But you've also shown exactly why you shouldn't have them – because you don't stop to think. You act first, justify later. React on impulse without considering the potential consequences.

"You have power here, Ellie – terrifying power – but you don't have the maturity to handle it properly. You've shown what you really are. You are just a child. Now. Hand. Me. Your. Bracers." Master Quinn spelled out his instructions.

Ellie thought long and hard, her heartbeat quickening with every moment that passed. Professor Fialova was right: they were scared of her. Very scared. Then she spoke her mind under her breath. "It was an accident. Kit Lamorna was just an accident." Before adding, "You're just jealous."

"I'm sorry?" Master Quinn said, equally quietly.

Ellie stood firm. "You're just jealous that I'm able to do things you can't even—"

Before Ellie could finish the sentence, Master Quinn moved his nose away from hers and, raising his wrists together, bound his Bracers and boomed, "ELEMENT 9. FLUORINE."

A deafening CRACK thundered from his wrists. A blinding, bright yellow light burst from both of his Bracers as Master Quinn snapped his arms upward, aiming toward the gaping void above. The energy surged out and as the Fluorine travelled, it instantly reacted with the moisture in the air, violently ripping itself apart, corroding anything in its path – the metal gangways high above, the concrete and stone walls, the glass panels in the upper windows of the atrium's ceiling.

The distant noise of falling glass slowly faded, and Master Quinn turned back to Ellie.

"Satisfied, Ms Ment?" he said, making his point abundantly clear by his tone alone. "Now hand me your Bracers," Master Quinn repeated.

"No," Ellie said firmly. "I am sorry about Kit Lamorna, but I can do good, I can make change. Isn't this what we're all here for? *Because* we can wield these Bracers. Shouldn't we be celebrating this?"

"There will be no celebration tonight. I sent a Glenmorgan member down here to make it known soon after you irresponsibly had Kit laying there writhing on the floor. And no, there is certainly going to be no celebration of you, but there will be a correction of another mistake."

Another blast of light.

Two blasts in fact.

This time they came from the wrists of the men now standing either side of Master Quinn. The pale-blue streams of Oxygen hit Ellie squarely in the centre of her chest, causing her to step back, and then again, and again, the force of the rushing air driving her back towards the wall.

"Stop it!" shouted Professor Fialova from the side as she

200

watched Ellie get pinned up against the side of the atrium. But it was no use. The two men breathing deeply, steadily, had no intention of breaking their flows.

Slowly, each torrent of Oxygen on Ellie's chest moved outwards, hitting her arms with a powerful blast, snapping them back against the wall.

"Professor! Kami! Help! Please help!" screamed Ellie, as Master Quinn steadily moved towards her, fixated on her raised wrists. There was no help coming. Kami and Reverend Cal stood shellshocked, unable to move at the scene that unfolded in front of them.

"ELLIE!" Michael shrieked and ran towards one of the men, lunging to tackle them off their feet.

Master Quinn, just moments away from Ellie's wrists, saw Michael fly through the air and turned.

"OXYGEN!" he barked. The stream of light and Oxygen clapped against Michael's shoulder, tumbling him back across the floor.

The attack on her best friend.

The momentary distraction of Master Quinn's fixation on her.

It was just enough.

Ellie forced her wrists inwards, carving away the smallest space from the oncoming streams. She had a fraction of a second, if that, before the blasts of Oxygen would catch up.

"ELEMENTAL BRACERS. CARBON. OXYGEN. CARBON DIOXIDE."

One Bracer blazed black, the other pale-blue, and using her palms to direct the streams, Ellie sent the smoky blue-grey light thundering from her wrists into a wall of power, meeting the Oxygen streams a metre in front of her. The denser Carbon Dioxide disrupted the air balance, holding the Oxygen back like a force field. Just.

The two men pushed harder.

Ellie too.

Master Quinn joined in.

Ellie was holding off the three streams, slowly, powerfully, pushing them back.

"I..." Ellie gasped, frantically looking towards Professor Fialova.

"I..." she started again, desperately trying to push the words out.

"I...can't breathe..." she finally wheezed, collapsing to the floor as her body fought to replenish itself with as much Carbon and Oxygen it could muster from the surrounding air.

Ellie's Bracers unbound themselves with a faint click and she slumped back against the wall, chest heaving.

The commotion had ended.

The blue flashes faded away from the room.

Master Quinn walked up and stood over Ellie. "Yes, you're good. But the world isn't changed by good intentions, Ms Ment. It's changed by those smart enough to endure long enough to see them actioned."

And with that, he knelt beside Ellie, leaning in to whisper, "And today, Ment, you've shown you're only a kid – a whizzle-whumping kid." With a measured slowness, he gently unclasped the Elemental Bracers from her weak wrists and took them from her.

## Chapter Fourteen

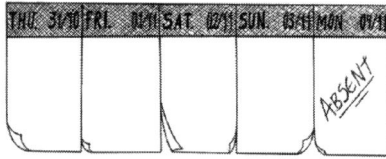

# The Science Of Being A Fallen Hero

For the first time since school records began, a blotch was marked against Ellie's name on Monday November 4th. The blotch read: ABSENT. The same again for Tuesday November 5th and all the way through to Friday November 8th. It was quite unprecedented.

It was true, at times in the past there were probably days when Ellie should have missed school – specifically, during a nasty bout of chickenpox almost exactly three years ago. But Ellie being Ellie convinced her parents that a 'mad, red-spotted scientist' was the perfect Halloween getup and, well, into school she went. Ellie's teachers became somewhat suspicious when Ellie had to keep up the costume for the week after Halloween for fear of revealing the actual cause of these red spots, but again, she was Ellie, and Ellie told her teachers that her Halloween-self had started an experiment and "true scientists don't abandon their experiments halfway through".

Incidentally, this ill-fated week of spots worked doubly well for Ellie. First, she didn't have to miss school when she absolutely should have. Secondly, the following week the entire class mysteriously came down with bouts of chickenpox and Ellie had a week of one-to-one teaching. How lucky!

When, however, Ellie declared to her mum and dad that she would also be missing school on the following week, they knew something was seriously wrong. The original excuse Ellie had given Mr and Mrs Ment was that she had a ballet injury. Her parents tried to enquire when on earth she took up ballet but Ellie had simply used Master Quinn's tactic of argument and made sure she turned her answer into something personal to them. "You wouldn't want me to miss *more* ballet by not fully resting my injury, would you?" And as their daughter had finally, somehow, begun a hobby that didn't involve destroying their house – something, dare they say it, 'normal' – and if resting her mysterious ballet injury meant so much to her that she was going to miss school…well then, rest away!

The truth was, however, that it's a strange thing having a new 'superpower' taken away from you. Especially when, just a few weeks ago, you had been planning how to change the world as part of an international secret science and environmental organisation.

Not that Ellie had anything to compare it to, of course.

But, as it turns out, losing a superpower takes far more from you mentally than any Elemental Bracers could ever summon. And more than anything, after all the events that had just unfolded, Ellie didn't know how she could face her teachers, almost all of whom were seemingly members of the Material Matter.

On the subject of Ellie's teachers, Phil and Seda Ment were pleasantly surprised as to how Hapsie School had shown particular interest in Ellie's absence. Within the first morning of her first day off school, a soft, calming voice had called her parents, wondering as to the whereabouts of Ellie. This same voice called again day after day, enquiring once again as to her wellbeing. Ellie's parents were unsure exactly how the school resources stretched to provide such attention to the well-being of all the school children who happened to be sick, but then again, it was well known that Hapsie School was regarded to have the best teachers and staff in the county, and clearly these standards stretched to whoever they must have employed as their receptionist too.

Little did they know of course that the enquiries were coming from the school's Head of Science, someone desperately concerned about Ellie, but knowing a doorstep check-in would get her into quite a bit of bother all around.

(It should be noted, at the end of the first week, Ellie's parents had tested the water with the 'school receptionist' as to the nature of Ellie's reason for being off school, and quite to their surprise they were told that if Ellie was saying her ballet injury needed rest, then as long as Ellie was generally well otherwise, they should adhere to the Ballet Book of Law Code 6.94, and allow Ellie to rest as described. Ellie's parents didn't have this Handbook, largely because it didn't exist, but the specific clause sounded very legitimate, so that was enough for them.)

Someone who absolutely was at school was Michael Upperton. Michael had little to no way of using the same tactics on his own parents, none at all.

Michael differed from his parents.

Michael's parents were incredibly proper.

Michael was not.

Michael's parents wore suits and collared shirts, even on the weekends. Michael would change out of his required school uniform on his way to school and slip on his favourite red HAPSIE Town football shirt.

Michael's parents received letters from the school about this so-called uniform truancy, and their punishment was to dock another week's worth from his already far-too-high pocket money. But unlike Michael's parents, Michael didn't need the newest, shiniest thing to be happy. His upcycling (or being resourceful, as his parents would try and explain to their also very proper friends) kept him very content.

Michael did however have a very valid reason or two for missing school himself. The first he couldn't really say – not because he was bound by any secret organisation's terms and conditions, but more because no one would believe him. If he told his parents he needed some time to rest after witnessing the events unfold at the Foundry Games, they would have had none of it.

The second reason was the very large purple-blue bruise on his left shoulder, the result of being blasted with a high-pressure burst of Oxygen. Oh, and that 5cm cut on his cheek from when he sort of went back in time (but actually didn't).

But as his father Theodore Upperton had told him, "You play with rubbish, son, you'll end up looking like rubbish." Followed swiftly by, "Now get dressed and go to school."

So off he went.

It was Michael, not Ellie's parents, not Professor Fialova, and certainly not Ellie herself, but Michael, who finally convinced Ellie to come back to school at the start of what would have been her third week off.

By the end of that week, Ellie really wished he hadn't done so.

It was worse than she could have possibly imagined.

When Ellie stepped into the Tithe Barn on her first day back, nothing was different. Nothing at all. And it was terrible.

Physical education with Ms Boden. The same Joanne Boden whom Ellie had accompanied to watch her tackle the fire tunnel and limestone bridge at the Foundry Games. Nothing,

nothing different. Ellie skipped and hopped as instructed over the dull, ashen grey bark and remains of the trees around the grounds, hung herself off the unnaturally drooped branches, and there was…nothing.

Art class with Master Quinn? Nothing, nothing unique. Master Quinn reluctantly called on her if she raised her hand (which admittedly was happening significantly less this week) and then continued to instruct the class as always, without much interest as to what their next assignment would be or how that would fit with the syllabus. There were no poignant remarks about her skill (or lack of it), no side-comment on how sticking around long enough was the key to making things happen, *or however he had put it*, Ellie thought.

Even the ludicrously planned field trip for maths class with Mr Fry, someone Ellie knew she had spotted on one of the large oak tables that first time she'd arrived at the Old Glove Factory…nothing. As the entire Falcon class crammed themselves inside the local estate agents, being asked by Mr Fry to add up bedrooms and toilets in the houses they saw on the noticeboard, there was no wink, no whisper, no knowing nod.

The most Ellie had to go on was a very calm, friendly, "Ellie, it's good to have you back. I hope you're well," from Professor Fialova as she sat down for her first science class that week, tucked away at the far end of the Tithe Barn. Maybe, just maybe, she had felt a soft touch on her back as the professor glanced over her shoulder to check her workings on a question about speed and velocity. Or perhaps, hopefully, an extra beat in her smile after Ellie answered a question correctly.

But given everything else, there was every chance, Ellie thought, that she was imagining all of it.

It was as if nothing had happened, as if it had been a dream. But it wasn't, and she had Michael to prove that.

"Why don't you just go to the Glove Factory and demand

to be let back in?" Michael asked, as the two sat on Ellie's bed on Friday after school.

"I don't think it works like that," replied Ellie. "I need to prove myself somehow. I guess I need to show them I'm responsible for my actions too, or something like that."

"Oh, right. Yeah. I wasn't really listening at that stage. You know, with having been blasted away and everything, if you know what I mean."

Ellie nodded at him. She knew exactly what he meant.

"Well, I see you at least took up some arts and crafts! I knew I'd rub off on you somehow!" said Michael, nudging and smiling at Ellie.

"What do you mean?" a confused Ellie asked.

"Er, your dreadful attempts at gardening," replied Michael, pointing towards the wilted, frail and barely growing plant pots on the windowsill. "You, um, decorated them? They're all…glittery."

Ellie looked across to where Michael was pointing. Sure enough, as the winter sun shone through the window, sharp glints of green and blue danced off the soil of the plant pots.

"I didn't…What on earth…?"

Michael was right. As Ellie moved her head from side to side, the soil seemed to shimmer. The smallest glint, but something. Ellie slowly moved her eyes across to the next pot plant. Nothing. No, wait – there! Again, a glint of green, blue. What was it? Something too small to see but catch it in the right light and it flickered before disappearing again into the soil.

Hold on.

Ellie sat back. "MICHAEL!" she exclaimed loudly. "DON'T. TOUCH. ANYTHING!"

"I HAVEN'T!" Michael protested. "Oh, come on! I know I did it that once and I've apologised. I—"

"SHUSHH!" instructed Ellie, putting a finger to his lips.

Michael shushed.

Ellie very slowly moved herself off the bed, muttering the word 'June' over and over. She was looking for something. "There! June!" she announced as she spotted a full jam jar in the corner of the room, one that Michael hadn't touched when he'd messed with them before. It had the corresponding month scrawled on a makeshift label. Even more slowly, methodically, without wanting to make the faintest disturbance in the water, she lifted it up and brought it in front of the window, allowing the winter light to stream through it.

"Michael! Do you see that?" Ellie nodded at the large jar. Her hands were locked around the glass to keep the water still.

Michael peered into the jar, through the water which was lit up beautifully from the streams of light behind. His eyes opened wide. He looked at Ellie then back at the jar. As he gazed with more detail at the still water inside the jar, his mouth opened. Ellie waited, hardly daring to breathe. There was silence, a realisation, an understanding between the two friends!

"Umm. See what?" Michael finally queried.

Oh. So no realisation or understanding then.

A very frustrated Ellie (thinking she was having a scientific breakthrough moment with her best friend) felt it very anticlimactic. "Michael, the water! It's been sat here for five months. Anything inside it should have settled by now, but look!"

Michael looked again. "Ellie, I'm seeing water, and a little bit of dirt at the bottom."

"It's cloudy, Michael! It should be crystal clear!"

Michael squinted. "I mean…barely."

He was right, to an untrained eye it just looked like water. But Ellie noticed the faintest haze as it was held to the light.

"Barely is good enough," she muttered. Before adding, "Another. Hold out your hands." And with that she gently placed the large jar of water in the outstretched palm of Michael's right hand. "Don't move a muscle," Ellie warned before hunting in her room for a jar that read August.

She carefully lifted a large jar of what once was hazelnut spread from the floor. She examined it in the light.

"What does this have to do with your glistening plant pots, Ellie?"

"It's exactly why they're shining. Here, hold this. Wait there. Don't move." She cautiously placed the second jar in Michael's left hand. And with that she scampered off the bed and out the door.

> (Now, I don't know about you, but the next time you're in the kitchen, grab two full jam jars and hold one in each hand as you stretch out your arms. See how long you can hold them for like that. One minute? Five minutes? Either way, after a while, no matter how light or small the jars are, the weight of them, plus the weight of your arms, start to weigh down on you quite considerably. Very considerably.)

Michael wasn't sure how long Ellie had left the room for, but he was in pain. A lot of pain. He had no intention of being scolded by Ellie again for ruining another, well, whatever this was, so he valiantly, courageously held his arms out, positively sure the jam jars were somehow getting heavier and heavier. At one point he let out a faint cry as his bicep muscles began to burn from the strain, a cry that alerted a passing Phil Ment who was just taking the washing basket downstairs.

Phil popped his head into the room to check everything was okay. "Oh, hi Michael!" he said, observing the eleven-year-old boy sitting on Ellie's bed with outstretched arms and two large jam jars in his palms.

Michael fractionally turned his head towards the voice, realising now that his neck was cramping slightly as he'd been tensing too much. "Er, hi, Ellie's dad."

"What are you doing?" enquired a cheerful, but very curious, Mr Ment.

"No idea." Michael would have shrugged but he wasn't allowed to move.

"Right you are! Well, good luck with that!" Mr Ment exited the room with a shake of his head, turning to bump into Ellie as she ran back in with a quick, "Hi, Dad!

"Sorry about that!" Ellie said to Michael as she crept back onto her bed. "Mum wanted to know how my day was. And I really didn't know how or what to—"

"Help!" a weak voice interrupted Ellie.

"Oh, right, sorry!" said Ellie, realising that her explanation could wait until Michael's hands were freed from his weight-training. She slowly took the jars back and placed them on the windowsill.

"Couldn't they have just been there all the time?" asked Michael, rubbing his aching arms.

"Yes," Ellie replied sheepishly. "Sorry about that. But watch this."

Just as careful as she had been throughout this entire exercise, Ellie unscrewed the metal lids of the jam jars, then from her pocket she took a small bottle of vegetable oil she'd borrowed from the kitchen.

Using a pipette, she sucked up some of the oil and dropped five drops into each jar. "If I'm right, Michael…well, just watch."

Michael and Ellie peered into each jar as the oil drops fell and began to swirl. As they did, tiny, minute, minuscule flecks of green and blue began to cling to the swirling oil. Just as poetically the oil began to rise to the top of the jar, carrying the flecks with

211

it.

"You see that?!" Ellie exclaimed.

"Where did they come from?" Michael wondered. "That's…that's magic!"

Oh dear, Michael. He was going to get a scolding from Ellie after all. "Magic?! Michael, I will personally glue your hands to a jam jar if you say that again. This is science!"

Ellie's eyes twinkled with excitement as she spoke. "Both these flecks and the oil are hydrophobic, which basically means they want to avoid water if they can. So when they meet, they stick together. Best buddies!"

Before Michael could ask *what* exactly was avoiding the water, Ellie had scooped some of the oil out of the top of the jar and produced a small fire-lighter she'd hidden under a book. She started pressing a flame up against the underside of the spoon.

"Do you smell that, Michael? Do you know what that is?" Ellie asked after a few minutes of the spoon heating up.

As small wafts of smoke began to rise from the spoon, Michael knew exactly what it was. The smell was very familiar. Only earlier that week, having been berated by his mother for ruining 'one of her best and finest winter gloves' by stuffing it with tissue paper and making some (very minor, he had thought) cuts, incisions and felt-tip markings to make it look more like an elephant when held upside down, Michael had wanted to make amends. So that very same evening he had decided to offer up an apologetic candlelit dinner for his parents. Of course, Michael was not allowed to touch the fancy candles that his parents kept in a drawer, so he had to make his own. Makeshift candles are difficult to create, especially when you don't have any wax or wick, and are left only with tissue paper and a toy recorder to act as a candle stick. As the tissue paper rapidly burned through and subsequently started melting the bright orange recorder, the fumes it gave off smelled exactly the same as the flecks Ellie was burning on the spoon.

"It's plastic!" exclaimed Michael.

"Exactly," responded Ellie.

"But why on earth is there plastic in your water?" Michael asked.

Ellie didn't need much time to think it over. The reasons had been running through her head since she saw the oil separate the plastic from the water. "Michael, if I'm right, then these jars must have been buried within a short distance of some plastic waste. The plastic has been slowly breaking apart into microscopic particles, which are ending up in our water system."

"Huh?" Michael said. "I thought the whole thing we're taught about plastic is that if you drop it in the ocean, it stays there for a thousand years."

"It's worse than that," Ellie explained. "It breaks down very, very slowly, releasing these microscopic particles into the water over those one thousand years."

"Crikey."

"Yeah…" said Ellie thoughtfully.

"So," pondered Michael, "if there's microscopic particles in the water from the plastic pollution. And our vegetables use the water to grow. And we eat the vegetables, and also drink the water…does that mean there's tiny bits of plastic inside all of us?"

"Yeah," she replied, as both of them began to realise the potential seriousness of this problem they had just uncovered, before adding, "Michael, do you still have that upcycled measuring wheel?"

Of course he had it. Michael never threw away his upcycles, otherwise they would just be rubbish again!

"It's in my bedroom," he replied, quite proud that Ellie remembered it.

Of course she had. As much as Michael thought it was

just a creative upcycle, he'd invented a full-on science and maths contraption, he just hadn't realised it!

"Let's get it and see how far these jars of water were buried from plastic waste." Ellie picked up her backpack, science pouch and logbook as they left her bedroom.

"But Michael," she said, stopping in her tracks, "Michael, if this theory is correct, then this is something big, and really serious."

Best of all, this could be her way back into the Material Matter.

## Chapter Fifteen

## Followed To The Letter

"So, let me get this straight," Michael said to Ellie as they trotted down the road on their ten minute walk to his house. "For the last year, you've been running an experiment on how plants grow depending on what type of water you feed them…"

"Yep," said Ellie, a little surprised and more than a little pleased that Michael had actually been listening at some point.

"But now, that exact same experiment is suddenly about these tiny plastic pollution flecks in the water, and has nothing to do with the plants growing?"

"Well, I mean, it is interesting why the plants from June to September aren't growing well, and whether that's linked," Ellie admitted. "But that's probably just my gardening skills, as you keep saying…so yes, ultimately, it's now an experiment about microplastics in our water." She panted slightly, struggling to keep up with Michael's pace.

"Right." Michael thought for a second. "So that's, like…totally different?"

"Well, I learned something new, and now the experiment has taken a different direction," Ellie explained, slipping into teacher mode. "We scientists say, 'we changed our hypothesis'."

"Huh." Michael pondered this. "So basically, that means you can never be wrong."

Ellie blinked. "What? No, that's not—"

"I mean, if every time your experiment doesn't work, you just change the reason you were doing it in the first place, then technically, you're always right," Michael said, unwinding the logic in his head.

"Well, it's not quite—" Ellie tried to object.

"So when people say, 'Ellie's always right when it comes to science', it's pretty unfair, really," Michael continued. "Because all you have to do is change the question to match whatever answer you've got." He grinned. "I mean, it's not that you're always right. It's just, by that logic, it's basically impossible for you to be wrong!"

"Much more fun like that, isn't it?" Ellie winked at Michael, who was obviously now wondering how he could apply the same logic when he played the wrong note on a musical instrument during a show or accidentally painted something badly in class.

"Oh." Michael stopped, looking up at his very large, very well kept house where they had just arrived. "Yeah, so, I actually can't go in."

"You can't go into your own house?"

"No. I mean, not until much later today," Michael said.

"Upcycle gone wrong?" Ellie questioned, already knowing the answer.

Michael nodded.

"No worries, I've got this. Your parents love me."

And that they did. Very much so. Without insight into Ellie's bedroom, specifically Ellie's Science Corner, to the Uppertons Ellie was everything their son wasn't. A top-grade student, very smart, and devoted to books. If they knew the truth behind Ellie's home experiments, they would likely see them as no different from Michael's own upcycles: 'a positively disruptive, house-wrecking activity'.

"Oh hello, darling!" announced Michael's mum as Ellie

rang the front doorbell and Michael hid behind a bush just to the side on their finely cultivated front lawn. "Oh dear," continued Gloria Upperton. "Oh dear, my dear, Michael isn't back from school yet."

"That's all right." said Ellie. "He asked me to get something for him from his bedroom."

"Oh?" enquired Mrs Upperton.

"Yes," said Ellie. "He needs some extra socks."

"How strange. Why?" wondered Gloria.

"Well, for his ballet practice this afternoon, of course."

"Oh!" said Gloria, a wide smile growing over her face. "My Michael? Ballet! How glorious, after all these years! Finally following my footsteps!"

At the same time, and quite unnoticed to Mrs Upperton, the bush to the right of the front door where they stood snorted indignantly.

*Excellent*, Ellie thought, grinning at the shrub as she walked into the front door. Ellie doesn't forget if you mess with her science; there will always be payback.

"Oh," came Gloria again. "Just be careful as you go up the stairs. Michael...you know..." she trailed off, before turning right into the kitchen.

Ellie walked through the grand entrance hall of the Upperton house, thinking (as she always did) that they could probably fit her entire house just in this one space.

At the bottom of the stairs she stopped. There was a very large old piece of thick orange foam blocking her way. Looking up, she realised why Michael might have decided to skip coming home for a few more hours. Down the entire run of the staircase was a row of old metal trays, clearly lifted from the skip behind the bakery, which, fastened together, acted as a massive slide. There was barely a foothold to the side to be able to walk up. The top metal tray was shifted to one side slightly, clearly an attempt by Mr or Mrs Upperton to remove it from its glued-down position. Without much success.

Ellie grinned, and holding onto the banister, carefully worked her way up the very little amount of actual staircase that was left.

Ellie always loved going into Michael's bedroom. It was such a shame she was rarely here. Michael much preferred to be at Ellie's house where the rules were more relaxed. But Michael's room, wow!

Firstly, it was huge, no different to every other room in the Upperton household. Secondly it was filled to the brim, top to bottom, with the most wonderful, creative and colourful inventions. To the immediate eye, it was trash – and of course, it had been once. Old food containers, end-of-life gardening equipment, endless bits and bobs Michael and Terry Tip had found at the Hapsie landfill. But under Michael's hands it was art, creations, works of Michael's brilliant mind! It was pure joy.

Ellie wished she could have sat and played, tried out everything, but there, leant against a shelf of upcycled toy planes, were the fishing rod, dustbin lid and cups that made up Michael's measuring device.

Holding it under her arm, Ellie headed back for the stairs and slid down the metal trays until she hit the orange foam with a quiet puff. She sauntered out the front door calling, "Bye Mrs Upperton!" as she went.

"Nice slide," she said to apparently no one as Michael tried to catch up behind her, making sure he remained unseen behind the various pots and plants that lined the garden path. "Oh, you might want to upcycle yourself a tutu," Ellie added, opening the front gate. "Now, let's get measuring."

For the next two hours Ellie and Michael weaved around Hapise, revisiting the locations where Ellie had planted her jam jars throughout the year, trying to find an order that would take them the least amount of time. Michael measured the distance between the holes and any plastic waste they could find on the ground around the area. Ellie logged it all in her notebook.

Having been excited to start her new school, she had planted the jam jars during the summer months in locations where she could catch a glimpse of it. Therefore, by the time they wove into Hapsie Forest for October's placements, only September's remained. Those had been planted along the old road through the forest, the very place where she had stood with Master Quinn and watched the school burn down with purple flames.

Ellie stood in the heart of Hapsie Forest, fixated on her logbook with a deeply scrunched-up face. As Michael shouted out the latest accurate measurement for an old hole which Ellie had determined must have been, "Thirty-four steps from Space Rocket, towards Big Ears, away from Large Lump," across from where they had found three large plastic bottles littered on the ground, Ellie's face grew even tighter.

"It's not going to work, Michael," she said eventually.

"What's that?" said Michael, who up until then believed that he, and his upcycled measuring device, were part of the breakthrough of a new scientific discovery.

"We have no idea if any of the plastic waste we've seen over the last two hours was there when the jars were. If any of this plastic was littered *after* the jars were collected, then our data is dud."

Michael sighed. "Did you not see it when you were digging the holes?"

"Do I remember the individual bits of plastic litter next to one hundred different random holes in the ground?" Ellie mocked. "Ten completed months up until now, ten jars and holes per month, equals one hundred holes. Even if I had been able to, I did all this in the dark and normally when it was raining."

"Oh." Michael sighed again. "That's a shame." He twirled his measuring device disappointedly.

"There's no control," explained Ellie. "We need some form of control."

"Huh?" said Michael, not understanding who needed to control what.

"We need somewhere, something, where we know there's always been plastic waste, and we know the water has been seeping through it. It will allow us to get a baseline," Ellie clarified.

The two looked at each other. Their eyes lit up.

"STEGO-HOLE!" they said in unison.

And they were right. A single location where the water at the bottom had passed through endless pieces of plastic waste, and importantly was trapped there!

Ellie and Michael immediately rushed away towards the road that divided the forest and led to their school, arriving at the exact place where Ellie had watched the school burn down.

Michael was at least twenty metres ahead of Ellie when he cried, "It's gone!"

"What do you mean, 'it's gone'?" said Ellie, catching up behind.

And sure enough, it had gone. Where Stego-hole used to be was now a perfect outline of a Stegosaurus, but this time instead of being a hole filled with Lucas Litter's plastic waste – aka: the perfect rainwater control for their experiment – instead it was filled with beautifully smooth fresh black tarmac.

"Gahhh!" exclaimed Michael. "I thought we were going to work it out, do something special. Arghhhh."

Ellie looked at a quite frustrated Michael, having not seen this side of him before. *Was this Michael getting excited about a science experiment?* she wondered. Well, she was not going to let it end here!

"Michael, it's okay, it's okay!" she blurted out, trying to calm Michael's very loud, verbal and surprising angst. "We just need more data, that's all. More data." Ellie was reassuring herself at the same time. "If the plan doesn't work, we're not wrong remember? We just change the plan."

"Right," Michael said slowly.

"Michael, you and I could be onto something big here. If plastic waste particles are seeping into our water, then, well it's…" She didn't know how to finish. She wanted to say, 'huge', 'groundbreaking', 'a major discovery'! Instead, Michael offered up…

"Scary?"

"Very. Very scary," agreed Ellie. "But we can't jump to conclusions. Right now, we need more data, and we'll need help getting it."

"From who? The Material Matter?" asked Michael.

"Exactly!" confirmed Ellie. "Well, I mean, eventually, but we're going to have to make the evidence much more watertight before we present it to them, otherwise they'll just think we're amateurs again. Kids."

"But we *are* kids," said Michael.

"Exactly! Excellent, Michael!" Ellie said happily, with Michael not entirely sure what he had been excellent about.

"We're kids, and we care! We just need more of us to get the data!"

"Got it!" said Michael, finally understanding.

"We need to get the message out to them, tell them to test their own water for microplastics and give us the data to compare it all. We compile the data, present it back to the Material Matter and let them do their thing to sort out the problem," said Ellie, before adding, "hopefully with me – I mean, *us* – as part of it!"

"In that case we need to go back to my house," said

Michael. "I have a plan."

Michael straightened his trousers, wiped his face with his t-shirt, then spat on his hand, running it through his curls. It made no difference, but at least Michael felt like it had and he felt a little more ready for what was about to happen.

He and Ellie stood at the front gate of his house. Michael took a deep breath and walked to the front door.

As he stepped inside, the familiar call of, "Michael Upperton, we need to talk!" rang out from upstairs. His mother proceeded to wedge her feet down the tiny gaps of what was left of the staircase and made her way toward him.

As she descended, cries of, "Preposterous!", "What were you thinking?", and "Your father…" could be heard between huffs and puffs, growing ever closer.

Michael's mum approached, ready to launch into another well-rehearsed lecture on respect for the house and the people who lived in it, before Michael did something that even took Ellie by surprise.

"Mother!" he announced, his voice suddenly different from his usual one – posher, more proper. "Mother. As you have always wished, I have joined the local ballet troupe!"

Gloria Upperton froze mid-step. The wind had been completely knocked out of her sails. I mean yes, she'd heard it from Ellie earlier, but hearing it directly from her own son? Many years ago Gloria had been a Prima Ballerina herself, until an ankle injury stopped her growing success. Could this really be true? Finally, her Michael picking up where she left off? Well, that news made her eyes well up with tears and her heart leap.

"You…you have?"

"Indeed," Michael replied confidently.

Michael's mum's eyes narrowed a little. She had known

her son for many years, so she knew that he could be prone to a white lie or two.

"Is that so? Tell me then, how was your first lesson?"

Ellie gulped.

Michael was unfazed.

"Oh, it was wonderful, Mother," he said smoothly, shaking out his legs as if they'd been working hard. "We started at the barre with some pliés and tendus, just to warm up – really focusing on turnout, you know? Then we moved into adagio work, which was all about control and extension, keeping the épaulement natural but elegant. Honestly, my port de bras felt a bit stiff at first, but I think I really found the flow by the grand battements. And then, of course, we finished with reverence – got to show respect to the art, haven't you?" He sighed dramatically. "I can still feel it in my calves."

There was a stunned silence, before Michael's mother quite uncharacteristically lunged forward and gave him a huge hug. "Thank you, Michael. Thank you. You'll love it, you really will!"

"I will. I'm certain of it," he confirmed. "You know, I was thinking about writing to a handful of academies, just to let them know in a year or so I'll be formally applying. I was wondering if you could maybe allow me to use your writing paper and fancy pens and inks?"

A stunned Gloria shook her head in disbelief and joy. "Yes, yes of course Michael. They're in my study, take what you need!"

"Thank you, Mother!" He nodded and strode to the other side of the entrance hall and through the grand doorway of his mum's study, making sure his head and shoulders were held high at all times, as that's what ballerinas did. Probably.

"How did you do that?" a shocked Ellie said to Michael as he rummaged through her mum's desk drawers to find a large stack of colourful writing papers and envelopes.

"Mum hasn't stopped harping on about ballet since I was a baby, showing me her old videos and what not. It's finally come in handy!" he replied, before adding, "Right then, we have paper, we have pens, let's get the message out!"

About an hour after they had started, Michael and Ellie folded up the final letters in Gloria's study.

Had they spent a little longer considering the contents of their letters, or researching who to send it to, then perhaps the letters would seem a little less rushed, their recipients a little more defined. As it was, they used Michael's knowledge of the local county schools from the various music and art competitions and festivals he'd attended over the years and decided to get the message out as wide as possible by sending letters to each year group.

Michael picked up the final letter.

Blockhurst School,
Avonshire.

YEAR 7 !!

PLASTIC EMERGENCY!!

Take action and make a difference now!
It might be harming us all!
                    THIS IS BIG!
If interested, write back and we'll
tell you how to help!
        — Ellie & Michael, Hapsie!

The first few letters Ellie and Michael composed had
described in detail the steps needed to test the water for
microplastic particles and measure where any plastic pollution
might be located near to the water source. However, due to the
time it took to write everything in full, the uncertainty of whether
this would even get pinned to a year group's noticeboard, and, of
course, some very sore fingers from writing so much, the pair
had opted for a much shorter note. They would only need to
write back in detail to the handful of children who replied.

They had also found it very handy that Michael's
mother's writing paper had a pre-printed address back to
Michael's house.

As they walked out of the study with two bags of letters
slung over each of their shoulders, Gloria Upperton clasped her
hands together in pure joy at how seriously Michael was taking

his new interest in ballet. With a nod and a firm, "To the future!" from Michael, they left the front door of the Upperton household and sprinted down the path towards the post office.

RATA-TAT-TAT! Ellie knocked hard on the wooden panel of the post office door.

No answer.

RATA-TAT-TAT! RATA-TAT-TAT! Michael joined in the knocking.

Mrs Totterwell finally unlocked the post office door and greeted them both. "Ellie? Michael?"

"We have some letters we need posting," said Ellie, before adding, "Right now."

"Ellie," Mrs Totterwell replied softly. "I'm closed. Can you come back tomorrow morning? It won't make a differ—"

"They are quite important. Very," chirped Michael.

Mrs Totterwell leant down to their height. "It's just that I've got to get to…well you both know where," she whispered.

The two stood there, unmoved by her words, looking expectant like puppies wanting their food. With a big sigh, Mrs Totterwell gestured them into the post office. Mrs Totterwell's second sigh was a little louder when she noticed the four large sacks of letters following them in.

"What on earth do you have in there?" she asked, laughing at the ridiculousness of the situation.

"Er…" they both said, looking at each other, before Michael had the bright idea: "Christmas cards."

"Highly important Christmas cards that absolutely must be sent no later than the 22nd of November?" Mrs Totterwell enquired, picking one of the envelopes out of the sack and twirling it in her fingers.

"Exactly," Ellie responded, hoping they wouldn't be kicked out straight away.

"I see. And how are you planning to pay for four bags of urgent Christmas cards?" Mrs Totterwell continued her questioning.

Ellie and Michael looked deflated. This part of the plan had completely slipped their minds. Michael didn't have any of his pocket money on him, and Ellie any pocket money full stop. There was a long awkward pause, broken eventually by Mrs Totterwell. "Michael, I see these letters are on official Upperton Law stationery. I assume that means you're posting letters on behalf of your mother and father. Should I charge it to their post office account?" winking towards Michael as she ended.

"No they're not—" started Ellie, who was just as quickly shoved in the side by Michael's elbow.

"Exactly, Mrs Totterwell," Michael responded, before adding, "And my mother asked for a bag of gummy worms as well."

Grinning, Mrs Totterwell replied, "Is that so? Well, maybe you leave them in the corner there and I'll deal with them on my return this evening?"

"You promise?" Ellie asked, without losing eye contact.

"I promise," Mrs Totterwell said.

Ellie's eyes now moved towards the side doorway, where, just a few weeks ago, her life completely changed when she walked through it and up the narrow stairs to the flat on the first floor. Mrs Totterwell noticed where her eyes had landed too. "She's already left, Ellie."

"Oh, right," said Ellie. "Well, thank you, Mrs Totterwell. Um, enjoy tonight." And with that she and Michael turned to leave.

"Ellie?"

"Yes?" asked Ellie, a small part of her wondering if she was about to be invited back to the Material Matter.

"You haven't told me what you want the postmark stamp

to read?" Mrs Totterwell prompted.

"Very Important Matter, You Must Open Straight Away and Read Immediately. Do it Right Now," Michael piped up, with only a vague knowledge of what or where a postmark goes or looks like but wanting to stress the urgency of the matter once again.

Mrs Totterwell smiled again. "On a Christmas Card? My, my, they must be lovely cards inside. But a little wordy. How about I just add 'Time-Critical'?"

Michael nodded, and lifting a bag of colourful gummy worms off the counter, he and Ellie left the post office.

As they walked down the cobbled road, Michael turned to Ellie. "So, what do we do now?"

"We wait, Michael. We wait," she responded.

"Oh," replied Michael, somewhat dejectedly, before adding, "That's a bit of an anti-climax then, isn't it?"

Ellie tried to offer some clarity. "Michael, science isn't all action and adventure. No matter what you've seen over the last few days and weeks, it's mostly waiting around – collecting and analysing data, thinking through processes…"

"Right," said Michael, deep in thought. "But," he continued, "if we had managed to get the water samples from Stego-hole, we'd be able to progress our thinking a lot quicker, right? You know, make some new hypo-thesis-thing?"

"Make a new hypothesis? Potentially. It certainly would have helped a lot!" said Ellie, loving her new science-focused friend, even if he was a little rough around the edges.

"Huh. Interesting." Michael was again lost in his own thoughts, chewing on a red and green gummy worm. Then he stopped and said, "Ellie! We've got to see Stefon. Now!"

# Chapter Sixteen

# Back To Back

"I really don't think this is a good idea," Ellie announced to Michael for about the tenth time over a period of about five minutes as they snuck through the gates of the Old Glove Factory, clambered through the freight lift and crept into the concrete building behind. Unfortunately for Ellie, no matter how much she wanted to protest further, she knew that she had to be quiet from then on.

"Through here," Michael gestured, having led Ellie exactly the same route that he remembered from his unauthorised entry before. Michael and Ellie clambered through a small gap in a blocked off stairwell and rolled under a final concrete block before they landed on an upper metal gangway of the atrium.

"My man! Upperton!" came a voice from a face looking down at them. "I was wondering when I'd see you again!"

It was Stefon Back, of course. Still as laid back as when they last met, still blissfully at ease with the fact he was chatting with not one, but now *two* illegal infiltrators into this secret science organisation.

"Oh wow!" he remarked, having looked Ellie up and down. "You've brought the infamous Kit Killer with you too!"

"Kit Lamorna's DEAD?!" exclaimed a stunned Ellie, in the loudest whisper possible.

"Well, no. It just sounds good." Stefon grinned, before noting that Ellie wasn't finding this funny at all. "Nice to meet you anyway. You both here for some quantum chaos?"

"Actually, yes," said Michael. "Can you help?"

"Sure, man! I was just about to step on back to see Galileo. It's going to be a clear night tonight, want to get some tips on how to use my telescope."

"Oh cool! That sounds…No, we actually have a place – or *time* – that we'd like to get to," said Michael, wishing he could also meet Galileo who, in addition to being a leading astronomer, also had been a pretty nifty artist and inventor.

"No problem my man, Galileo can wait!"

Stefon led Ellie and Michael across the gangway and through a chamber door.

"WOAH!" exclaimed Ellie as she entered a Reaction Room for the first time. "What is this place?"

"This is where I was trying to get you to the other day, just after you blew up your room," said Michael. "They use these rooms to practise their Elemental Bracer Wands."

Ellie gave Michael a quick scowl for the use of that word 'wand', then looked around, marvelling at the strange metallic space. Taking in for the first time the entire room – walls, floor, and ceiling – lined with scorched and dented silver metal plates, as if it had endured countless experiments, some more successful than others. In the centre stood the set of targets, their surfaces charred and marked. Ellie ran her hands along the edges and studied the large glass boxes on the steel tables – some filled with swirling, colourful gases, others eerily empty. The feeling of loss of not having her Bracers firmly clasped to her wrists right now spread back over her.

"Where are we heading? Romans? Saxons? Want to go back and play along with Ethel again?" said Stefon, rolling up his sleeves to reveal his dad's Bracers, before raising and lowering both his eyebrows in quick succession to Ellie.

"Hapsie Forest, October 1st," said Ellie.

"All right, history of Hapsie time. I've done a few of these. I checked out the building of the clocktower earlier this week actually. So, what time in history are we heading for?" said Stefon.

"This year. Hapsie Forest, October 1st, at about 2am," Ellie confirmed.

Michael interrupted Ellie. "Wait, isn't that when...?"

"Yeah," said Ellie.

"Why would we go back to then?" asked Michael.

"We need a point before Stego-hole was filled in. It's the only day I know for sure it was wet," Ellie explained.

"It's wet almost every day!" exclaimed Michael.

"But I know for certain it's fresh then. Trust me, it will be great data."

"Hold on, hold on. This year, as in about a month ago?" asked Stefon.

Ellie nodded.

"So yeah," muttered Stefon, cringing a little. "It doesn't really work like that.""

"What do you mean?" asked Michael. "It's in the past, so it must have an echo, right?"

"Well, yeah, I mean, theoretically it does. But in practice it's just a big old mess. You see, man, anything within the last forty years or so, the echoes haven't settled yet, they're too new, raw. It's..." Stefon tried to think of a good way to explain it.

"Let's pretend you are standing in a big open field, and you shout real loud. Your voice gets lost in the open space. But if you put your head in a bucket and shout the same, your voice is trapped, bouncing back at you. It's really deafening, right?"

Ellie and Michael hadn't recently placed their heads in any buckets and shouted but could imagine the scenario.

231

Glad that his on-the-spot analogy seemed to be working, Stefon continued. "So that's a bit like what's happening here, but with time and echoes. The field is your passage of time, when you shout everything's been able to spread out, settle down due to all the space you're giving it. The bucket is more recent times, everything is happening, it's raw, it's...loud."

"Ah," said Michael, realising his amazing plan to hurry their science along was quickly falling away from him.

"Never mind, Michael," said Ellie. "It was an excellent idea. It doesn't matter that we can't do it. We'll just wait for the letters to come back."

"*Can't do it?* Oh, we can do it." Stefon raised an eyebrow at Ellie. "We're going back, I'm just saying – hold onto your britches, 'cause it's gonna be a wild, vibrant ride!" He grinned before adding, with a bit more seriousness, "But yeah, man, we can't hang around there for long. Whatever you gotta see or do, make it quick."

"Vibrant? So, it's not going to be black and white like before?" asked Michael.

"HA!" Stefon laughed, and with that he grasped Ellie and Michael by the arms and shoved his hands down by his side. "Ready? Good! Don't forget to close your eyes for this bit. We don't want half of your body observing today's state while the elements are trying to reform into last month!"

Before Ellie or Michael could fully process that rather unsettling statement, Stefon took a deep breath, his grip tightening slightly. Under his breath, he began to mutter:

"Step up, take one step back, we are travelling to the past to the world of white and black...sort of."

As the words left his lips, the Elemental Bracers on his wrists flared to life – first with a slow, pulsing glow of alternating white and black, then flickering faster and faster until the entire room was strobing with intense bursts of blinding light and deep, consuming darkness. The very air around them seemed to hum, vibrating like a plucked string. The metal walls of the Reaction Room warped and shimmered, as though struggling to decide which reality they belonged to.

"Huh…" Stefon muttered, suddenly thoughtful over the roar of energy, "I wonder if this will work with three people? I hope all parts of us make it!"

Before either Ellie or Michael could protest, Stefon yanked them backward. The flickering light pressed against their closed eyelids, shadows and brightness flashing through in rapid succession.

And then…silence.

Before BLAAHHHHH RARRRRRRR CRKKKKKKKK

Ellie, Michael and Stefon cowered down on the soaked soil, rain hammering down on them. The noises around them were deafening, but it was nothing compared to when they tried to open their eyes.

Waves of colour so bright, so intense, throbbed around them, forcing them to keep their eyes shut, or squint at best.

A cry came from Ellie's right.

"YOU!" burst out Stefon. "YOU! SAID WET!" he shouted over the downpour. "YOU DIDN'T SAY A FULL-ON RAINSTORM!"

He was laughing. Stefon was laughing! Rain pelted his face as he shook his head. "Man, you gotta be more specific next time! I'd have put on my coat!"

How was he enjoying this?

TCHCHHHHH KKKKRRRKKKK came the noises around them as another wave of intense saturated colour wrapped around them, making the orange leaves on the ground burn bright before throbbing back into the early-morning darkness.

233

"I drank way too much soda at the movies one time!" Stefon hollered into Michael's ear. "Missed the big twist 'cause I had to run to the bathroom!" Rain pounded against them as he kept yelling. "So I figured I'd just step on back later that night to catch it again." He let out a loud laugh before shouting through the water smashing against his lips. "Never – and I mean never – try just a few hours before! That was insane, man! I lasted like, thirty seconds before I had to bail!"

"WHAT?!" cried Michael, as the rain drops burst into bright blue in front of him, not expecting to be receiving an anecdote about someone's trip to the cinema at a time like this.

Crackling through the disturbance, Ellie saw it first.

Stego-hole.

Filled with Lucas Litter's plastic. Just as it had been on that night.

Then Michael saw it too. "Ellie, do it now! Get the sample." His voice faded in and out before it reached Ellie, but she didn't need Michael's reminder.

Tearing off her soaked backpack, Ellie yanked out her science pouch, the fabric jumping between blue, yellow and red, before resting back to green. Grabbing a test tube and slamming her backpack over her shoulder, she ran over to Stego-hole as a CLANNGGGKCKKKKKK of sound almost ripped her off her feet.

Driving the test tube into the hole, Ellie managed to get a sample of water from the bottom, deep under the plastic, and pressed a cap over it to secure it in.

"ELLIE!" screamed Michael from behind. Ellie turned around, fighting through the wind, rain and warped vision to see him. He wasn't hard to miss, his HAPSIE football t-shirt shrieking its red. "ELLIE! If you've got it, let's go!"

"All done? Awww. This was fun," said Stefon, the boy who seemed not the least disturbed by the goings on around him.

"It reminds me of that time I saw the Krakatoa volcano erupt in 1883. That was loud, man!" Stefon joyfully screamed through the spinning brightness and then darkness. "Or that time – wait!" Stefon stopped. "Where's she off to?"

Michael looked back to see Ellie sprinting away from them in the direction of the school.

Three hundred paces away from Stego-hole, Ellie saw two figures, then after a blinding SCREEETCHHHH she heard…

"But how could this have happened? It's…"

Ellie heard herself. Ellie saw herself. That was her! Squinting through another colour blast she saw herself next to Master Victor Quinn.

Another voice could be heard. It was gruff, oscillating between blaring loud and desperately quiet, but Ellie remembered it well.

"It's almost Halloween. Blasted tricksters! It's whizzle-whumping kids."

CHHHHHHHH ZPPKKKKKKKK

And with that, Master Quinn limped off into the distance, chucking the end of a bag of nuts down his throat as he left.

Ellie watched.

"Go home, Ellie. I'll make sure this is taken care of."

Ellie thought for a moment about what happens if you meet yourself in this quantum scenario, and then concluded it was only an imprint of her past, a visual echo, so probably (hopefully) it would be fine.

"HI!" Ellie screamed through the darkness to her imprint.

Ellie's imprint, reasonably shocked there was another voice, turned back to see…herself.

"Umm, hello? Are you…?" started Ellie's imprint.

235

"YEP! I'm you. You're me. Crazy, right?" before not wasting any time. "Can I borrow your raincoat?" said Ellie to the imprint of herself.

"Er…I sort of need it. It's raining," said a very confused Ellie imprint.

"Ellie," said Ellie, to the imprint of herself. "Ellie, I'm a future version of you, appearing through a Quantum Superposition Echo. The particles making up this moment exist in multiple possible states, and by interacting with them in just the right way, I have been able to collapse them temporarily into a projection of the past without actually altering history. And I'm doing this to find out why the school is burning down with purple flames."

Everything in our world has an explanation for how it happens. The beauty of life lies in the fact that, eventually, even the strangest peculiarities can be explained. And right then, right there, Ellie had provided a perfect explanation to Ellie's imprint as to why this particular oddity, (i.e. seeing herself) was occurring to her.

Ellie's imprint got it. To her, it made total sense.

"That adds up." She took off her raincoat just as Michael and Stefon arrived.

"Ah! Stefon, Michael, meet my imprint, Ellie. Ellie, meet Stefon, and of course you know Michael."

"Hi," said Ellie's imprint to her best friend from the future.

"Er, hi, Ellie" said Michael to Ellie's imprint, before noticing the school roaring in flames in front of them. "Are those flames…are those flames purple?"

"YES!" Ellie and her imprint said together.

"I thought that was just the colour distortion," Michael said.

"No. They're really burning purple. I can't explain it,"

Ellie's imprint answered.

"You will be able to soon but I need a closer look," said Ellie.

"Ellie, we really gotta go!" Stefon shouted as a blast of sound and colour ripped past them. "This is getting way too unstable!" And he was right, waves of colours were now rippling through the sky, screams of ear-splitting echoes ricocheting off the trees around them.

"I need one more minute!" Ellie yelled, and she sprinted towards the burning school.

Michael turned to Stefon, petrified of what this could mean.

Stefon was laughing again. "She's real feisty isn't she! I can see why you're friends with the Kit Killer!"

"I *kill* someone?" suddenly asked a shocked imprint of Ellie.

"Oh. No. Just severely maim them. But that's like a good few weeks away, and it was mostly an accident." Stefon grinned. "Come on, Michael, we'll need to all be together when we return. Don't want to leave someone behind now, do we?"

Michael and Stefon rushed after Ellie, with Michael politely telling Ellie's imprint goodbye, and that he looked forward to seeing her soon.

As Ellie's imprint watched them disappear into the torrential rain she smiled. With the rain dripping down her woolly jumper, she gave her fist a mini pump accompanied with a, "Yay! Go me!"

Michael and Stefon dodged a bolt of bright green that shot from the ground before ducking past a wave of TCHHHHHHHHHHHH that could blow out an eardrum.

THUMMMPPPPPP

It wasn't a sound wave this time. The boys clattered into Ellie who was standing still as she watched the school burn.

"LOOK!" she said.

Everyone looked.

Through the flickering light, the throbbing colours, the trio could see not just Master Victor Quinn, but Mr Fry their maths teacher, Mr Neebles (English), Joanne Boden (PE), and Greg Hoggett too. As they looked around further, they could see about fifteen Material Matter members surrounding the school – although most were too blurred or absorbed in waves of colour to make out properly.

All had their wrists crossed.

Elemental Bracers bound.

All firing streams of glowing blue light and elements directly into the school.

CHHHHHHHZSKKKKKKKKKKKK roared the noise around them as an explosion of colour knocked them off their feet.

Michael said it first.

"They're trying to put the fire out! Water blasts!"

"Yes..." murmured Ellie, before looking across at Master Quinn, a man deep in concentration who was growing weaker and weaker by the second as the elements were drained from him, Bracers clearly drawing on the Hydrogen and Oxygen from the trees and plants around to produce the water, wilting them, blackening them as he summoned all his energy to fight the fire.

The Material Matter were here, trying to save her school.

"WE'VE GOT TO GO!" shouted Stefon as his face turned bright green then red, suddenly sounding significantly less playful, before a deafening buzz hit their eardrums.

"One more moment!" Ellie shouted back. She was striding through the mess of colour and sound to Master Victor Quinn, letting the sounds and colours hit her as she walked.

"MASTER QUINN!" she shouted.

A dazed, confused man turned to her.

"Ellie? What? No! I told you to go home. I…" said a tired Master Quinn, breaking the bind on his Elemental Bracers to face her, not knowing that he was speaking to a future version of the Ellie he had met just a few moments ago.

"Master Quinn. With everything that's happened recently I probably won't have the courage or opportunity to say this…" she hesitated, "… but I want to thank you for trying to save the school." And with that she extended her hand.

Master Quinn, stunned and disorientated, hesitated, but accepted and shook it.

Ellie was mid smile when – THWACKKKK!!!

Stefon and Michael tackled her away from Master Victor Quinn. As they did, he split into a thousand strands of light, the echo breaking apart before forming again, this time back to his bounded Elemental Bracer position.

Stefon shouted for them all to shut their eyes and muttered under his breath as the world zapped around them.

"One step back. Here I'm done. Back to the present, echoes, be gone! Quickly!"

With it, he hurled Michael, Ellie and himself backwards as his Elemental Bracers blinked bright white light and darkness across the scene, strobing violently just like on their arrival.

There was silence. There was calm. There were two soaked and dishevelled boys and one soaked and dishevelled girl in a green raincoat sprawled across the floor of the Reaction Room, holding tightly to each other.

Slowly, Ellie got up, while the boys remained flat on the floor.

Michael looked up with a groan. "Where are you going?" he asked.

"My imprint got an explanation," Ellie said, turning back to the boys. "Well, now I need mine."

# Chapter Seventeen

# The Reaction

Ellie had a question that needed asking but hated the fact she already knew the answer. An explanation she had to hear, but dreaded its likely consequence. And there was only one person she could direct her question to.

As she peered over the steel gangway high in the rafters of the atrium, the arched windows – grimy with dirt and veiled in dust – were level with her eyeline, allowing the last streaks of muted sunlight to seep through. Below her, the crisscrossing girders and gangways, some still marked with the blackened scars of Master Victor Quinn's demonstration weeks before, formed a tangled web leading to endless doorways, corridors and rooms beyond the walls of the atrium.

Far beneath, where the towering bookcase met the ground, Ellie could just make out the large oak tables bathed in the dim glow of industrial lights hanging above them, where large open-flamed lanterns provided a reading light by each chair.

The tables, the chairs, the surrounding area were full. The chatter of almost a hundred voices rose up to meet her before faintly bouncing off the rooftops and disappearing as they lost their energy. This is where Ellie had to be.

But – and this was a big BUT – when you're set on asking a question, maybe making a statement, fully focussed on your mission at hand, there's nothing more infuriating, completely exasperating, than the sheer annoyance of, well, getting lost. It really knocks you off your stride. And sadly for Ellie, as she ran down the first steel gangway and took a left turn into a brick wall, she suddenly realised that she had absolutely no clue as to how to get to the ground floor from her elevated starting position.

She raced through the labyrinth of corridors, rooms and pathways of the Material Matter's Hapsie headquarters. This undiscovered world, bit by bit, began to reveal itself to her – to skip and dance upon this young, curious mind.

A right turn and a duck under a badly placed girder in her path, a hangover maybe from the Old Glove Factory's distant past, she was met with two large, very new, glass sliding doors. Pulling them open, Ellie gasped. It was as if someone had reached inside her head and pulled out her dream list of equipment and supplies – a room so full of everything she had ever wanted, she felt she could likely conduct any science experiment she could ever imagine. Row upon row, shelf upon shelf of apparatus, kits, instrumentation, swabs, solutions…everything a questioning scientist – young, old, new, experienced – could ever want.

Ellie's feet suddenly stopped wanting to run. There was no one else inside so she slowly walked down a row, eyeing up every beaker, cylinder, scale, pH meter. Her hand reached out to a row of headtorches in every size shape and colour, and very deliberately, but completely by accident of course, found that she had shoved one into her backpack. This was incredible.

*Should I replenish my science pouch while I'm here!?* she thought. Then she laughed. With this in front of her she'd no longer need a science pouch, she'd need an entire laboratory! There probably was one! Right down the next passageway no doubt!

No matter which way Ellie turned, twisted, ducked or descended, she could not avoid uncovering the uppermost layers of this secret world – a realm dedicated to everything she loved and desired. Passing by further Reaction Rooms, some far bigger than the one she, Michael and Stefon had just occupied, some only the size of a store cupboard, she stopped again at another door. An old wooden door. There was something interesting about it. It didn't fit its hinges or fully shut. Above it was a tattered sign simply reading, 'Wayfinder'.

Ellie found her legs wouldn't run again, too tempted to enter. Once again, and quite by mistake of course, she pushed it open and crept inside. Again – empty.

*Excellent*, thought Ellie.

It wasn't the biggest room and there were only a handful of dull lights which helped break through the darkness. The old brick of the glove factory peppered each wall as orange and brown dust settled on the floor from years of compression.

Across the walls and on top of the chest-high desks lay maps, charts and diagrams inscribed onto scrolls and old papers. Ellie walked up to one desk where the words 'Smugglers Passage' were scrawled at the top of a large piece of brown parchment. Ellie recognised the look and feel of the aged paper. It was the same material as the one Master Quinn and Ms Boden had held when deep in discussion at the front of the railcar. Below the title was an endless stream of lines with dots interspersed along them. It looked like the nervous system of the human body, spreading out in every direction, lines coming off other lines, weaving over each other. Many of the dots had crosses through them, more had question marks, and then a few had labels.

Ellie recognised some of the names, 'Foundry', 'Penruth', 'Glenmorgan', but there were many others that meant nothing to her. It dawned on Ellie that her twenty or so minute journey to the Foundry was barely a glimpse into what lay in those tunnels.

Then on the walls, more traditional maps, maps that showed the world, maps which were pinpointing—

"Huh?" Ellie muttered out loud. "What *are* they

243

pinpointing?"

Key events? Other Material Matter headquarters maybe? She wasn't sure, she knew she didn't have time to investigate, but she wanted to. She desperately wanted to know more about what lay around her, but as if pulling her legs with her arms, she forced them to guide her out of the room.

From the frantic start, Ellie's pace had slowed dramatically. Still descending as best she could, down towards the explanation she knew she needed, her mind kept being drawn into each new room and corridor she passed. She almost stopped again at two heavily locked green iron doors which read, 'Archives'; her feet almost turned themselves back into the Matdev laboratory where Kami had shown her their revolutionary new work. But bit by bit, slower step by slower step, she made her way downwards.

As Ellie walked past the vertical farm, once again gaping up at its sheer enormity, her mind raced with that same jolt of excitement she had experienced the first time she entered these walls. What more could be achieved from the bright minds that made up the members of the Material Matter? What incredible science could she be unlocking this evening had they trusted in her potential, rather than classed her as dangerous and irresponsible following her mistake at the Foundry Games? Oh how she could help the world with the power held here in this building!

Still deep in thought, Ellie came to the edge of another gangway. She was now only a few metres above the oak tables. People were moving, dispersing. Whatever the day had brought was now over and everyone was starting to say their pleasantries and slowly diffuse into the archways and corridors around. Ellie peered over the rail to see their faces.

She caught a glimpse of Mr Fry and Mr Neebles, two of the Hapsie School teachers she had just seen in the echo, at the fire. Across the hall, Joanne Boden – no longer just an imprint, no longer firing her Bracers into the school blaze – was laughing and chatting as if nothing had happened. By the wall was Greg Hoggett; he had witnessed the fire burn purple too.

And there was Master Quinn, striding towards the freight elevator. Why had he never spoken to Ellie about the fire? Why did they all ignore the fire? A fire that burned purple. A fire that burned down their school.

Fury fumed, flared, flashed inside her. Without thinking, Ellie tried to scream, "F—" but her voice caught, strangled by nerves. "F—" she forced again, her throat tightening. Then, finally, the air ripped through her vocal cords. She screamed into the atrium below—

"F…F…FARMERS!"

Now, it's fair to say, this choice of word surprised Ellie just as much as it did the hundred or so people below her. And with that, it's also very accurate to say that two hundred or so eyeballs turned to look up at the gangway above their heads where an eleven-year-old girl stood in a soaking wet green rain jacket and matted wet hair. A girl they recognised immediately of course, a girl named Ellie Ment, a girl who had only a few weeks before caused havoc at the Foundry Games, and the subsequent – let's call it kafuffle – that led to her removal from the Material Matter inside this very room.

A girl that should absolutely not be standing on the first floor gangway of their secret headquarters observing this gathering and screaming the word, "Farmers!" Let alone something less unusual.

The silence that followed Ellie's cry likely would have lasted a little longer had two boys not tumbled themselves onto the same gangway, in pursuit of that same girl.

"Ellie! Wait!" cried Michael as he caught up with her, before turning to see the many faces below him and following it

245

up with an, "Oh crikey!"

Two men stood up, the same two men who had forced Ellie against the wall the last time she stood in this room. In unison, they locked their wrists together, pointing the sapphire glass faces of their Elemental Bracers towards the trio.

"Wrists!" one shouted through the silence. "Show us your wrists!"

Ellie heard a gulp and a mutter from Michael of something that sounded distinctly like, "Oh, come on. Not again!"

Ellie shouted back, "You took them from me. I'm not wearing them. I don't have them!"

The call came again, this time louder, more forceful. "Show. Us. Your. Wrists!" They were scared of her.

Ellie raised her arms, her sleeves sliding back to reveal her bare, empty wrists and outstretched palms.

"And you two boys," came the instruction from the other man, gesturing with his locked palms to the left and right of Ellie.

Michael and Stefon glanced at each other. If Michael moved, Stefon would have to as well, and Stefon's own secret would be revealed. Michael held his arms squarely by his side and closed his eyes before repositioning his feet. First it had been water to the face, then an Oxygen blast to the shoulder. He was hoping this next one would stay above the belt too.

"Felix," came a composed voice from below, as a firm hand was placed on the shoulder of the man barking orders. Michael opened one eye. "That's my son you're talking to, and probably one of his only friends right now. I'd appreciate it if you didn't threaten them like that. Now, please, lower your Bracers." Before he added a final, "Please."

Looking to his right, the man shared a nod with Orban Back and lowered his Bracers.

"Anyway, I have my Bracers on me," Mr Back went on.

"Stefon isn't wearing any. He sadly doesn't have the mind for them." He looked up towards his son, never losing eye contact with Stefon for a second.

Both men had dropped their Bracers. Michael finally took another breath. Silence filled the atrium. Ellie, Michael and Stefon stood looking down at the gathering before Stefon leaned into Ellie and whispered, "I think it's your turn to speak."

Ellie felt the heat rising under her shirt collar, her forehead turned damp, her mind went blank. Here was the ultimate test. A hundred people stared at her. All of them wanted answers, and as it always did in tests, her mind was letting her down.

"Farmers," she said again, softly but firmly. Then she paused, taking three long deep breaths.

Stefon leaned into her once again. "Yeah, you're just repeating that word again. We're gonna need a little more…"

As Ellie exhaled for the third time she said, "Farmers don't fertilise their fields in winter." Another pause, more breaths. "Do they? Do they, Master Quinn?" she said, this time a lot louder.

Master Quinn was staring at her.

Ellie stared back.

"Farmers don't fertilise their fields in the winter. Which means the wetlands shouldn't have had any fertiliser runoff. Therefore, the wetlands shouldn't have had an algae bloom. It wasn't farmers, was it?" Ellie took one more deep breath, before quietly, so only Stefon and Michael could hear, she said, "It was you. You burned the school down."

Softly, just for Ellie's ear, Michael whispered, "Er, Ellie, we literally just saw it. They were all trying to put the fire out. They were shooting it with water."

Ellie's response wasn't so quiet, not so private. This time the whole room would hear it.

"Really, Michael?" she said, turning to him. "*Water?* It was pouring down with torrential rain. They didn't need more water!"

Ellie's frustration wasn't really with Michael, but Michael didn't know that and he sank back into his soaked t-shirt, as Stefon briefly gave him a face to indicate that he too thought that the blue light streams from the Elemental Bracers of the Material Matter were water.

"You couldn't even shake my hand properly, could you?" Ellie's voice rang through the atrium, her gaze locked onto Master Quinn. "You could barely grip my hand. Could you?!"

Master Quinn glared, sharp and unwavering.

"I sent you home," he said. "I never shook—" He stopped mid-sentence. His brow furrowed. "She shouldn't have been there," he gruffed quietly to the room. As Master Quinn spoke, his left hand absentmindedly traced over his right. From across the room, Stefon tilted his head.

"After the exam, in the Tithe Barn, Michael's mouth," Ellie continued. "You weren't caring about Michael at all. You were worried about what you had done! If Michael had had a drink, there would be far more questions. Wouldn't there?"

"Ellie, what on earth are you on about?" asked Michael, desperately trying to follow along as always.

Ellie looked at Michael, then swung her rucksack off her shoulder, opened it, and rummaged about inside. After a few moments she pulled out a crumpled piece of paper and held it up to the room. "*This.* This is what I'm on about."

Ellie held up her pencil and charcoal-soiled drawing – the one of the scientist in the lab coat looking through the microscope. Michael looked too. Stefon also. Everyone looked. What they saw was a black smudged, charcoal-covered mess, that vaguely resembled a human blob of uneven jelly.

Stefon turned to Michael and mouthed, "Is that a

person?"

Michael shrugged.

"I think it's time for you to go now, Ellie," came the stern voice of Master Quinn from below, "before you embarrass yourself any further. Before you waste any more of our time with dumb, childish demonstrations."

Ellie didn't respond. Instead, she scrunched up her drawing in both hands, stepped forward, and leaned over the gangway above the oak tables.

She stretched out her arm, then let the ball of paper drop.

All eyes followed it fall.

All eyes watched as it landed directly on top of one of the oak table's open-flamed lanterns below.

All eyes saw the paper ignite in a burst of purple flames before its blackened embers vanished into the base of the lantern.

"You're right," Ellie said, her voice eerily calm as it carried through the atrium. "I am dumb. You literally told me the answer. The problem was, I believed you. I believed it was the farmers. I believed it was fertiliser runoff."

She took a step back, exhaling slowly.

"A weak grip is a sign of Potassium or Magnesium deficiency – but your fingers didn't tremble when I shook your hand, Master Quinn. Not like mine did after I fixed the wetlands. At 2am on October 1st you were short on Potassium, not Magnesium. But why?"

The silence in the atrium deepened.

"Because you had a problem. The rain. The torrential rain. You needed something that would keep the fire burning, something that wouldn't be drowned out. Yes, Potassium would react violently with water in the air, but it wouldn't create the heat needed to melt a school down. So you needed something else.

"You needed a chemical compound that would add Oxygen to the flames, something that would make it burn hotter,

249

stronger, unstoppable – even in the storm.

"The trees around the school weren't just wilted from the heat. They were drained. Their Nitrogen stripped away, because one person alone wouldn't have had enough Nitrogen. Even all of you together wouldn't have had enough."

Ellie turned to Michael and spoke like a friend comforts their best friend.

"If you'd eaten or drunk anything slightly acidic, like a swig of my lemonade on the way home, or some gummy sweets, the charcoal on your face would have fizzed and popped. It would have been excruciatingly painful. That's why he wiped you down with his dry handkerchief. Because that charcoal on your face was mixed with a residue of exactly what was used to burn down the school, exactly what could have given away the secret.

"The light pink of Potassium looks like Hydrogen. The soft blue of Nitrogen looks like Oxygen. Together, the same colour as water."

Ellie swallowed. "So no, Michael, it wasn't water they were shooting. It was Potassium Nitrate. A chemical compound that would oxidise the flames, make them roar, even in the wettest conditions – but also make them burn purple."

At this point Ellie could have turned to the room, made a grand Sherlock Holmesian statement about how they all started the fire; but she didn't, she didn't care.

The Material Matter burned down the school, that was clear. But that was old news to her now, and anyway, she knew everyone else in the room knew it too. There was no secret here.

But you see, Ellie had a question that needed asking but hated the fact she already knew the answer. Ellie had an explanation she had to hear – but dreaded its likely consequence. And there was only one person she could direct it to.

She spotted a small circular staircase at the end of her gangway, leading down to the ground floor. She strode to it, heart

250

hammering, as she scanned the room.

One by one, the faces in the atrium came into focus. The people who had watched. Who had stood silent. Unmoved.

She had an explanation for the *how*. The proof. The undeniable facts.

But *why*? Why burn down a school? Why cover it up?

Yet, somehow, that didn't matter, not for Ellie. She knew that the answer would come in time. The *why* always follows if you know the *how*. Eventually.

But there was one question burning in Ellie's mind. The thought had been swirling heavier than the storm-drenched jacket clinging to her skin, ever since she left the echo.

Ellie pushed through the bodies and then suddenly stopped rigid. Without turning, she quietly, in a hushed whisper, asked:

"Did you know?"

Kami gulped.

# Chapter Eighteen

# A Calculated Response

"Ahem," wheezed a voice from the back.

A familiar rotund man, with a thick round nose and a crescent of brown hair retreating rapidly towards his thick neckline, pushed through the crowd. "Ahem," he said again.

A slightly out of breath Greg Hoggett shoved his way to where Ellie stood.

"Brilliant!" he said as he arrived in front of her. "Brilliant, brilliant, brilliant!"

He waited for a reaction from Ellie. But none came.

"The dramatics, there! Watching that paper fall, and PUFF, up in purple flames...Brilliant! Loved it! Gosh, science!"

Still no reaction, other than the same stare Ellie had given him since his head had popped up.

"You know, that's the type of mind we need round here. I told them that. I told them all that. The girl who can summon Fluorine from her Elemental Bracers after just one week. Chlorine after two days! That's exactly who we need! Don't eject her, embrace her, she has a mind of—"

"Gold?" interrupted Ellie, reminded of Greg Hoggett's inquiry on the railcar on the way back from the Foundry Games. "A mind who could help you make Gold?" she said, before ending her interest in Greg Hoggett and turning to face Kami.

"Why didn't you tell me?" Ellie asked again under her

breath, this time firmer, this time meeting Kami's eyes, and once again getting no immediate answer.

"Concrexio can change the world, Ellie," blurted out Greg Hoggett, but this time his voice was different. It was sincere, serious. "*We* can change the world. *You* can change the world. But you can't change the world if you're not given the chance to change the world. In that sense I guess Concrexio and Ellie Ment are exactly the same. Both brilliant, both with the utmost potential, but both reeling from their mistakes. Ellie Ment, someone who is truly excellent, but banished for her perceived danger and immaturity. Concrexio..." He paused and looked around. Was he looking for permission? If so, who from? "Concrexio, something that is also truly brilliant, but almost lost forever, for the same reason.

"Ellie, Hapsie School was Concrexio's advertisement to the world. A new material that can convert waste materials back into new, recycled, durable construction materials. It would replace polluting concrete. Concrexio found a use for all that plastic waste terrorising our lands and oceans, but..." Greg Hoggett trailed off.

Ellie was listening now, her mind momentarily moved away from Kami. "What was the danger?" she asked.

"It was so silly. So simple, really. Everything was perfect...but we didn't cure the plastic properly, we didn't seal the product properly. As the endless Hapsie rain hit the school walls it was seeping, oozing small plastic particles of itself back into the environment."

"My jars," Ellie muttered.

"There was going to be an inspection the following day. If they had discovered what was happening, if news had spread, the backlash would have been catastrophic. No one would ever trust the material again. Its danger to the environment, the product's apparent immaturity, would have stopped it from ever seeing the light of day," Greg explained.

"Which is why you couldn't wait," said Ellie, voice slightly lowered. "You burned the school down to destroy the evidence of your mistake."

"If we hadn't burned it, the world would have set fire to Concrexio's potential anyway. A single failure would have doomed its progress. Destroying the evidence was the only way to protect the future of the material and give the world an opportunity to repurpose all that plastic waste that smothers us!"

Ellie wasn't moved, but Greg Hoggett realised why.

"Ellie, you're not following because you don't know what happened afterwards. We fixed it! We fixed the mistake, Ellie! It no longer seeps! Concrexio is perfect!"

"Perfect?" Ellie echoed.

"Yes! A material born from what would otherwise be waste plastic that's as strong as concrete, as durable as steel! We fixed it!" Greg smiled, proud of his work, the work of the Material Matter.

"And now you'll release it? Give it to the world?" asked Ellie, now very interested.

"Exactly! Now we can sell it to construction companies all over the world, it will change everything! They will only know about the fixed version, the world will only see the fixed version, it will—"

"Wait...*sell?*"

Greg Hoggett found the word that Ellie had plucked out of his sentence a little strange. "Yes, exactly. It's our gift to the world!"

"It's not a gift," Ellie scorned. "You said you're selling it."

Greg, quite taken aback that the conversation was still focussed on this one little word, tried to reason, "Um, yes. Of course, we developed a product that—"

"There are trillions of pieces of waste plastics suffocating our oceans. There's rivers, lands and beaches drowned in plastic waste, animals dying from ingesting it, and within these walls you're sitting on a product that can take all this waste plastic and repurpose it. And you're going to *sell* it…for *profit?*"

"Er…" stumbled Greg.

"It's like telling the world you've cured cancer, but only for those who can afford it! How's that going to change the world? The ones that can afford it are already going to be fine!"

"Ellie, that's how the system works! Another step towards greater good!" Greg insisted.

"But the system doesn't work, DOES IT?" Ellie fired back. "If the system worked, the planet wouldn't be in this mess! You say the Material Matter is the planet's only stand, free from outside influence. You claim to be unbeholden to voters, shareholders, corporations – only doing good because you only need to do good, because you want to do good. But you're the same. You're just the same! If you're playing inside the system, you're bound by the same rules, the same constraints, the same restrictions as the system." Ellie pondered for a moment, gathering her thoughts, and then proceeding slowly, more quietly.

"It's worse. You're totally unaccountable, hiding away in secret, burning down a school because you believed it to be a step towards the greater good. Hiding the evidence to fix a mistake. To make a profit. Where does that stop? Who stops you?"

Ellie turned around to look towards the freight elevator.

"You blamed the kids. On that night, you said it was kids. It wasn't the kids. We kids are the ones having to deal with this mess. We didn't cause it! You have a solution to a global crisis. And instead of simply doing what's right, you *sell* it?" She threw her words across the room towards Master Victor Quinn before turning back to Greg Hoggett.

256

"How do you even sell it anyway? You're a secret organisation!"

"Ah well, yes. But Greg Hoggett's Construction Ltd isn't," Greg replied, thinking he was being helpful.

Ellie was distraught. "You're just the same. You could just be doing pure good, but you—"

"And do you think all *your* actions would be pure good, Ellie?" said Master Quinn as he stepped forward. "You think you don't need to play by the same rules and laws as the rest of us? You think a simple ideology of doing pure good will change the world for the better?"

Ellie stuck her chin in the air.

"Tell me. The wetlands. How *did* it revitalise itself when I visited again the following morning?" Quinn asked.

"I… I…" Ellie started.

"You…you used Magnesium to encourage the growth of the other vegetation, to smother the algae?" Victor said, finishing her sentence, mocking her nervousness. "Oh, very good. That's good. Ellie Ment, doing uncompromised good." Quinn enunciated each word to the entire atrium, punctuating them with a slow, deliberate clap, before continuing. "Brilliant. Of course! Unless, of course, you're the wilted vegetation under your feet – the very plants you stripped the Magnesium from to feed your ambition of doing good. Everyone's good has consequences, Ellie. Yours may not have been consequential there, but it was just one wetland. Try changing the world."

Master Victor Quinn took another slow step forward. "Ment, pure good doesn't exist. Everything has a consequence. Perfect doesn't exist. Give Concrexio away for free and we can't fund new research from the brightest minds, new research that will help the world even further. We need money to do all this." He gestured at the high-tech secret lab. "Dilute a market overnight with a product that replaces everything? Overnight the concrete industry loses thousands of jobs, people out of work, the system breaks down, chaos and anarchy line the streets. Nothing moves forward.

"But progress does work. And here we make progress – good progress, excellent progress for the world. Feed Concrexio into the system and the system has time to adapt, to change, those jobs can move over naturally. Actual change can happen, progress happens. But our actions to better the world are no freer from unintended consequences than yours, Ment, than anyone's."

"So you think the system breaking down is worse for the planet than the planet itself breaking down?" Ellie snapped back.

"Oh come on, Ment!" a highly irritated Master Quinn roared back. "Don't be such a whizzle-whump! You think you'll make progress with perfection? Grow up. Childish ideology won't change the world."

Ellie went to reply just as ferociously, but just as she did—

"No," came a voice beside her.

Ellie turned.

"No," came the voice again.

A single word. A single syllable. And yet, somehow, it hit Ellie harder than anything Master Quinn or Greg Hoggett had said.

"I didn't know," said Kami. "I didn't know about the fire. I was told it was an accident, vandals."

Ellie turned. All the colour had drained from Kami's face, her hands clenched at her sides. She wasn't lying, Ellie could see that. There was no flicker of hesitation, no tell-tale shift in her stance. Just the simple, unflinching truth.

She didn't know.

Ellie's breath caught in her throat. Her mind had been racing, calculating, turning over every possibility of how she would react when she heard the answer from Kami – but not this.

If Kami had known, if Kami had hidden the secret from her, it would have been simple. So simple. If Kami had known, she would have been just another name on the list of those who compromised their potential. Another person who had decided to work within the system, rather than change it.

But she didn't. She hadn't.

Which meant, what? That they were still equals? Why did this matter to her so much?

Ellie felt herself exhale, before Kami made her hold her breath again.

"But you knew," Kami said, her voice low and steady. "You knew about the purple flames. You knew that Quinn was there. And you didn't tell me? You chastise me in front of everyone for not telling you? But you knew something, too! Because you're better? Because you're smarter?" Her volume increased with every word.

The seconds ticked on. Ellie stood there in silence. If Stefon had been near, no doubt he would have leant into Ellie to nudge her onwards.

But it was Kami who spoke again. "I agree with them, and you should too! Ellie, look around you. Look at what we have here. Look at what can be done at the Material Matter to change the world for the better. It's not just the materials produced here that will save the world; it's the most brilliant minds! The new energy they're developing at Glenmorgan, ecosystem restoration in Penruth, and all the outposts across the world – all of them want to help. Endless options to fight the big problems further. It's happening, Ellie, right here, right now! Progress is happening."

Kami took a breath.

"They were right to burn the school down, because I

259

agree, you've got to be in the game, taking action. Shouting from the sidelines gets you nowhere. And now Concrexio is still in the game, ready to better the world."

Kami looked at Greg Hoggett who nodded. She stared towards Victor Quinn who didn't react. How could he react when he knew what was coming next? Ellie Ment knew about them, she knew about their cover-up, and he knew this bright mind could one day help them further, however flawed he found her ideologies right now, however dangerous her potential was if uncontrolled.

Kami continued, "You're brilliant, Ellie, you know that, everyone here knows that. You can stand outside and yell about how the rules should change, how the system should be different, or you can come inside and change them." Kami smiled. "Ellie, there's a reason we fill balloons with Helium, not Hydrogen. Because not everything has to explode in people's faces in order to rise."

Was Kami right? The world was built on laws and rules and to make change you must work within them, respect them, navigate their path. Some compromise over here, can make great change over there?

Everything Ellie had seen, every corridor she had just wandered, every passageway that led to new undiscovered opportunities, the bountiful resources of the Material Matter. The power of the Elemental Bracers. It all led to one undeniable truth.

The Material Matter wasn't just talking about saving the world.

They were actually doing it. Finally, someone was doing something.

And here – here in this place, Ellie could do it too.

"Ellie..." Kami prodded, softer this time.

Ellie looked up at Michael and Stefon on the gangway.

Michael sheepishly shrugged. He'd follow Ellie to the end of the world and back. Stefon grinned down at her.

Ellie looked back at Kami and gave the smallest of nods. She knew where her future lay.

# Chapter Nineteen

# A Jarring Christmas

**P**hil Ment stepped back to admire his handiwork.

"Yes," he muttered to himself with an agreeable nod. "This will do just fine."

Around Ellie's dad, the Ment household had been transformed into a winter wonderland, and the final string of plastic reindeer he had hung over the lintel of the front door finished it off nicely. Or at least, that's what he was saying to himself.

The true test would come when Aunt Melicia – Phil's sister and Ellie's aunt – arrived to celebrate with them in two weeks' time.

Aunt Melicia was a stickler for perfect Christmas decorations, even more so than she was for the Christmas dinner itself. And with her being a chef and restaurant owner, Phil had decided that he could at least win on one front this year.

So, there it was: a true winter wonderland of festive decorations, from the moment you stepped through the front door to the waving Santa Claus who greeted you from your bedside table.

As Phil took one last look at his garland of prancing reindeer, he let out a little, "Uh…"

Something was off. What was it? The reindeer were perfectly level at each end, he'd measured it to the millimetre. Mr

Ment took a step back.

"What the?" he suddenly said out loud. Because there, hanging on the coat stand by the door, was Ellie's green rain jacket, and next to it, was Ellie's green rain jacket. That jacket had been his when he was a child. He knew it well.

Ellie's dad examined both jackets. Identical. How come there were two?

"Seda?" Phil called to his wife upstairs. "Did Ellie get another rain jacket?" He continued before she had a chance to answer. "Yes? No? Maybe? I've no idea what that girl gets up to. Go ask her yourself, I think she's in her room with Michael."

Taking a closer look at the duplicate raincoats once again, Phil turned and headed up the stairs to ask his daughter how she had managed to get her hands on a second coat identical to the one he'd been bought more than thirty years ago…

But it's lucky he did – because if he'd stayed a few moments longer instead of bounding up the stairs, he might have been a little more surprised when the raincoat to the left began to disintegrate. The fabric shimmered, then dissolved into the air, unravelling into swirling plumes of pink, green, blue, yellow, and black gas. The colours danced in the air for a fleeting moment before fading, each element slipping back into its rightful quantum state – until dispersing until nothing remained at all.

"Ellie! Ellie!" Phil started calling at the top of the stairs, before gently knocking on her door and going in without waiting. "Ellie—" Phil stopped. There was no Ellie and Michael. There were no jam jars, bags of soil, pot plants. There was barely any science equipment at all. Well, there was, but it was tucked neatly into the corner of a room, into a clearly defined Science Corner.

"Er, Seda," Phil called again. "They're not here. Actually nothing—"

"Then she's probably at ballet again," Seda Ment called from across the landing. "She's been there a lot lately, with

Michael. They really need to give our family a demonstration when Cousin Cassie is here. Cassie does ballet too."

She paused before adding, "At least Ellie seems to be making a new friend or two, by the sounds of it. So that's nice."

And Ellie's mum was somewhat right,

> (Well, at least about the new friend bit, but certainly not the ballet bit, of course. Oh, and also her assumption that Cassie did ballet too. No, as it turned out, Cassie had been using the same excuse to her mum whenever she wanted to hang out with her friends at the shopping mall for the fourth and fifth consecutive days. Which, together with Michael, would make for a very amusing demonstration that Christmas. But that's a separate anecdote entirely.)

Down the country lane away from Ellie's house, across town, into a large hall, up a metal staircase, and into a very special room full of the most wonderous things, Michael and Stefon sat on the floor while Ellie perched on the edge of Michael's bed.

Well-used upcycled toys, inventions and the like were scattered across the floor, but in the middle, jars. Endless jam jars of all shapes and sizes. But they were empty, at least of water (and certainly of jams). Instead inside each one lay a small tealight candle, and Stefon, Michael and Ellie were busy painting and decorating them.

"Done another!" Ellie exclaimed happily, turning her jar to show the two boys her work of art.

"Er…" They both hesitated in unison.

"That's a lovely…" Michael began.

"Snowman?" attempted Stefon.

"Santa?" tried Michael.

"Snowstorm?" struggled Stefon, squinting at the silvery

white splat with flecks of other colours dotted between.

"Mess?" ended Michael, with all three laughing.

"No, you broken beakers! It's a Christmas scientist in a festive lab!" said Ellie, laughing at the absurdity of how little it looked like any of the words she had just said.

"Riiiiiiiiiiiight." Stefon nodded.

"Do you think you'll give one of these to any of the teachers?" asked Michael. "I'd love to see Master Quinn's face if you handed it to him. You could tell him it was a festive wetland Magnesium blast."

"Nothing will beat his face when you just walked out. That was priceless!" said Stefon, reflecting on the events from just a few weeks ago. "I mean, you sort of left us hanging, up on the gangway and all, but as you disappeared up the freight elevator…well, I've never seen a grimace so big! What an exit!" Stefon smiled and shook his head.

"What about giving a tea light to Professor Fialova?" Michael suggested.

The mood shifted. Ellie's face fell.

"I haven't spoken to her since that day," she admitted. "I mean, we've had a few classes, but school ended for the holidays before we could have a chance to chat." Ellie frowned. "I suspect she's pretty mad at me. She trusted me, gave me the Bracers, and then I just let her down."

"You know, you could probably still change your mind?" prodded Michael.

"No Michael, I made the right decision. If I'm going to make a difference, a *real* difference, I need to do it my way. It needs to be done the right way."

"And because I want to be totally clear – what is that way, again?" enquired Stefon.

Ellie scrunched up her face. "I'm not sure yet. But not that way."

"Right. And again, just so I'm totally clear here. Endless resources, collaborating with the brightest minds, producing new materials and concepts that can change the way we look at energy, waste, biodiversity...just to be totally clear, that's *not* the right way?"

This was the spark Ellie needed. "Change doesn't mean sitting in a hidden room, making deals in secret, bending the truth whenever it's convenient. That's not change, Stefon. That's just playing by the same rules that broke everything in the first place.

"The Material Matter has the power to stop plastic waste from poisoning our oceans. Instead, they're going to sell it to the highest bidder.

"Change comes from fighting for what's right, out in the open, where everyone can see. Where people – normal people, not just a select few – get to decide their own future.

"So no, Stefon. That's not the right way. The right way is messy. It's hard. But if I have to choose between changing the world their way, or actually fixing it, then I choose to fix it."

Stefon and Michael had stopped painting their Christmas jam jars. This had all turned rather serious.

"So you're saying the Material Matter, are, like, evil?" asked Michael.

"No!" exclaimed Ellie. "No, not at all! That's not what I'm saying. They're good, they're doing great! What they have and I'm sure will develop, it's amazing. It will improve things. They're just..." She trailed off. "They're just not doing enough. Or how they are doing it won't change enough. Quickly enough."

"Right," said Stefon. "Well, there's you. There's me. There's Michael. I guess that's a start. We could just about start a band or something."

"I don't think Ellie should be doing that," Michael interjected with a grimace, "especially if we're trying to get more people to join us."

He received a polite scowl from Ellie.

"Oh and jam jars, we've got a hell of a lot of jam jars. I'm sure they'll be very helpful." Stefon chuckled, eyeing up the sea of glass that stretched across Michael's room.

"Now, now!" said Ellie firmly but fondly. "These jam jars did a pretty good job at uncovering a cover-up from a worldwide secret organisation."

"Oh yeah. On that. Did you ever test the sample? Were there plastics in the water from Stego-hole?" said Michael.

"I did. Before it vanished. There were lots," replied Ellie.

"Was it from Concrexio or Lucas Litter's Stego-hole stockpile?" asked Michael.

"I dunno. When we took the sample we didn't know about the school leaking plastics, so we couldn't control for that. But sadly, I suspect both. We're going to need to look into that more."

"Wanna go get another sample?" Stefon suggested with a grin.

"No!" Ellie and Michael shouted in unison.

"I'm NEVER going back to anything within the last forty years with you! That was carnage!" added Ellie, as Stefon laughed.

"Wait," said Michael. "You still can? I thought your dad would have taken the Bracers off you after he found out you had them that day."

"Yeah, I mean, he was pretty mad about having to lie for me with the Bracers, but hey – on the bright side, I took him back to see a Louis Armstrong jazz concert. And man, I don't know if it was watching his favourite musician live or realising this whole Quantum Relativity thing can be manipulated like this with the Bracers, but he got over it real quick. Turns out he now knows I do have a mind for something after all," said Stefon, grinning broadly. "The only rule is I have to take him somewhere cool every few months."

268

"Do you miss them, Ellie?" asked Michael.

"Who?" replied Ellie.

"Your Elemental Bracer Wands, doofus," said Michael.

"I miss not being able to blast you with water for calling them wands," joked Ellie, not fully sure if she was joking or not. "It's science, Michael, not magic".

"Sure, but science *is* magic, right?" Michael reminded her. He received an approving nod from Ellie. "Exactly. Anyway, you shouldn't need fancy gadgets to make a real difference. So I don't need them either."

"Ethel Smyth and the suffragettes did it mostly with placards and pure grit!" added Michael, pleased with himself that he could add 'history buff' to his growing list of skills.

"So what do we do now? You know, to make a difference?" Stefon asked, bringing the question back around to that pertinent question.

Luckily for Ellie, who didn't have a fully fleshed out answer, the doorbell went.

"Race you to the door?" Michael challenged Stefon and Ellie, and with that they all leapt out the room and slid down the metal baking trays that were still fastened on the Upperton staircase.

As they reached the bottom it was Michael who noticed it first. "Ellie, look!" he cried. Because there, on the centre of the doormat, was one of the letters they'd posted at the end of November. A perfectly folded green envelope.

"Someone finally replied!" exclaimed Michael, having totally forgotten about all the letters until this point.

"Eyyyyy!" said Stefon brightly. "Look at that, the band is expanding, we're now four strong! That'll make a difference."

Ellie reached down, picked up the envelope and opened it. If Ellie and Michael had been expecting some positive words, such as "I'm in!", "Show me what to do!", or maybe, "Let me know more!" then they would have been bitterly disappointed.

Instead, it simply read:

*Titanium Thorium. Boron Argon Nitrogen.*
*Nitrogen Oxygen Tungsten.*

"Oh great!" said Michael loudly. "Our only reply and it's someone trolling us with science jargon."

Ellie scrunched up her face for a good two seconds, pocketed the letter, looked up at the boys.

"We've got to go."

# Chapter Twenty

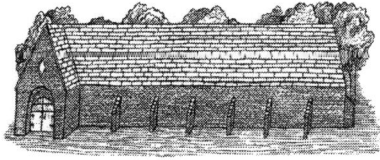

# The Answer That Solved Everything

Ellie had sprinted so quickly out of the Upperton front door that she didn't even have time to find her hat and gloves, or put on the warm winter coat she had arrived in. This was particularly unfortunate for all three of them as the snow had been falling while they were painting their jam jars and had decided at this moment to pick up its flurry into a blizzard.

"Where are we going?" cried Michael, desperately trying to catch up with Ellie.

"And why so quickly?" Stefon followed up, panting.

"The letter!" Ellie shouted through the flakes which were (gently) battering their face and jumpers. "It was code."

"I gathered that," puffed Michael, "but what did it say?"

"Simple," cried Ellie as she turned a corner into a country lane. "The elements were Titanium Thorium, Boron Argon Nitrogen, Nitrogen Oxygen Tungsten. All you need to do is make a sentence with their atomic symbols from the periodic table!"

"Right," said Michael. "Understood!" he continued, continuing to run alongside the others. Before finally adding "And that would be?"

"Tith. Barn. Now," replied Stefon, having worked it out through his knowledge of the periodic table and also by using his fingers. "What's a Tith?" he added.

"I'm guessing it means Tithe," said Ellie. "There's no atomic symbol that's just an E."

"Got ya!" said Stefon, panting. Before he added, "And what's a Tithe Barn? Is it far away?"

Michael, pleased this was the type of question he could answer, had the chance to interject. "You'll be spending a lot of time in it after Christmas! And it's exactly 184 metres and 20 centimetres away."

The trio stomped over the snow-covered fresh tarmac of what was once Stego-hole.

As Ellie, Michael and Stefon arrived at the stone entrance vestibule to the Tithe Barn, two figures came out to greet them.

"Professor Fialova!" exclaimed Ellie. And without missing a beat immediately began to apologise. "Listen, I'm so sorry, I didn't mean to put you in an awkward position, I—"

"What on earth are you talking about, Ellie?" she reacted. "From what I hear you were absolutely brilliant. You really stood up to them."

"Wait, you're not angry?" said Ellie.

"Angry? Not at all!" replied Professor Fialova. "Plus, your little distraction gave me the perfect opportunity to slip off and take care of an errand I had been meaning to do for a few days. But enough about that." She grinned. "I'm just glad Lucas delivered my note to you. I was quite sure it would end up being dropped somewhere along the way. Asking Lucas wasn't the cleverest choice of mine, but he was up here feeding the birds so…well, I think I may have given the birds a break from eating the odd sweet wrapper or two," she added, as the three children tried to catch their breath.

"Mrs Totterwell and I thought it best we do this here," Professor Fialova continued. "We weren't particularly sure that Michael's parents would appreciate it."

"What do you mean?" asked Michael.

"Hello Stefon, lovely to see you here too. I think you all better take one more deep breath, and then come with us." Professor Fialova walked them through to the vestibule, where Mrs Totterwell was standing at the doors that led into the Tithe Barn.

At this point, Professor Fialova stopped. "What's through these doors, well, I just…I just hope you're all ready for it." She gave a nod to Mrs Totterwell.

Mrs Totterwell pushed open both large barn doors.

There were no desks, no chairs. They had been moved to the side.

There were no dividers, they had been taken away.

Instead.

Piles. No, mountains.

Hundreds. No, thousands.

Of letters.

Endless letters and envelopes. In stacks reaching upwards high towards the wooden beams of the barn. Of all different colours. Stretching back throughout the Tithe Barn in each and every direction. Heaps upon mounds of hand scrawled notes. Stacks upon batches of…replies!

Three sets of wide eyes on legs walked into the Tithe Barn, weaving through the endless masses of letters. Every now and then you'd see a reused letter on Upperton stationery, but beyond that it was a boundless mishmash of homemade leaflets and papers.

Michael bent down and picked one up. It simply read, "I'm in. Sincerely, Adah". And then her address scrawled underneath.

Stefon lifted another. "Show me what to do? Gabby". This time with her address stamped neatly below.

Ellie turned to Professor Fialova and Mrs Totterwell. "I…I don't understand."

"Well. It seems everyone really liked your Christmas cards, Ellie." Mrs Totterwell giggled. "And apparently they liked them so much they told all their friends, who told all their friends, who, I'm guessing, told all their friends too."

"Crikey! We're absolutely not ready for this at all!" said Michael, handing Ellie a letter.

Ellie opened it and read out loud. "What can we do to make proper change? Hamish and Rufus!"

She took a step back and stood by Michael's side as Stefon walked around picking up more and more letters, opening them, reading them.

"Ellie, what does this mean?" Michael asked.

"Kids," replied Ellie. "It means there are kids everywhere that are like us, Michael. That want change. Like us. Yes. Kids. Whizzle-whumping kids," she added with a smile to her best friend. He returned it.

"Ellie." The soft voice of Professor Fialova spoke from behind. "Ellie, about that distraction you caused the other day. Listen, I really, really shouldn't be giving you this, but…" and with that Professor Fialova pulled a small dark brown leather satchel from under her coat. It was tattered and scratched. She opened it and inside lay two…well, at first glance they looked like watches.

But Ellie knew exactly what they were this time. She reached in and picked one up. It was weighty, there was real substance as she looped it over her wrist and adjusted the clasp on the band to secure it tightly. The clasp snapped shut. As it did, a tingling sensation, a small vibration flowed lightly down her arms and up into the palm of her hand, then vanished. For a brief moment a sense of tiredness came over her, then just as quickly as the tingling, that vanished too.

It felt good, it felt very good.

From across the hall an American voice popped up. "I

thought you said you shouldn't need fancy gadgets to make a real difference, Ellie!"

Ellie considered Stefon's words, let them swirl around in her mind. Then she clasped on the right hand Bracer, brought her wrists together in front of her, and summoned, "Elemental Bracers. Hydrogen. Oxygen. Give me water."

A blast of blue light shot across the Tithe Barn, hitting Stefon gently in the chest and face, so he was soaked to the core.

"You shouldn't need them," said Ellie, as Stefon spluttered. "But they can certainly help."

Michael keeled over in laughter.

With the two boys preoccupied, Ellie turned back to Professor Fialova. "Professor Fialova, I do need to ask. Were you at the school? Did you help burn it down too?"

"No," replied Professor Fialova, simply.

"Oh." Ellie felt a wave of relief rush over her.

"But I also didn't do anything to stop it, Ellie. So does that make it any better?" Professor Fialova added, posing her ethical dilemma back to Ellie.

Ellie didn't have the answer, but did have a second burning question.

"Whenever anyone has seen me with these, they…they seem to recognise the Bracers."

"Yes," Professor Fialova replied again.

"Why?"

"They're Dr Higton's."

"The geography head?" Ellie responded, taken aback. "Then…then why do I have them? Doesn't Dr Higton need them?

"For that, you'll have to ask Dr Higton directly," said Professor Fialova.

"But how? They're missing."

"So you'd better go and find them!" prompted Professor

Fialova with a pointed look and a tap on Ellie's shoulder, before heading over to give Stefon her jacket to warm up.

Ellie stood still, thinking about Professor Fialova's words. Were they a request? A challenge? Then she turned to Michael and said, "Want to see something fun?"

And before Michael could reply she brought her wrists together. The two outer crowns of the Elemental Bracers closest to each other snapped together once again. Ellie felt the ripple of vibrations run up both arms, before crying out loud, "Elemental Bracers. Oxygen."

A force of light cracked out from the sapphire glass faces on each wrist and Oxygen shot out in a great force, blowing envelopes and letters to the rafters of the Tithe Barn. Taking deep breaths, Ellie began to control their swirls, using her outstretched fingertips to separate, organise, order, while whirlwinds of new Oxygen streams picked up more and more and more letters.

Michael and Stefon ran around laughing, catching flying letters, stuffing them into their pockets, dancing under the flurry of paper. Ellie slapped a letter into Michael's face and sent a rush of envelopes to swipe out Stefon's legs, while very deliberately making sure Professor Fialova and Mrs Totterwell were free of any obstruction as they watched the letters circle.

Ellie had one thought repeating over and over in her mind: *Things are about to get very interesting indeed.* Then, just as she was trying to separate the colours of a pile of letters—

"PROFESSOR FIALOVA!" came a cry from the door.

Everyone turned. The letters fell to the ground. "Lucas," Professor Fialova said calmly. "Lucas, thank you for delivering my message. But I—"

"It's the birds," Lucas interrupted her.

"What about the birds?" asked Professor Fialova.

"They've stopped chirping, and they're...they're on the

ground. They won't fly. Maybe they *can't* fly."

"How do you mean?" said Mrs Totterwell.

"I don't know. It might be to do with the sky," Lucas continued.

"What's wrong with the sky?" asked Ellie, very confused.

"It's green," Lucas said slowly. "It's neon green!"

Ellie looked at Michael, who turned to Stefon. Professor Fialova and Mrs Totterwell shared a confused look. And then they all rushed out of the large doors of the Tithe Barn, through the vestibule, to the outside.

Sure enough, it was no longer snowing. The birds were sitting silently on the ground around the Tithe Barn, and the sky, the sky was a vibrant, neon green.

It was green above the burned remains of the Hapsie School.

Bright green above the Tithe Barn, and all the way down the forest road, past Stego-hole.

It was green over Ellie's house, over the river, over the cobbled streets of the post office.

The neon green could be seen over the old railway too, above the Old Glove Factory.

But.

And just because we found ourselves there, anyway.

Not everyone had noticed the green sky just yet.

Deep, down an old rusting freight elevator shaft.

Inside a large atrium.

Along a metal gangway or two.

Inside a room the size of your average classroom, lined entirely with silver metal plates, across the walls, floors and ceiling, a beam of explosive, pale blue light burst out from two wrists. The force blasting the owner backwards across the room, landing with a hard thud on the metal floor behind them. Snacks blown into the air.

Dazed and confused, they looked up, where a man smiled and his gruff voice simply said, "Finally. Very well done, Kami."

*Hold on to your beakers, Ellie will be back...*

**Scan the QR code above or visit
EllieMent.com to stay up to date.**

# The Periodic Table of Elements

| 1 | 2 | 3 | 4 | 5 | 6 | 7 | 8 | 9 | 10 | 11 | 12 | 13 | 14 | 15 | 16 | 17 | 18 |
|---|---|---|---|---|---|---|---|---|----|----|----|----|----|----|----|----|----|
| 1 H Hydrogen | | | | | | | | | | | | | | | | | 2 He Helium |
| 3 Li Lithium | 4 Be Beryllium | | | | | | | | | | | 5 B Boron | 6 C Carbon | 7 N Nitrogen | 8 O Oxygen | 9 F Fluorine | 10 Ne Neon |
| 11 Na Sodium | 12 Mg Magnesium | | | | | | | | | | | 13 Al Aluminium | 14 Si Silicon | 15 P Phosphorus | 16 S Sulfur | 17 Cl Chlorine | 18 Ar Argon |
| 19 K Potassium | 20 Ca Calcium | 21 Sc Scandium | 22 Ti Titanium | 23 V Vanadium | 24 Cr Chromium | 25 Mn Manganese | 26 Fe Iron | 27 Co Cobalt | 28 Ni Nickel | 29 Cu Copper | 30 Zn Zinc | 31 Ga Gallium | 32 Ge Germanium | 33 As Arsenic | 34 Se Selenium | 35 Br Bromine | 36 Kr Krypton |
| 37 Rb Rubidium | 38 Sr Strontium | 39 Y Yttrium | 40 Zr Zirconium | 41 Nb Niobium | 42 Mo Molybdenum | 43 Tc Technetium | 44 Ru Ruthenium | 45 Rh Rhodium | 46 Pd Palladium | 47 Ag Silver | 48 Cd Cadmium | 49 In Iridium | 50 Sn Tin | 51 Sb Antimony | 52 Te Tellurium | 53 I Iodine | 54 Xe Xenon |
| 55 Cs Cesium | 56 Ba Barium | 71 Lu Lutetium | 72 Hf Hafnium | 73 Ta Tantalum | 74 W Tungsten | 75 Re Rhenium | 76 Os Osmium | 77 Ir Iridium | 78 Pt Platinum | 79 Au Gold | 80 Hg Mercury | 81 Tl Thallium | 82 Pb Lead | 83 Bi Bismuth | 84 Po Polonium | 85 At Astatine | 86 Rn Radon |
| 87 Fr Francium | 88 Ra Radium | 103 Lr Lawrencium | 104 Rf Rutherfordium | 105 Db Dubnium | 106 Sg Seaborgium | 107 Bh Bohrium | 108 Hs Hassium | 109 Mt Meitnerium | 110 Ds Darmstadtium | 111 Rg Roentgenium | 112 Cn Copernicium | 113 Nh Nihonium | 114 Fl Flerovium | 115 Mc Moscovium | 116 Lv Livermorium | 117 Ts Tennessine | 118 Og Oganesson |

| 57 La Lanthanum | 58 Ce Cerium | 59 Pr Praseodymium | 60 Nd Neodymium | 61 Pm Promethium | 62 Sm Samarium | 63 Eu Europium | 64 Gd Gadolinium | 65 Tb Terbium | 66 Dy Dysprosium | 67 Ho Holmium | 68 Er Erbium | 69 Tm Thulium | 70 Yb Ytterbium |
|---|---|---|---|---|---|---|---|---|---|---|---|---|---|
| 89 Ac Actinium | 90 Th Thorium | 91 Pa Protactinium | 92 U Uranium | 93 Np Neptunium | 94 Pu Plutonium | 95 Am Americium | 96 Cm Curium | 97 Bk Berkelium | 98 Cf Californium | 99 Es Einsteinium | 100 Fm Fermium | 101 Md Mendelevium | 102 No Nobelium |

## ABOUT THE PUBLISHER

The Clean Planet Foundation is the not-for-profit arm of the Clean Planet Group, working to educate and take action for the sustainable use of plastics and the reduction of carbon emissions. The Foundation believes that everyone deserves better and initiates projects to mitigate the impact of the plastic and climate crises across the UK and beyond.

## ABOUT THE AUTHOR

When Bertie's not writing about Elemental Bracers and science going bang in the early hours of the morning, he spends his working days as co-founder and CEO of the Clean Planet Group. Together with his team, they're building advanced recycling facilities to tackle the plastic waste crisis, developing breakthrough technologies, and launching diverse environmental projects via the Clean Planet Foundation. Stephens now lives between England and Czechia with his wife and almost-three-year-old, Oskar – who, incidentally, was very happy to hear his big green balloon made it into Ellie's story.

## ABOUT THE EDITOR

Lil Chase is an author with six books written under her own name and countless others under various pseudonyms. She's created everything from lift-the-flap board books, hilarious teenage dramas, to the whole history of human existence in just 48 pages. She's worked as an editor at Working Partners Ltd and Hachette creating stories for millions of child readers. Lil lives in London with her family and their dog, Dougal. She has her own writing corner, but would love her own science corner too.

Learn more about the Clean Planet Foundation:

cleanplanet.com/foundation